Evidence-Based Treatment for Alcohol and Drug Abuse

PRACTICAL CLINICAL GUIDEBOOKS SERIES:

Evidence-Based Treatment for Alcohol and Drug Abuse

A Practitioner's Guide to Theory, Methods, and Practice

Paul M.G. Emmelkamp
Ellen Vedel

Routledge
Taylor & Francis Group
New York   London

Routledge is an imprint of the
Taylor & Francis Group, an informa business

Routledge
Taylor & Francis Group
270 Madison Avenue
New York, NY 10016

Routledge
Taylor & Francis Group
2 Park Square
Milton Park, Abingdon
Oxon OX14 4RN

© 2006 by Taylor and Francis Group, LLC
Routledge is an imprint of Taylor & Francis Group, an Informa business

Printed in the United States of America on acid-free paper
10 9 8 7 6 5 4 3 2 1

International Standard Book Number-10: 0-415-95286-7 (Softcover) 0-415-95285-9 (Hardcover)
International Standard Book Number-13: 978-0-415-95286-6 (Softcover) 978-0-415-95285-9 (Hardcover)
Library of Congress Card Number 2006012723

Library of Congress Cataloging-in-Publication Data

Emmelkamp, Paul M. G., 1949-
   Evidence-based treatments for alcohol and drug abuse : a practitioner's guide to theory, methods, and practice / Paul M.G. Emmelkamp, Ellen Vedel.
      p. ; cm. -- (Practical clinical guidebooks series)
   ISBN 0-415-95285-9 (hb. : alk. paper) -- ISBN 0-415-95286-7 (pb. : alk. paper)
   1. Substance abuse--Treatment. 2. Evidence-based medicine. I. Vedel, Ellen. II. Title. III. Series.
   [DNLM: 1. Substance-Related Disorders--therapy. 2. Behavior Therapy--methods. 3. Evidence-Based Medicine. WM 270 E54e 2007]

RC564.E46 2007
616.86'06--dc22   2006012723

Visit the Taylor & Francis Web site at
http://www.taylorandfrancis.com

and the Routledge Web site at
http://www.routledge-ny.com

To Lotte, Esther, and Julie

Contents

Preface

Research in the past decade has shown that substance abuse and substance dependence are clearly treatable disorders. The field has witnessed the introduction of evidence-based psychological and specific pharmacological treatments. Unfortunately, many of these empirical supported therapies are still not widely applied by practitioners. In fact, many of the treatment approaches currently used in the addiction field are clearly not evidence-based.

This volume is intended to give basic information about what one needs to know when working with patients abusing substances. We intend to inform substance abuse treatment practitioners, mental health professionals, and students about the latest developments in the field in order to provide the clinician with valid and practical guidelines applicable across a variety of treatment settings and patient groups. The opinions expressed herein are the views of the authors and do not necessarily reflect official guidelines. Further, in every individual case, the practitioner should evaluate whether the interventions proposed here match the needs of the patient.

The book provides necessary background information on defining characteristics, classification, and prevalence of substance use disorders. The latest advances of fundamental research in the addiction field are discussed in a palatable way for students and clinicians. This means that substantial selectivity was exercised concerning topics to be included. In selecting the relevant literature, our primary aim was to provide the practicing clinician and the student with an up-to-date understanding of the epidemiology, etiology, and course of substance abuse disorders that are relevant to clinical practice. In addition to describing phenomenology and etiology, the book provides a guide to the assessment and treatment of abuse and dependence of alcohol, stimulants (e.g., cocaine, amphetamines), opiates (heroin), hallucinogens (LSD), cannabis/marijuana, and party drugs (e.g., ecstasy). Illustrative case histories were added to further clarify phenomenology, assessment, and treatment procedures.

The therapeutic approaches described in this volume are all grounded in empirical research. We do not advocate one particular approach, but present the evidence currently available. Treatment procedures with no or little empirical support, however, were omitted (e.g., psychoanalytic approaches, system-theoretic approaches). Further, the emphasis is on adult substance-abusing patients. Our intention was to provide a systematic account of evidence-based treatments, as little constrained as possible by the unsubstantiated assumptions of traditional psychotherapy schools. We examine a range of evidence-based treatment alternatives, and discuss the factors that might help the clinician to decide which treatment will best match the clinician's patients' needs. Similarly, the pros and cons of medication are described in an objective way, thus enabling the clinician to decide whether or not drug treatment may be useful in particular cases.

In the chapters on clinical application, scientifically supported therapies for substance use disorders are described in detail and guidance is given on how to plan and implement specific techniques. Vignettes of patients are presented and each case study conceptualizes the problem, the treatment approach, and the goal of therapy and discusses the overall course of therapy. Patient–therapist dialogues are presented where these are informative.

We tried to put the emphasis on real clinical patients rather than on research subjects in academic settings. This means that we describe the treatment of polydrug users as well as the treatment of patients who not only are substance abusing but also have other psychiatric disorders including personality disorders.

The present text is directed to both the practitioner and the researcher. The book will be useful in the training of therapists and counselors and of interest also to experienced practitioners. Researchers will find in the book a comprehensive and critical evaluation of research in the field. The extensive bibliography should assure the book's usefulness as a reference source. We hope that the book will appeal to a wide audience of practitioners, students, and researchers in psychology, social work, and psychiatry.

We would like to thank several people and institutions for helping bring this book together. First, we wish to thank the patients with whom we have worked over the years in addiction and mental health centers. To protect the privacy of our patients, case material has been altered in such a way that there is no resemblance to individual cases. Further, we express our profound gratitude to the staff of the Netherlands Institute for Advanced Study in the Humanities and Social Sciences (NIAS) in Wassenaar, who helped to gather much of the material discussed in this book, when Paul Emmelkamp was a fellow at the NIAS. In addition, preparation of this book was facilitated by Grant 31000016 from Zon-Mw (Health Research). Finally, a married co-authorship has the advantage and disadvantage of being able to discuss the material 24 hours a day. We thank Lotte, Esther, and Julie for keeping each other busy and providing the necessary amounts of coffee.

CHAPTER 1

Description of Substance Abuse and Dependence

PHENOMENOLOGY

The purpose of this chapter is to provide an overview and a synthesis of the information available on the clinical picture of substance-use disorders, the epidemiology of these disorders, comorbidity with other mental disorders, and current etiological models. Further, we will describe the course of these disorders and the detrimental consequences associated with chronic substance abuse. Finally, we will provide an overview of diagnostic measures that are relevant for clinical practice.

Research into substance-use disorders has increased enormously over the last decade, particularly in the field of brain chemistry. It would be impossible to explore all these issues within a single chapter. Rather than inundating our readers with a list of all the current controversies in the field, we have chosen to write a fair and balanced overview of the current state of research. This is intended to assist practitioners in understanding the problems of substance abusers and in diagnosing and planning treatment for their patients.

In recent years, the term *addiction* has been popularized to refer to any kind of compulsive behavior such as pathological gambling, sex addiction, Internet addiction, work addiction, and compulsive eating. Although some of the issues discussed here are also relevant to non-substance-abusing addictions, we limit our scope to substance abuse and substance dependence. Moreover, since we target clinicians working in addiction centers and mental health centers, we will limit our discussion to those kinds of substance abuse and dependence that are primarily seen in these settings, such as the abuse of alcohol, opioids, cocaine, amphetamine, party drugs, and cannabis.

A Description of the Clinical Picture

In contrast to common perceptions, substance-use disorders are seen in people from all layers of society. Substance abuse is not restricted to the homeless, the poor, or the destitute. People from all walks of life can become addicted to substances, although certain substances are more likely to be (ab)used by the middle and upper classes (e.g., party drugs), while others are more likely to be popular among the lower classes of the society (e.g., heroin, crack cocaine). In the United States, 1.6 million people with full-time jobs are heavy alcohol and drug users (Substance Abuse and Mental Health Services Administration, 2004). Likewise, there are many well-known citizens including film stars, pop stars, politicians, and Nobel Prize winners who have acknowledged that they had a substance-use disorder at some time.

Substance-Use Disorders: Abuse and Dependence

The system laid down in the fourth revised edition of the *Diagnostic and Statistical Manual of Mental Disorders*, or *DSM-IV-TR* (American Psychiatric Association, 2000), distinguishes substance abuse from substance dependence and focuses on the maladaptive patterns of use leading to clinical significant impairment, and not on actual quantities and frequencies of use.

The *DSM-IV-TR* lists specific criteria that, if met, warrant the diagnosis of substance abuse (See table 1.1). It is striking that fulfillment of only one criterion is sufficient to warrant the diagnosis; extraordinarily, this means that a student who skips class several times because of a hangover meets the *DSM-IV-TR* criteria for such a diagnosis.

TABLE 1.1   *DSM-IV-TR* Criteria for Substance Abuse

A. A maladaptive pattern of substance use leading to clinically significant impairment or distress, as manifested by one (or more) of the following, occurring within a 12-month period:
1. Recurrent substance use resulting in a failure to fulfill major role obligations at work, school, or home.
2. Recurrent substance use in situations in which this is physically hazardous.
3. Recurrent substance-related legal problems.
4. Continued substance use despite having persistent or recurrent social or interpersonal problems caused or exacerbated by the effects of the substance.

B. Symptoms do not fit the criteria for substance dependence for a particular class of substance.

TABLE 1.2   *DSM-IV-TR* Criteria for Substance Dependence

A. A maladaptive pattern of substance use, leading to clinically significant impairment or distress, as manifested by three (or more) of the following, occurring at any time within a 12-month period:
   1. Tolerance, as defined by either of the following:
      a. A need for markedly increased amounts of the substance to achieve intoxication or desired effect.
      b. Markedly diminished effect with continued use of the same amount of the substance.
   2. Withdrawal, as manifested by either of the following:
      a. The characteristic withdrawal syndrome for the substance (criteria sets for withdrawal are listed separately for specific substances).
      b. The same (or a closely related) substance is taken to relieve or avoid withdrawal symptoms.
   3. The substance is often taken in larger amounts or over a longer period than was intended.
   4. There is a persistent desire or unsuccessful effort to cut down or control substance use.
   5. A great deal of time is spent in activities necessary to obtain the substance (for example, visiting multiple doctors or driving long distances), use the substance (for example, chain-smoking), or recover from its effects.
   6. Important social, occupational, or recreational activities are given up or reduced because of substance use.
   7. The substance use is continued despite knowledge of having a persistent or recurrent physical or psychological problem that is likely to have been caused or exacerbated by the substance (for example, current cocaine use despite recognition of cocaine-induced depression, or continued drinking despite recognition that a ulcer was made worse by alcohol consumption).

According to the *DSM-IV-TR*, an essential characteristic of substance dependence is a cluster of cognitive, behavioral, and physiological symptoms indicating that the individual continues to use a particular substance despite significant substance-related problems. The formal criteria for substance dependence are listed in table 1.2.

Since only three endorsements are required, it is possible for a person to meet the current diagnostic criteria for substance dependence without having any physical symptoms of dependence (tolerance and/or withdrawal). However, continued heavy substance use is often associated with the development of tolerance and withdrawal. The intensity of response to a substance often diminishes as the same dose is administered repeatedly. As this tolerance develops, increasing doses are needed to produce the same desired effects. Substances that produce tolerance often produce, more or less synchronically, withdrawal as well. The withdrawal symptoms of the various substances vary greatly but usually include physical reactions such as nausea, sweating, palpitations, and cravings for the withdrawn substance. Consequently, many theoretical models have suggested that drug tolerance and withdrawal symptoms are both manifestations of a common underlying mechanism. The two effects both stem from the same general homeostatic system that underlies physiological adaptation.

Different substances are associated with various degrees of tolerance. Furthermore, not all drugs produce the physical dependence syndromes of tolerance and withdrawal. Individuals using alcohol and heroin as well as those who make *heavy* use of cocaine often develop substantial levels of tolerance. On the other hand, amphetamines and hallucinogens do not appear to produce such physiological dependence and withdrawal signs.

The severity of the dependence is an important factor in evaluating the disorder, as it can be important in determining the appropriate level of care. For example, in the case of heavy binge drinking and cocaine use three times per week, outpatient counseling may be sufficient. On the other hand, in the case of heavy daily alcohol use and the presence of high levels of tolerance and withdrawal symptoms, specialized treatment including medically supervised detoxification will be necessary.

The criteria for substance abuse described above are problematic in that the direction between substance-use disorders is one way. Someone who is defined as a substance abuser can go on to develop behavior that warrants the label *substance dependence*, which often happens. However, someone having been classified as substance dependent cannot ever again merely be classified as a substance abuser. Clearly, the disease model of substance abuse, which holds that a substance-dependent person cannot recover from dependency, influences this: once dependent, always dependent (Blume, 2004). However, epidemiological data indicate that many of those who at one point were classified as meeting the criteria for substance dependence in fact go back to what should only be classed as substance abuse. For example, users of alcohol can alternate periods of heavy drinking with periods of abstinence or controlled social drinking.

Individuals can become psychologically dependent on a substance without developing physiological dependence. Physical dependence is related to physical changes that allow tolerance to build up and cause withdrawal symptoms. In contrast, psychological dependence is related to the need to use substances for psychological needs—for example, relying on alcohol or drugs to cope with stress. In clinical practice, it is often difficult to distinguish between physical and psychological dependence, as in many patients these processes are interdependent.

Alcohol

In early theories on addiction, it was believed that once addicted to alcohol, individuals were unlikely to be able to control their drinking and were at great risk of dying from medical complications. These pessimistic views were based on evidence from alcoholics seen in clinical settings who were unable to stop drinking of their own accord. Drinking until severely intoxicated (loss-of-control drinking) is an important concept in the disease model of substance abuse. According to this disease model, the ingestion by alcoholics of even a small amount of alcohol triggers a physical demand for alcohol that overwhelms their ability to control subsequent drinking. This is expressed by the Alcoholics Anonymous slogan, "One drink, one drunk." There are no epidemiological arguments to suggest that the loss-of-control drinking model is widely applicable. There is evidence that former heavy drinkers are quite able to become social drinkers or controlled drinkers (Vaillant, 1996). In other words, one single drink does not inevitably lead to loss-of-control drinking in former heavy drinkers. Moreover, extensive epidemiological community studies have shown that many individuals who drink heavily do not develop alcohol dependence.

The effects of alcohol on alcohol nonabusers are directly associated with blood alcohol concentration (BAC) levels. Mild euphoria is usually felt at levels of 30 mg/dl. At higher BAC levels, intoxicated individuals may experience "black-outs"—that is, an inability to remember what occurred during the drinking period. In general, the same intake in units of alcohol will result in a higher BAC level in females than in males. This is not only related to a difference in body weight, but is also primarily attributed to the female body being less effective in breaking down ethanol. Even after relatively low doses of alcohol, withdrawal symptoms (such as a "hangover") are common. In alcohol-dependent persons, seizures may occur during withdrawal of alcohol. Chronic alcohol consumption leads to adaptive changes in the brain, which presumably are related to the development of tolerance, withdrawal, and dependence and alcohol abuse can lead to substance-induced anxiety and depressive symptoms. These symptoms usually disappear within a few weeks after abstinence.

Two alcohol dependence subtypes have been defined in the literature, described as types A and B (Babor et al., 1992) and types 1 and 2 (Cloninger, Sigvardson, & Bohman, 1996), respectively. Although there are some differences between both typologies, there is evidence that overall, indeed two types of alcoholics can be distinguished. One type (type 1/type A) is characterized by later onset, less severe dependence, fewer childhood risk factors, and less psychiatric impairment. In contrast, familial alcoholism, early onset, greater severity of dependence, multiple childhood risk factors, and higher incidence of antisocial personality traits characterize the other type of alcoholics (type 2/type B). It is thought that the latter type may be more genetically determined than the former.

Another clinically important distinction is between continuous drinkers and those who drink excessive amounts of alcohol periodically. Some people regularly drink the same amount of alcohol each day while others are indulged in frequent periods of binge drinking alternated with moderate or even no alcohol use in between these periods.

Cannabis

The term *cannabis* refers to marijuana as well as hashish. Marijuana is a combination of chopped-up dried flowering tops, leaves, and stems of the hemp plant, or *Cannabis sativa*. Hashish is the brown or black resin from the flowering tops of the same plant, shaped into small rocks. Cannabis is usually smoked, and inhalation produces a state of relaxation and mild euphoria often accompanied by heightened perceptual acuity and intensified sensory inputs. These effects can last up to three hours after taking the drug. The active ingredient in cannabis is delta-9-tetrahydro-cannabinol (THC). The effects of cannabis vary greatly depending on the dose and the quality of the drug as well as the users' experience with cannabis and their expectancy about the effects of the drug. It is increasingly being acknowledged that cannabis it is not a safe recreational drug as it was once thought to be. A clinical perception that cannabis use is harmless may be based on lack of knowledge about recent developments in the potency of marijuana. Currently, cannabis contains much higher levels of THC compared to twenty years ago and data indicate a substantial increase in the potency (concentration) of THC in marijuana since the early 1990s (ElSohly et al., 2000). Smoking cannabis can increase the heart rate and has been associated with an increased risk of heart attack.

Although the *DSM-IV-TR* does not mention cannabis withdrawal, there is increasing evidence that it is associated with restlessness, irritability, anger, and sleep problems. Budney, Hughes, Moore, and Vandrey (2004) recently proposed diagnostic criteria for cannabis withdrawal syndrome. Ten percent of people who start using cannabis will develop dependence, and frequent use is associated with a higher risk of dependence. Long-term use of cannabis damages short-term memory. The use of cannabis is sometimes associated with violence, but less frequently so than alcohol (Dawkins, 1997). Common street names for cannabis are *grass*, *herb*, *skuck*, and *weed*.

Opioids

Opiates are a subclass of opioids that are alkaloids extracted from opium. Besides heroin, commonly abused opiates include morphine and codeine. Heroin use leads to immediate feelings of euphoria, a "rush," accompanied by a warm flushing of the skin, dry mouth, and a heavy feeling in the user's arms and legs. Effects appear within 10 seconds when injected, but take slightly longer (10–15 minutes) to be felt when smoked or inhaled (snorted). Chronic heroin use produces tolerance and withdrawal symptoms. In multiple substance users, cocaine use is often related to continued use of heroin (see, e.g., Pérez, Trujols, Ribalta et al., 1997). Street names for heroin include *smack*, *H*, *skag*, and *junk*.

Cocaine

Cocaine is usually taken by inhalation though the nose (snorting) but can also be dissolved in water and injected. Cocaine produces euphoric effects after a few minutes, and this lasts from 15 to 30 minutes. Small amounts of cocaine make people energetic, and talkative, which explains why it sometimes is described as an "antidepressant" drug. Larger amounts of cocaine intensify euphoria but can also induce anxiety, restlessness, bizarre aggressive behavior, and paranoia. The smokable form of cocaine is called *crack cocaine*, and gets its name from the crackling sound it makes when it's smoked. Crack cocaine produces a more rapid and intense "high" lasting from 5 to 10 minutes, sometimes described as orgasmic. Following a period of intense euphoria an unpleasant period of restlessness, hyperarousal, and insomnia is accompanied with craving (high desire) for more cocaine and often leads to use of sedating agents such as alcohol, heroin, or sedatives or hypnotics to counteract these effects (Rounsaville, 2004).

Dependence takes longer to develop if cocaine is snorted, whereas if smoked or injected the drug can lead to dependence within months or even weeks. Some time ago, it was held that tolerance was not an aspect of cocaine abuse. It has become increasingly clear that tolerance and withdrawal, the latter typically characterized by symptoms of depression, fatigue, and disturbed sleep, are also associated with prolonged cocaine use. It is currently considered that heavy use will result in tolerance.

Common street names for cocaine are *coke, C, snow, flake, white lady, blow, candy,* and *Charlie.* Crack cocaine goes by the names *freebase, rock, gravel,* and *Roxanne.* Cocaine or crack combined with heroin, or crack and heroin smoked together, is called a *speedball.*

Methamphetamine

Methamphetamine is a powerful stimulant that can be smoked, snorted, orally ingested, or injected. An intense rush is felt at varying times depending on how taken: immediately if smoked or injected, after 5 minutes if snorted, and after 20 minutes if taken orally. The effects of methamphetamine can last up to 12 hours. Chronic methamphetamine use can result in cardiovascular problems including increased blood pressure and increased risk of stroke. An overdose can lead to convulsions and hyperthermia that are fatal if not treated immediately.

Methamphetamine is commonly known on the streets as *speed, meth, chalk,* and *Tina.* In its smokable form, it's often called *ice, crystal, crank, glass, fire,* and *go fast.*

Ecstasy

Ecstasy (3,4-methylenedioxymethamphetamine, or, more commonly, MDMA) is a stimulant with psychedelic effects. It is taken orally, and its effects last up to six hours. Ecstasy is often used at all-night dance events called "raves" so that the user is able to dance for longer periods of time. The psychological side effects of ecstasy use include anxiety, depression, confusion, and paranoia. Potentially dangerous physical effects include increased heart rate and blood pressure, heart and kidney failure, hyperthermia, and dehydration, all of which can be fatal under certain circumstances. However, only a small proportion of drug-related emergency admissions are ecstasy related. In animals, administration of Ecstasy has been found to be associated with a significant depletion in the neurotransmitters serotonin, dopamine, and norepinephrine. Repeated systemic administration of MDMA leads to widespread degeneration of presynaptic serotonergic axon terminals resulting in low levels of serotonin and its major metabolites and low densities of serotonin reuptake sites throughout the brain. There is growing evidence that these toxic effects may also occur in humans (Green, Mechan, Elliott, O'Shea, &

Colado, 2003). Presumably, these processes cause damage to parts of the brain associated with thought and memory processes. A number of studies demonstrate low memory performance in ecstasy users (Gouzoulis-Mayfrank et al., 2005). Some other street names for MDMA/ecstasy are *XTC*, *Eve*, and *A'dam*.

Hallucinogens

The most common forms of hallucinogens are LSD (lysergic acid diethylamide), psilocybin (the active ingredient in "magic mushrooms"), and mescaline. The most common effects from hallucinogens are feelings of euphoria and altered auditive and visual perceptions, which usually, but not always, are experienced as pleasant. LSD is also referred to as *acid*, *boomers*, and *yellow sunshine*.

Polydrug Use

Drug users often use a combination of alcohol and/or drugs. This is often to counter the unpleasant side effects or withdrawal symptoms of one drug by using another. Experienced chronic substance abusers know from experience and advice from other users how to combine and phase their drug intake to achieve optimal positive effects. For example, they may start with crack cocaine in order to get a rapid kick and then follow this with heroin to alleviate the low and depressed feelings that follow. Alcohol is often used to enhance the effects of amphetamines and cocaine and may be used by heroin users when heroin is unavailable.

EPIDEMIOLOGY

The National Epidemiologic Survey on Alcohol and Related Conditions (NESARC) and the National Household Survey on Drug Abuse are large epidemiological studies in the United States that examine the problems of alcohol and drug abuse. The Epidemiologic Catchment Area Study and the National Comorbidity Survey (NCS) are large U.S. community studies that address the prevalence of mental disorders, including substance-use disorders. Most of the epidemiological data discussed here are taken from these large community studies.

The NESARC (Grant, Stinson et al., 2004) found 12-month prevalence rates of 2% for drug-use disorders and 8.5% for alcohol use disorders. In 2002, 9.4% of the U.S. population were substance abusers or substance dependent, of which 1.4% involved drug and alcohol dependence/abuse, 1.7% drug dependence/abuse, and 6.4% alcohol dependence/abuse (Substance Abuse and Mental Health Services Administration, 2002).

Alcohol

The lifetime prevalence of alcohol dependence is generally three times as high among males than among females. In the United States, the average person of 14 years or older consumes 2.77 gallons of absolute alcohol annually. Binge drinking, usually defined as five or more alcoholic drinks in a row, is a common form of alcohol abuse and is associated with many health and social problems. Binge drinking among individuals of 18 years or older is estimated at between 14.7% and 21.6%. Young men with low self-esteem, who drink primarily for oblivion, are particularly at risk of becoming binge drinkers.

Cannabis

Cannabis is the most commonly used illicit drug. In the United States, cannabis accounts for 75% of all illicit drug use, but this is not reflected in the number of admissions to addiction treatment centers. In 2002, 40% of Americans over the age of 12 had used cannabis at some time in their life and 11% of Americans had used it in the past year.

Cocaine

Cocaine use in the United States has been a widespread problem. In 1982, 8.5% of adults and 28% of adolescents used cocaine. Although the use of cocaine declined in the United States after 1985, cocaine dependence continues to be a problem. The use of crack cocaine became more common around 1986 and its use is still on the rise. Based on the National House Survey on Drug Abuse, cocaine addiction continues to be an important health problem, with an estimated 1.7 million cocaine users in the United States (Substance Abuse and Mental Health Services Administration, 2002). In Europe, the prevalence of cocaine use and dependence is much lower than in the United States, the United Kingdom having the highest rate (Haasen et al., 2004). Cocaine is typically used in the context of the party scene; opiate addicts often use it as a secondary drug to counter the side effects of opioid use.

Methamphetamine

The widespread availability of amphetamines has made this a popular drug in the United States. In 2002, over 5% of people over the age of 12 reported that they had used methamphetamine at least once. The use of methamphetamine in the last year has been estimated as: 0.9% of 12- to 17-year-olds, 1.7% of 18- to 25-year-olds, and 0.4% of those 26 years and older.

Opioids

It is estimated that 1.4% of people in the United States over the age of 12 have used heroin at least once in their lifetime (National Survey on Drug Use and Health, 2001). However, heroin use is mainly restricted to a small group of habitual drug abusers. Nevertheless, there is reason for concern since the initiation of new drug users under adolescents was rising in 1999 and reached its highest level since the early 1970s. Further, a steady increase in emergency department referrals associated with heroin use has been seen in the past decade.

Polydrug use

Epidemiological and clinical studies reveal that many individuals use multiple substances. In samples of users from the community, a combination of alcohol and cannabis was the most common. In clinical samples the use of multiple substances is even more common. In opioid-dependent individuals, accompanying cocaine dependence is the most prevalent current and lifetime substance-use disorder, followed by alcohol and cannabis dependence.

COMORBID PSYCHIATRIC DISORDERS

Comorbidity, or *dual diagnosis*, refers to the coexistence of two or more mental disorders. In the current context, it is used to describe the co-occurrence of substance-use disorders on the one hand and other mental disorders (including personality disorders) on the other. The presence of comorbid psychiatric disorders in substance-using populations has been increasingly recognized. Dual diagnosis of mental and substance-use disorders are common in clinical studies (Mertens, Lu, Parthasarathy, Moore, & Weisner, 2003) and community samples (Grant et al.,

2004; Kessler et al., 1996; Regier et al., 1990), but is highly prevalent among specific populations such as those of inmates and the homeless. Approximately half of the individuals in the community with a lifetime alcohol- or drug-use disorder also meet criteria for at least one other lifetime mental disorder, while about half of individuals with a lifetime mental disorder also have a history of alcohol or drug abuse or dependence. Studies of clinically referred samples reveal even higher rates (50–90%) of comorbidity of substance-use disorders and other psychiatric disorders. Thus, in clinical cases, comorbidity is the rule rather than the exception and is a pervasive clinical problem. Clinicians regularly encounter cases in which substance abuse should be an important factor in diagnosis and treatment, but in mental health settings many fail to recognize these disorders.

In the general population, substance-use disorders are especially prevalent in adults with antisocial personality disorder, bipolar I disorder, and schizophrenia, and less so in depression or anxiety disorders (Regier et al., 1990). Multiple comorbidity is an especially strong predictor of substance abuse, and persons with three or more psychiatric disorders are 14 times more likely to be drug dependent than persons without these diagnoses. In substance-abusing adolescents, high rates of co-occurrent psychiatric disorders have been reported, of which conduct disorder (32%-59%) and mood disorder (35%-61%) are the most prevalent. Other less prevalent disorders include anxiety disorders and attention deficit hyperactivity disorder, or ADHD (Wise, Cuffe, & Fischer, 2001).

Most people with dual diagnoses report the onset of substance-use disorder later than the onset of other mental disorders. Prospective studies confirm this temporal order, but with some mental disorders (e.g., anxiety and depression) the risk relationship is reciprocal, with these mental disorders predicting increased risk of later substance abuse, and vice versa.

In the 1990s, 40% of adults with co-occurring mental and substance-use disorders received some treatment in the health care sector (Kessler et al., 1996). Generally, patients with both substance disorders and other mental disorders are more persistent and severe (Brady, Krebs, & Laird, 2004; Brady, Rierdan, Peck, Losardo, & Meschede, 2003; Margolese, Malchy, Negrete, Tempier, & Gill, 2004), and have less positive treatment outcome and prognosis (Ouimette, Gima, Moos, & Finney, 1999) as compared to patients with only one disorder. The risk of suicide is very high among persons with co-occurring mental and substance-use disorders, especially for individuals with bipolar disorder (Dalton, Cate-Carter, Mundo, Parikh, & Kennedy, 2003; Kelly, Cornelius, & Lynch, 2002).

Etiological Models for Comorbidity

A number of etiological models for comorbidity have been introduced. Generally, three etiological pathways can be distinguished to explain the comorbidity between substance-abuse disorders and other mental disorders, which have clear implications for treatment planning.

The first pathway assumes that common causes, either genetic or environmental, lead to the onset of both types of disorder. Regarding genetic cause, in a study by Kendler, Prescott, Myers, and Neale (2003) who analyzed comorbidity in twin pairs, separate internalizing (major depression, generalized anxiety disorder, phobia) and externalizing (conduct disorder, antisocial personality disorder, alcohol dependence, drug abuse and dependence) genetic factors explained most of the comorbidity of individual disorders.

As for the common environmental factor, physical and sexual abuse is common in substance abuse and in many mental disorders as well (see, e.g., Langeland, Draijer, & van den Brink, 2004). Two-thirds of all women and over a quarter of all men entering addiction treatment report a history of sexual or physical abuse (Pirard, Sharon, Kang, Angarita, & Gastfriend, 2005). High rates of abuse have also been reported in anxiety disorders, borderline personality disorder, and schizophrenia.

The second pathway, that of alternative causal models, holds that mental disorders lead to the onset and/or persistence of substance-use disorders. A few examples are listed below.

In *impulse-control disorders*, as antisocial and borderline personality disorder, disinhibition to experiment with drugs might lead to substance abuse.

In the case of *conduct disorder*, subsequent substance abuse might be accounted for by increased exposure to drug use.

Patients may use substances to regulate *anxiety* and/or *mood*. This self-medication model holds that patients use specific substances to alleviate specific symptoms. It has been suggested that particular kinds of mental disorders are associated with particular kinds of substances, such as mood disorders with substances that have antidepressant effects, and anxiety disorders and schizophrenia with substances that have anxiolytic effects, thus representing attempts to self-medicate mental disorders. A study addressing this issue, however (Aharonovich et al., 2001), did not find a strong match between type of mental disorder and type of drug used.

In the third pathway, according to the toxicity hypothesis, alcohol- and drug-use disorders are viewed as causing the comorbid mental disorders. For example, cannabis use may induce panic or mood disorder, or heavy cocaine use may have brain-kindling effects that cause panic attacks. This causal relationship can also be indirect; for instance, divorce as result of alcoholism could induce the onset of a major depressive episode.

The models discussed above implicitly assume that causality is one-directional. In clinical practice, substance abuse may be both a cause and a consequence of another mental disorder, and a mental disorder may be both a cause and a consequence of substance abuse, thus creating a vicious circle. In individual cases, multiple pathways of association between substance abuse and other mental disorders might be acting simultaneously in both directions.

Substance Abuse and Psychosis

Substance-use disorders are extremely prevalent among persons with the most disabling psychiatric conditions. The lifetime prevalence of substance abuse or dependence in psychotic disorders is about 40–60% (see, e.g., Regier et al., 1990). Comorbidity of substance abuse and psychosis is associated with being male, single, and of younger age, and with conduct disorder or antisocial personality disorder (Kavanagh et al., 2004). Generally, individuals with psychosis tend to have poly-substance abuse and dependence. Substance-use disorders are especially prevalent in persons with schizophrenia (Kavanagh et al., 2004; Regier et al., 1990). Given their vulnerabilities, it does not come as a surprise that many of them became addicted to drugs and alcohol, which are often used as self-medication.

Case Example

Arnold, a 32-year-old male diagnosed with schizophrenia, was referred to our clinic after he, induced by the use of alcohol and illicit drugs, had experienced a psychotic episode during which he tried to commit suicide by setting himself on fire. After being detoxified and prescribed antipsychotic medication, Arnold was discharged from the clinic and offered treatment on an outpatient basis. Although aware of the negative effects of alcohol and drugs on his condition, Arnold was reluctant to give them up. Walking the streets and using alcohol and drugs together with other users was the only way he knew how to engage in some form of social interaction, to counter his feelings of isolation and loneliness.

Exposure to cannabis use (and especially heavy use) during adolescence and young adulthood increases the risk of psychotic symptoms later in life (Arsenault, Cannon, Witton, & Murray, 2004; Smit, Bolier, & Cuijpers, 2004; Macleod et al., 2004). As many as 15% of cannabis users report psychotic symptoms directly after use. However, transient psychotic reactions to cannabis have to be differentiated from psychotic disorders such as schizophrenia. We do not know whether cannabis causes psychosis. An alternative hypothesis is that (pre-)psychotic patients use cannabis for self-medication, which would imply that those with a predisposition for psychosis are particularly at risk. A number of recent studies investigated prospectively whether cannabis use, at baseline, increases the risk of subsequent development of psychotic symptoms. Cannabis use in young people moderately increased the risk of developing psychotic symptoms. The risk for the onset of symptoms was much higher for those who began use at an early age and with a predisposition for psychosis. Frequent use of cannabis was associated with higher levels of risk in a dose-response relationship. A Munich study (Henquet et al., 2005) showed that predisposition psychosis at baseline did not predict cannabis use at follow-up. This refutes the self-medication hypothesis, which suggests that individuals turn to cannabis use in order to relieve psychotic distress.

Thus, it seems that cannabis use primarily precipitates psychosis in those who are at increased risk, but it still cannot be ruled out that cannabis use causes psychotic disorders in people who would not have developed a disorder in the absence of cannabis use. Finally, Van Nimwegen, De Haan, Van Beveren, Van Den Brink, and Linszen (2005) have suggested that adolescence is a period with specific changes in the brain that increases the probability of the onset of both psychosis and substance abuse in vulnerable adolescents.

Substance Abuse and Anxiety Disorders

High comorbidity rates have been found both in community and clinical studies for anxiety disorders and substance abuse, especially alcohol abuse (Grant et al., 2004). In the NCS study (Kessler et al., 1997), 35.8% of males diagnosed with alcohol dependence also met the criteria for a comorbid anxiety disorder, as opposed to 60.7% of females. In alcoholic patients seeking treatment, Schneider, Altmann, Baumann, and Bernzen (2001) found an overall rate of 42.3% with anxiety disorders. The most prevalent were social phobia (14%), agoraphobia (13%), and panic disorder (5%). Substance-abusing patients with anxiety disorders abuse alcohol, benzodiazepines, cocaine, and cannabis, and many of these comorbid patients report a history of emotional and physical abuse (Schade et al., 2004). In a study on treatment-seeking alcoholics, childhood abuse was associated with post-traumatic stress disorder, social phobia, and agoraphobia (Langeland et al., 2004).

Anxiety disorders often predate alcohol- or drug-use disorders (Kessler, 2004; Merikangas Mehta et al., 1998; Schade et al., 2004). Among female alcoholics, substance abuse secondary to phobia is particularly common, with over 30% of all female alcoholics reporting an earlier phobia (Helzer & Pryzbeck, 1988). However, in a number of cases the risk relationship is reciprocal, with anxiety disorders predicting increased risk of later substance abuse, and vice versa. Many individuals endorse the belief that alcohol reduces anxiety. Secondary substance abuse in anxiety disorder patients may be attributed to anxiety that promotes the use of alcohol and drugs as a form of self-medication. Substance abuse as self-medication is prevalent among patients with agoraphobia and social phobia. Many individuals use alcohol or drugs as self-medication, which is confirmed by studies showing peak substance use on high-stress days. Further, a number of studies have shown anxious people to be more likely than others to report using alcohol as a means of coping with social stress (Carrigan & Randall, 2003). Symptoms of anxiety and panic are common after heavy drinking and during withdrawal and should be distinguished from primary anxiety disorders.

Although panic attacks and other anxiety symptoms are also common among cannabis users, studies have not yet addressed the association between cannabis use and anxiety disorders. Cocaine abusers have an increased risk of panic disorder (Anthony, Tien, & Petronis, 1989). Patients dependent on heroin or cocaine have been found to have more often social phobia than individuals in the general population (Zimmerman et al., 2004).

Case Example

Bert, a 54-year-old electrician, was referred to an addiction treatment center by his general practitioner because of alcohol dependence. Bert was not very happy about this referral. For the past five months he had contacted his GP repeatedly because of spontaneous, unexplainable attacks of palpitations, sweating, shortness of breath, and the sensation of fainting. Bert was afraid these were signs of an oncoming heart attack. However, instead of being referred to a hospital, Bert's GP referred him to a counselor.

High rates of comorbid post-traumatic stress disorder (PTSD) and substance abuse have been reported in a number of epidemiological studies. In a community sample of substance-abusing women (Stewart, Pihl, Conrod, & Dongier, 1998), about 42% reported histories of physical assault, and about 47% reported histories of sexual assault. In substance-use-disorder populations, rates of 30–58% have been reported for lifetime PTSD and 20–38% for current PTSD (Stewart, 1996). In the United Kingdom, 38.5% of substance-abusing inpatients met criteria for current PTSD (Reynolds et al., 2005). A number of explanations have been proposed to explain the co-occurrence of PTSD and substance-use disorder, of which three are plausible. First, the co-occurrence of substance-use disorder and PTSD may be accounted for by a third factor such as a common genetic pathway or early childhood trauma. Second, it is common for victims of violence to be under the influence of alcohol or drugs at the time of the attack, thus enhancing the risk for victimization. Third, alcohol and drugs may be used as self-medication to forget traumatic memories, to manage sleep disturbance, and to prevent nightmares. Most studies on order of onset suggest that exposure to traumatic events and PTSD symptoms indeed precede, rather than follow, the development of substance-use disorders (Stewart, 1996), thus supporting the self-medication hypothesis.

Substance Abuse and Mood Disorders

Major depression moderately predicts substance abuse. One in four persons with major depression is a substance abuser (Kessler, 2004). In studies on opioid abusers, major depression is the most common current and lifetime Axis I codiagnosis (see, e.g., Kidorf et al., 2004). The comorbidity of depression with drug-use disorders is typically stronger than with alcohol-use disorders. In epidemiological studies, depression is more strongly associated with substance dependence than substance abuse. The strongest association between depression and substance abuse is reported for amphetamine dependence (Swendsen & Merinkagas, 2000).

Although there is generally strong consensus that substance abuse and depression often co-occur, the direction of this relationship is still under debate. DelBello and Strakowski (2003) provided evidence for three etiological models to explain the association between substance-use disorders and mood disorders. Based on a comprehensive literature review they found support for the idea that mood disorders may be a cause of substance dependence, substance dependence may be a cause of mood disorders, and both disorders may share a common risk factor. Thus, substance-use disorder and depression are risk factors for each other.

As far as the relationship with specific substance-use disorders is concerned, there is slightly more support for the notion that alcoholism precedes depression than for the notion that depression precedes alcoholism. This point is illustrated in the work of Schuckit et al. (1997), which studied patients meeting criteria for co-occurrent alcohol dependence and major depressive disorder. In their study it was noted that about 60% of patients had an alcohol-induced mood disorder, whereas 40% experienced an independent major depressive episode. However, in opiate-dependent men, there is some evidence that mood (and anxiety) disorders more often precede substance abuse (Swendsen & Merinkagas, 2000).

Results with respect to comorbidity of major depression as a risk marker for substance abuse in adolescence are inconclusive. In an epidemiological survey, a progression from depression to substance abuse during the transition from adolescence to young adulthood was demonstrated (Lewinsohn, Rohde, Seeley, Klein, & Gotlib, 2000). Comorbidity with major depressive disorder did not act as a predictor for substance abuse in the Cornelius et al. (2004) study. In the Cornelius et al. study, however, negative affect was cited by subjects as one reason for relapse to drug abuse. Further, early marijuana use predicts subsequent major depression and may be associated with an increase in suicidal ideation, especially among adolescents (Rey, Martin, & Krabman, 2004). On the other hand, continued substance abuse on its own may lead to depression as well, thus creating a vicious circle.

Substance-use disorders are especially prevalent in persons with bipolar I disorder, of whom 61% either abuse or are dependent on substances (Regier et al., 1990). In this large epidemiologic study, individuals with bipolar disorder had the highest lifetime rates of alcohol use (46%) and drug use (41%) disorders of individuals with Axis I disorders. Similar results were found in the more recent NCS study. Only the comorbidity rate of substance-abuse disorders and antisocial personality disorder was higher. In patients with bipolar disorders, 14–65% had lifetime substance-use disorders (Sherwood Brown, Suppes, Adinoff, & Rajan Thomas, 2001). Substance abuse has been associated with an earlier age of onset of bipolar disorder and more severe subtypes of bipolar disorder, such as rapid cycling, dysphoric, and mixed states and increased risk of suicide (Levin & Hennessy, 2004). Bipolar disorder often predates alcohol- or drug-use disorders (Merikangas, Mehta, et al., 1998; Kessler 2004. A genetic linkage between substance dependence and bipolar and antisocial personality disorder has been proposed (Winokur et al., 1995; Kendler, Jacobson, Prescott, & Neale, 2003).

Substance Abuse and Borderline Personality Disorder

Given the defining characteristics of borderline personality disorder, which include self-damaging impulsivity (e.g., compulsive sex, substance abuse, binge eating), it does not come as a surprise that high comorbidity has been reported between borderline personality disorder and substance abuse. The median reported prevalence rates of substance-abuse disorder in borderline patients is 67% and the median prevalence rate of borderline personality disorder within substance-abuse populations is 18% (Van den Bosch et al., 2001). Additionally, individuals diagnosed with borderline personality disorder are likely to initiate substance use and abuse at a younger age than nonborderline individuals, resulting in more severe substance-use disorders (i.e., more severe physical dependence) and more adverse emotional and social consequences (Lejuez, Daughters, Rosenthal, & Lynch, 2005).

Case Example

> Helene, a 37-year-old woman who taught history at a university, entered an inpatient addiction treatment program after a failed suicide attempt (alcohol in combination with sleeping pills). Helene had been using cannabis on a daily basis for years and during weekends drank between 20 and 30 units of alcohol after her boyfriend broke off their relationship; she decided—in an impulse—to quit her job. However, in the days after, panicking about the consequences of having quit, she started drinking heavily and tried to kill herself.

Although the exact factors underlying the etiology and course of borderline personality disorder are unknown, it is generally held that borderline personality disorder is the result of both biological vulnerabilities and environmental stressors (e.g., emotional and physical abuse, or sexual trauma). It is hypothesized that shared etiological factors may account for the high comorbidity between borderline personality disorder and substance-use disorders, including impulse disinhibition and adverse family upbringing (Trull, Sher, Minks-Brown, Durbin, & Burr, 2000).

A genetic/biological predisposition to impulsivity and a family history of mood disorders and impulsivity are important etiological factors in both substance-use disorders and borderline personality disorders, and are likely candidates to account for this comorbidity. Indeed, impulsivity consistently has been shown to be a biologically based, heritable characteristic with emergent psychological properties linked to the development and maintenance of borderline personality disorder and substance abuse (Lejuez et al., 2005). A second possible pathway to comorbidity of substance-use disorder and borderline personality disorder may be due to a history of (persistent) traumatic childhood experiences (i.e., physical and sexual abuse), which may lead to self-harm (Tyler, Whitbeck, Hoyt, & Johnson, 2003) and substance use (McClanahan, McClelland, Abram, & Teplin, 1999). For these individuals, self-harm and substance abuse may serve as a coping strategy to deal with negative feelings.

Substance Abuse and Antisocial Personality Disorder

There is an extremely high comorbidity between substance abuse and antisocial personality disorder, higher than with any other mental disorder. In the NCS community study, the odds ratios for comorbidity between antisocial personality disorder and substance-use and drug-use disorders were 11.3 and 11.5, respectively. Also, in the epidemiological data from the NESARC reported by Grant et al. (2004), substance-use disorders were highly related to antisocial personality disorder. As in the case of borderline personality disorder, this is partly due to the defining characteristics of antisocial personality disorder, including impulsivity and reckless disregard for safety of self or others. Comorbid alcoholism is much more often found to be primary and associated with antisocial personality disorder among men (Hesselbrock, Hesselbrock, & Workman-Daniels, 1986; Roy et al., 1991).

Substance Abuse and Childhood Disorders

To some extent, nearly all childhood psychiatric disorders are associated with substance abuse in adulthood, the prevalence being particularly high in externalizing and in mood disorder. Of adolescents applying for treatment of substance abuse, 35% have a comorbid externalizing disorder, conduct disorder being the most common disorder, followed by ADHD (Rowe, Liddle, Greenbaum, & Henderson, 2004).

Generally, conduct disorder precedes alcohol abuse (see, e.g., Kellam, Brown, Rubin, & Ensminger, 1983). This might be due to specific risk factors (e.g., impulse dysregulation) or to easy exposure to drug-use opportunities. Longitudinal studies show that cannabis use in early childhood is a predictor of later conduct problems. There is no evidence that ADHD—in the absence of conduct disorder—increases the risk of drug use (Kim-Cohen et al., 2003). In ADHD in adults, there is an increased risk of substance-use disorders when compared to the general population (Wilens, Biederman, & Mick, 1998).

ETIOLOGY

There exists a range of theoretical explanations for substance abuse and dependence. One of many ways of broadly categorizing these explanations is by distinguishing genetic and neurobiological models, classic learning models and craving, and personality and cognitive social learning models. Each of the models proposes a way of understanding substance abuse, and focuses primarily on how substance abuse and dependence develops.

Genetic Vulnerability

Although psychological researchers have tended to emphasize the social and cultural influence on familial transmission of substance dependence, there is growing evidence that individuals may inherit increased vulnerability to develop substance dependence. The most convincing information concerning the role of genetics in substance dependence is available with respect to alcohol.

A number of studies suggest that substance dependence runs in families. Merinkagas, Stolar et al. (1998) found that relatives of individuals with an alcohol disorder (abuse or dependence) were more than twice as likely to be diagnosed with an alcohol disorder as compared to relatives of nonabusing control patients. Similarly, Nurnberger et al. (2004) found a twofold increased risk of alcohol dependence in relatives of alcohol-dependent individuals. About one-third of alcoholics have at least one parent who abuses alcohol and the risk of becoming an alcoholic is higher for males than for females: one out of four sons of alcoholic fathers is likely to become an alcoholic himself.

Family studies, however, do not allow us to distinguish between genetic and environmental influences. Studies of adoptees raised by nonalcoholic foster parents reveal that adopted boys whose biological fathers are alcoholics are just as much at risk of becoming alcoholic as boys who are raised by their alcoholic biological father. Twin studies have found that concordance rates for alcohol dependence are higher among monozygotic twins than among dizygotic twins. Heritability rates are the same for men and women, with approximately one-half to two-thirds of the variance accounted for by genetic factors (Knopik et al., 2004; Liu et al., 2004; McGue, 1999). Thus, there is substantial evidence that alcohol addiction has a clear genetic component, but this does not mean that other factors are not important. It should be stressed that the majority of children who have alcoholic parents do not themselves become alcoholic.

There is little evidence of a specific genetic component in other drug dependencies, although it is generally assumed that certain people are more susceptible to substance abuse in general (Hesselbrock, Hesselbrock, & Epstein, 1999). Neither Karkowski, Prescott, and Kendler (2000), nor Kendler Jacobson, Prescott, and Neale (2003) found evidence of specific substance abuse related to heritability. Environmental experiences unique to the person largely determine whether predisposed individuals will use one drug or another. Furthermore, the fact that many individuals are dependent on multiple substances makes it less likely that these people are genetically predisposed to being dependent on one specific substance.

Many theories have been put forward to explain what exactly is inherited, such as substance sensitivity (to, e.g., ethanol), heritable personality traits (e.g., novelty seeking, low harm-avoidance, impulsivity), vulnerability to substance-induced damage to the brain, deficit in brain neurotransmitters (e.g., serotonin, dopamine), or hyperexcitability in the central nervous system motivating substance abuse. For example, there is some evidence that the genetic influence may not just be limited to substance abuse, but could be a part of the genetic transmission of comorbid psychiatric disorders such as mood disorder and antisocial personality disorder (see, e.g., Kendler, Jacobson et al., 2003). In a U.S. military veteran male twin sample (Fu et al., 2002), the interrelationships among antisocial personality disorder, major depression, alcohol dependence, and cannabis dependence almost entirely reflected common genetic (rather than common environmental) effects. Genetic effects associated with antisocial personality disorder were a major determinant of the common genetic risk among depression, alcohol dependence, and cannabis dependence.

The Neurobiology of Addiction

Apart from genetic predisposition, other biological factors also play a significant role in the etiology and development of substance abuse. These include intrauterine exposure to substances because of maternal substance abuse, the biological mechanisms involved in developing drug tolerance (and its associated withdrawal symptoms), and the neurological effect of different substances on brain activity.

There is now substantial evidence that alcohol and drug use can create changes in brain chemistry and synaptic transmission. Substances (e.g., alcohol, cocaine, and heroin) produce pleasurable effects by increasing the concentration of dopamine in the brain. Such an increase is caused by the mesocorticolimbic dopamine pathway (the "pleasure pathway"), which is considered to be the center of psychoactive drug activation in the brain. There is now considerable evidence that the hippocampus (for learning and memory), the amygdala (for emotion regulation), and frontal cortical areas of the brain are affected by substance abuse. The orbitofrontal cortex and the anterior cingulate gyrus are the frontal cortical areas most frequently implicated in drug addiction. These regions are neuroanatomically connected with limbic structures, and studies have shown that they are activated in addicted subjects during intoxication, craving, and bingeing, and likewise they are deactivated during the process of withdrawal (Volkow et al., 2004).

Presumably, long-term substance use reduces the brain's ability to produce its own dopamine, which means that chronic drug users become increasingly reliant on drugs to experience feelings of pleasure. Normal activities are no longer sufficient to induce these feelings. The other groups of neurotransmitters involved in substance dependence are endorphins and serotonins. For example, stimulants such as cocaine and methamphetamine have been found to activate the dopamine, norepinephrine, and serotonin systems. Alcohol is believed to affect several different neurotransmitter systems, whereas other drugs typically affect one specific transmitter system more strongly than others. For example, cocaine affects the dopamine system, and heroin the opioid system (Mozak & Anton, 1999).

Recent research indicates that changes in the neurochemistry of the brain resulting from chronic or heavy substance abuse may cause anxiety or depression. This reinforces substance abuse, as the abuser will take drugs to relieve these feelings. For example, many stimulant users will continue to use cocaine, amphetamines, or methamphetamine to alleviate the feelings of depression that occur when the drugs wear off. Whether the changes in neurochemistry of the brain are permanent or (partially) reversible is not clear yet. There is evidence that such alterations in neurochemistry may persist for years.

Conditioning and Craving

Conditioning processes play a significant role in the etiology and development of addictive behaviors and substance-abuse disorders. Addictive behaviors are viewed as learned habits that are reinforced by rewards according to operant conditioning principles. Addictive substances stimulate the pleasure centers in the brain, thus providing positive reinforcement for substance use. Although the positive reinforcement of substances is a physical phenomenon—for example, becoming high on cannabis or heroin or the euphoric kick of cocaine—in many cases substance abuse is also reinforced because it ameliorates unpleasant feelings. This latter process is called negative reinforcement. Taking alcohol or illicit drugs reduces anxiety and tension, which facilitates drug-taking and so, on subsequent occasions when the individual experiences stress and anxiety, he will be more likely to take alcohol or drugs to relieve tension. Initially, alcohol and drugs are used to relieve emotional discomfort, to reduce stress and anxiety, and to improve mood. However, as tolerance builds up, substance abusers require greater amounts of alcohol and drugs to achieve distress relief, and thus an addictive cycle is created. The substance abuse itself creates additional work and relationship problems, which again increase stress and this increases the need for substances and thus reinforces the addictive cycle.

Classical conditioned stimuli are held partially responsible for the emergence of craving. Craving, defined as the intense desire to use alcohol or drugs, is elicited as reaction to substance-related stimuli (drug paraphernalia, environmental cues). These stimuli are termed cues and the reactivity these drug cues elicit is generally considered to be a conditioned drug response. Siegel (1983) has suggested that drug cues might serve as conditioned stimuli for a compensatory response (opposite in direction to the unconditioned drug effect) that compensates for the impending unconditioned drug response. This compensatory response would probably be an aversive state and may be interpreted as craving. The cue-reactivity paradigm assumes that stimuli paired reliably with the administration of a drug (e.g., seeing injection needles, visiting someone from the "drug scene," being in a bar, socializing with "drinking buddies," smelling alcohol), and also mood states (anxiety, anger, depression) become conditioned stimuli and therefore are able to elicit conditioned craving in the absence of administration of the actual drug (i.e., the unconditioned stimulus).

Case Example

> Thomas, a socially anxious male, was hospitalized because of severe alcohol dependence. After four weeks of abstinence, he was asked to fill out several questionnaires in order to assess depressed mood and social phobia. Filling out the forms, Thomas became anxious, which elicited a craving for alcohol. He was quite overwhelmed by these sensations, this actually being the first time he experienced craving during hospitalization. This made him somewhat reluctant to continue the assessment of his anxiety and mood state.

Cue reactivity experiments with abstinent individuals who had been physically dependent on opiates indicated that exposure to cues associated with a certain drug led to drug-opposite responses resembling withdrawal symptoms, but results with abstinent alcoholics are inconclusive (Niaura, Rohsenow, Binkoff, Pedraza, & Abrams, 1988).

Craving may only be subjectively experienced, but it is also reflected in psychophysiological measures (e.g., skin conductance, heart rate, salivation, and skin temperature). More recently, regional blood flow changes in specific brain areas have also been found to be associated with craving (Goldstein & Volkow, 2002). The conditioned drug responses can also be behavioral (as in drug-seeking behavior). Many addiction theories assume that craving is associated with the activation of a hedonic emotional state and this motivates actual drug-seeking behavior. Craving is not only involved in the initiation and maintenance of drug dependence but is also a central part of relapse (Tiffany & Conklin, 2000).

More recently, cognitive accounts of craving have suggested that the information pertaining to drinking and drug use resides in memory networks. When primed by cues (drug paraphernalia, environmental cues), these networks activate information related to drinking or drug use, including the expected outcomes of substance abuse and the emotions associated with such abuse. Whether theories are primarily based on conditioning or cognitive theories, these theories of craving generally presume that urges vary widely among individuals. For example, it is questionable how relevant the craving model is for alcohol dependence. Ames and Roitzsch (2000) have found in an inpatient sample that 64% of inpatients did not experience any craving. A meta-analysis on substance abusers has revealed that alcoholics had a significantly smaller craving effect size when compared to cigarette smokers, cocaine addicts, and heroin addicts (Carter & Tiffany, 1999).

Psychological Vulnerability

Substance abuse has often been conceptualized as a result of intrapersonal conflicts, and some have suggested the existence of an addictive personality. Originally, this view dates back to the psychodynamic proposition of the oral personality. According to the psychoanalytic view, alcoholics are characterized as individuals who have suffered conflict at the oral stage of psychosexual development and have remained fixated in this stage.

What evidence is there for a "substance-abusing personality"? Recent theorists hold that addicts are characterized by specific personality traits, including low self-esteem, high novelty-seeking, impulsiveness, emotionality, and antisocial traits. Although most of these traits have been found to be related to substance abuse in a number of individuals (see, e.g., Holahan, Moos, Holahan, Cronkite, & Randall, 2003; Wills, McNamara, Vaccaro, & Hirky, 1996), there are many more individuals with the same personality traits who do not become addicted. In one meta-analysis, the relationship between three personality traits and the use, misuse, and abuse of marijuana was investigated (Gorman and Derzon, 2002). The results of this meta-analysis suggest that negative affect, emotionality, and unconventionality do not play a direct role in the etiology of marijuana use and abuse. Thus, it does not appear to be possible to predict, based on personality traits, who will become dependent and who will not. Furthermore, a substance abuser's personality may be as much a result as a cause of the addiction. Thus, personality psychologists do not have much to offer in the way of understanding addictive behaviors. Although there is some evidence that specific personality traits are related to the development of substance abuse and dependence, the specific contribution of personality to this process is probably minimal.

Social Learning

Studies investigating whether parental rearing practices influence drug use in children indicate that the parental rearing style of drug-abusing patients is characterized by high maternal and paternal control and low maternal care, a pattern characteristic of an "affectionless control" rearing style (Emmelkamp & Heeres, 1988; Torresani, Favaretto, & Zimmermann, 2000). The social learning and cognitive models of addiction represent a number of constructs influenced primarily by social learning theory (Bandura, 1977, 1997). The key social-learning concepts include environmental stimuli (stressors), modeling of substance abuse, coping skills, self-efficacy, and outcome expectancies.

In recent years, *expectancy* has emerged as a key concept in psychosocial models of substance abuse. People's beliefs about the effects of alcohol and drugs on behavior, moods, and emotions predict substance abuse in adolescents and adults (Goldman, 1994). Expectancies can involve beliefs about the positive and negative effects of using alcohol or drugs. The decision to drink or use drugs is assumed to be driven partly by the positive expectancy that the substance will result in certain desirable consequences, such as getting high, tension relief, or improving mood. Young children have predominantly negative beliefs about alcohol (see, e.g., Johnson & Johnson, 1995). Once children start experimenting with alcohol in early puberty, expectancies start to shift from negative to positive and subsequent drinking experiences will further shape the development of expectancies (Aas, Leigh, Anderssen, & Jakobsen, 1998). In substance-abusing clients, positive expectancies are difficult to change, and remain often latent even after a person has been abstinent for some time.

Another important concept is *self-efficacy*. Self-efficacy is the person's belief that he or she is able to accomplish a task—that is, to control substance abuse, or to be able to cope with a high-risk situation. Substance abusers are often characterized by low self-efficacy in high-risk drinking or drug-using situations. Low self-efficacy is predicative of increased lack of control with respect to substance use triggered by particular situations (Blume, 2004) and is associated with poor treatment outcome.

These more general social learning constructs have been adopted into more specific, integrative models, the model with clear clinical applications being the relapse model by Marlatt & Gordon (1985). This model of the relapse process is partly based on the assumption that substance abuse and dependence is a habitual, maladaptive way of coping with stress. In Marlatt & Gordon's model, the presence of a high-risk situation and the lack of social support threaten an individual's sense of control and increase the risk of relapse. If an individual does not have adequate coping responses in his or her repertoire or these coping responses are not used, he or she experiences a decrease in self-efficacy and an increase in positive-outcome expectancies for the administration of the substance. These positive outcome expectancies lead to a "lapse": using some alcohol or drug. Many people show occasional lapses from total abstinence. When a lapse leads to cognitive dissonance ("I quit drinking, and yet I took a beer"), guilt and the feeling of being weak ("I have no willpower"), and having failed ("I am a failure," "I just can't do it"), this in turn increases the likelihood of additional substance use, and full relapse. This process has become known as the *abstinence violation effect*, in which minor transgressions are perceived as giving in to the old habit. Marlatt and colleagues emphasize that the client's emotional and attributional response to an initial lapse is more important than the specific characteristics of the high-risk situation associated with this lapse (Larimer, Palmer, & Marlatt, 1999).

COURSE

Substance use evolves over time, usually starting with alcohol and then progressing to cannabis, sometimes followed by hallucinogens in college years. In the United States, 50% of students in grade 6 reported having tried alcohol or illicit drugs. In the United States, one-third of students start using marijuana while in college (Rey et al., 2004). In Australia, the average age for first-time cannabis use is 15.5.

General population studies on adolescents show a steady increase in the prevalence of alcohol use and other substances between the ages of 12 and 18. Youthful experimentation is common. Most adolescents use alcohol or illicit drugs at some point and experience some substance-related problems but do not necessarily progress to more serious substance abuse or dependence. Expectations about the effects of alcohol constitute an important reason for continued and heavy drinking of alcohol. Adolescents who start to drink alcohol with positive expectations about its effects are most likely to increase their consumption of it (Smith, Goldman, Greenbaum, & Christiansen, 1995). As people get older, substance use usually becomes more moderate. There is some evidence that *early* cannabis use facilitates the progression to using drugs such as heroin and cocaine independent of genetic factors (Fergusson & Horwood, 2000).

There is no evidence that adolescent drug use itself predicts mental health problems in later adulthood. Increased polydrug use over time, however, does increase the risk of mental health problems—especially suicide ideation and psychosis. Further, *increased* cannabis use, in particular, has consequences for mental health in the long term (Newcomb, Scheier, & Bentler, 1993).

For most people, the predictive basis for later substance abuse is established by the time they finish high school. Those who continue to use illicit drugs do so less often than when they were younger. The majority of young adults stop using illicit drugs altogether. Life transitions such as marriage and parenthood have a strong effect on the levels and incidence of substance use. Thirty-five-year-old married individuals and parents are less likely to use cannabis or cocaine, or to drink heavily. Cannabis use and heavy drinking are less common among 35-year-old college graduates than among those who never attended college (Merline, O'Malley, Schulenberg, Bachman, & Johnston, 2004). Older people do not use alcohol as much as younger people, and they hardly use illicit drugs. However, this may change in the future as the current population ages. On the other hand, elderly people are more likely to abuse legal drugs such as hypnotics, sedatives, anxiolytics, and painkillers.

It is rather difficult to specify a typical course for substance dependence. Age of onset varies widely. However, persons who begin drinking regularly before age 14 are at least three times as likely to develop alcohol dependence than those who did not drink until they were 21 (Grant, 1998). Similarly, individuals who start using cannabis at the age of 16 years are at increased risk of being diagnosed as cannabis dependent by age 21 (Fergusson, Horwood, Lynskey, & Madden, 2003). Addictions tend to develop over time, and periods of problematic use and related impairments often occur for many years after criteria for dependence or abuse have been reached. There is considerable evidence that in most individuals the course of substance abuse is not progressive. Usually, periods of heavy use are alternated with periods of relative abstinence or unproblematic use, even in individuals with a history of substance dependence (Anglin, Hser, & Grella, 1997; McKay & Weiss, 2001). For example, in a longitudinal study, the course of alcohol abuse was studied prospectively among adolescent males, who were followed from 1940 until around 1990 (Vaillant, 1996). The average age of onset of alcohol abuse was around 35. The number of males who continued to abuse alcohol went gradually down after the age of 40, and a substantial proportion of alcohol-abusing men (around 30%) succeeded in returning to abstinence or controlled drinking.

ASSOCIATED PROBLEMS

Substance abusers usually have other problems besides the need for alcohol and drugs. Substance abuse and dependence is associated with a host of psychiatric, medical, legal, social, relationship, and employment problems. It is often not the addiction itself, but the financial, social, and medical complications that lead substance abusers to seek treatment. Long-term abuse can have devastating effects on many areas of a person's life. Most research has been done on the impact of alcohol abuse.

Sexual Functioning

Although many drugs can increase desire, they usually impair sexual performance (see, e.g., Johnson, Phelps, & Cottler, 2004). This is the case for alcohol as well as heroin and chronic cocaine. Initially, cocaine usually enhances sexual desire, but long-term performance is negatively affected. A relative recent new party drug called GHB (gamma hydroxybutyrate) is often used to enhance sexual feelings, but long-term effects are yet unknown.

Relationship Problems

Substance abuse is associated with marital problems (Emmelkamp & Vedel, 2002), and excessive alcohol use is one of the most frequent causes of divorce in many countries. The divorce process and associated social problems can exacerbate substance abuse. Substance-abusing couples do differ from nonabusing couples in that they report more domestic violence. There is some evidence that specific behaviors of the spouse can function either as a cue or reinforcer for drinking or drug-taking behavior.

Within a behavioral framework, substance abuse is assumed to have a negative effect on communication between partners and marital satisfaction, and has also been linked to other marital issues such as domestic violence and sexual dysfunction. Research has differentiated families of alcoholics from healthier control families in that the former typically manifest poor communication, organization, problem solving, conflict management, and affect regulation processes. However, comparing alcoholic couples to nonalcoholic but distressed couples revealed that similar dysfunctional processes characterized the latter group (O'Farrell & Birchler, 1987).

Problems in Children

Substance abuse is often associated with impaired parenting and the inability to care for the child. There is ample empirical evidence for increased risk of child neglect or abuse by parents who are substance abusers. As compared to non-substance-abusing mothers, substance-abusing mothers show less maternal affection, are less responsive to the needs of their babies, are inconsistent in their disciplinary practices, and are short tempered with their children (Donohue, 2004). In both the United States and the United Kingdom, crack cocaine use by the mother is more closely associated with child abuse than is any other substance (Street, Harrington, Chiang, Cairns, & Ellis, 2004).

Children of substance-abusing patients have a high risk of getting psychological problems themselves. Girls are more likely to suffer from anxiety, eating disorders, depression, and low self-esteem. Boys are particularly at risk to display antisocial behavior, which eventually may result in themselves engaging in substance abuse (Edwards, Marshall, & Cook, 2003).

Social and Legal Problems

Excessive alcohol use is associated with several types of criminal behavior. In the United States, 40–50% of all murders, over 50% of rapes, and over 50% of deaths resulting from car accidents are alcohol related. These figures show that a large number of alcohol abusers will come into contact with the justice system. However, it does not follow that alcohol addiction always leads to severe maladaptive behavior.

The social problems experienced by heroin users are great. The lives of most heroin and polydrug users are increasingly centered on obtaining drugs. As addicts become more desperate for drugs, they resort to lying and criminal behavior to obtain the drug, even those individuals without premorbid antisocial personality traits. Some will become dealers in order to finance their addiction. A substantial number of female heroin addicts turn to prostitution. Moreover, problems with housing, employment, and the law are common among cocaine users, especially among crack cocaine users. Furthermore, crack cocaine is often associated with promiscuous sexual behavior, often with unknown partners and sometimes in exchange for money or drugs.

A number of studies suggest that alcohol or drug use is associated with domestic violence, particularly marital violence. For example, an analysis of episodes of domestic violence showed that 90% of the assailants reported having used alcohol or other drugs on the day of the assault (Brookhoff, O'Brien, Cook, Thompson, & Williams, 1997). Research on violence in alcoholics indicates that the frequency and quantity of the alcohol consumed is often proportional to the severity of the assault (Fals-Stewart, Klostermann, O'Farrell, Yates, & Birchler, 2005).

Notably, using alcohol and drugs is also associated with a greater chance of being the victim of violence (El-Bassel, Gilbert, Wu, Go, & Hill, 2005; Smith, 2000). Women may particularly initiate or increase their substance use to cope with the distress of experiencing violence by their partner (Kilpatrick, Acierno, Resnick, Saunders, & Best, 1997). This holds for heroin, cannabis, cocaine, and crack, but not for alcohol

(El-Bassel et al., 2005). Couples who are both substance abusers are at a higher risk of marital violence. Conflicts about money and sharing drugs often lead to arguments that escalate to partner violence. Some substance abusers become homeless. Many of them have children who live elsewhere, usually with relatives, less often in foster care.

Health Consequences

Heavy alcohol use and illicit drug use are associated with many negative effects, including greater likelihood of injury, illness, poor health, and even an increased risk of suicide.

Up to 30% of heavy drinkers develop *cirrhosis of the liver*, a potentially fatal disease. Another serious alcohol-related liver disease is *alcoholic hepatitis*. Further, chronic heavy alcohol use is associated with hypertension, cardiovascular diseases, and particular forms of cancer. About 50–80% of persons diagnosed with alcohol-use disorders display subtle to severe deficits on neuropsychological tests (Bates & Convit, 1999); these deficits included mental confusion, and impairment in abstract reasoning, (short-term) memory, attention, problem solving, and cognitive flexibility. Heavy alcohol use can cause brain damage well before liver damage is detectable. Some cognitive deficits (e.g., mental confusion) are reversible after detoxification but others can last for months, even years.

Withdrawal following excessive use of alcohol over a long period can produce an acute psychotic reaction called *alcohol withdrawal delirium* (delirium tremens), which may last from 3 to 6 days and has a high risk of mortality (10%) if not appropriately (pharmacologically) treated. The symptoms of alcohol withdrawal delirium include

intense autonomic hyperactivity (profuse sweating and tachycardia)
mental confusion characterized by incoherent speech
disorientation
extreme restlessness
hallucinations, often of crawling animals

Auditory and visual hallucinations may also occur in the context of heavy alcohol consumption, in which case the diagnosis of *alcoholic hallucinosis* may be considered (Tsuang, Irwin, Smith, & Schuckit, 1994). In patients with paranoid or grandiose delusions after a period of heavy drinking, the diagnosis of *alcohol-induced psychotic disorder with delusions* may be considered. Both disorders seem to be unrelated to schizophrenia and the prognosis is generally good when the patient is abstinent.

Older alcoholics are at risk of developing *alcohol amnestic disorder*, or *Korsakoff's syndrome*, which is characterized by severe memory impairment, especially in the short term, and the inability to plan; new learning is impaired. These patients are inclined to confabulate, filling in memory gaps with reminiscences and fanciful tales. They may come across as delusional and disoriented, but this is usually related to their efforts to fill gaps in their memory through confabulation. It is now generally assumed that alcohol amnestic disorder is caused by a vitamin B deficiency and other effects of malnutrition. A variant of this disorder is the *Wennicke syndrome*, which is characterized by mental confusion, an unsteady gait, and problems with short-term memory, which are less severe than those associated with Korsakoff's syndrome. Nevertheless, immediate medical treatment is required given the risk of irreversible brain damage and death (Thomson, Cook, Thouquet, & Henry, 2002).

Expectant mothers who drink during pregnancy have a higher risk of stillborn babies or babies with birth defects or brain damage. Although the risk is higher for the babies of heavy drinkers, alcohol is never safe during pregnancy. Mothers who drink heavily during pregnancy put their babies at risk of developing *fetal alcohol syndrome*, which is characterized by mental retardation and specific facial disfigurations.

Despite all the negative effects of alcohol abuse, it should be noted that small amounts of daily alcohol have been found to be associated with a lower risk of coronary disease.

A number of medical complications may occur in individuals who use drugs. In opiate users, an overdose is common and requires immediate medical attention. Approximately half of all illicit drug users report at least one nonfatal overdose during their lifetime. In New York City, deaths due to drug abuse currently rank among the five leading causes of death in 15- to 54-year-olds. Complications of drug overdose include pulmonary edema, cardiac arrhythmia, rhabdomyolysis, and cognitive impairment. More than 90% of heroin overdose victims who receive emergency medical care while still exhibiting pulse and blood pressure survive, although neurological and other physical effects of overdose become more severe if hypoxia is prolonged (Tracy et al., 2005). Other medical complications of opiate use are respiratory depression and effects on the gastrointestinal system such as nausea and vomiting.

Many injection-drug users have been infected with hepatitis B or C, which may result in chronic liver disease. Large doses of amphetamines and cocaine can result in serious medical complications including ischemia or myocardial infarctation (Weaver & Schnoll, 1999). With crack cocaine there is especially a heightened risk of a cerebral infarct. When stimulants are smoked, pulmonary complications are common.

Cocaine can induce transient psychotic symptoms, such as paranoia, that typically resolve with abstinence. The term *cocaine-induced psychosis* has been used to describe this syndrome, and is quite common among cocaine-dependent individuals. In addition, chronic cocaine use is often associated with *cocaine-induced delirium*. In cocaine-dependent individuals, two-thirds reported transient psychotic symptoms; cocaine-induced hallucinations were endorsed by nearly as many cocaine users as were cocaine-induced delusions (Cubells et al., 2005). In methamphetamine users, delusional states including paranoia and hallucinations may occur as well.

Over the past decade, research has emerged showing that a substantial number of drug abusers suffer from impairments across cognitive domains (Rogers and Robbins, 2001; Vik, Celluci, Jarchow, & Hedt, 2004). In chronic cocaine abusers, cognitive domains—such as those of attention, memory, decision making, and problem solving—are often impaired (Bolla et al., 2003; Tucker et al., 2004). The negative impact of chronic excessive drug use on brain structure and function is supported by neuroimaging data (Volkow, Fowler, & Wang, 2003). Although some drug-induced damage is reduced after detoxification, as long as the drug use stops, the extent and the rate of cognitive recovery are highly variable, and improvement may be minor in terms of clinical relevance (Bates, Voelbel, Buckman, Labouvie, & Barry, 2005).

Substance users are more susceptible to various physical problems because of poor diet. Illicit drug users are even more likely to become ill as they have the added risk of HIV infection and AIDS through the use of unsterilized needles and the potential for unprotected sex. Moreover, unsterile needles can also lead to infection with hepatitis C. It is estimated that injection drug use is a factor in one-third of all HIV and more than half of all hepatitis C cases in the United States. Heroin, methamphetamine, and cocaine use are associated with detrimental effects on the fetus and the newborn child.

Long-term daily consumption of cannabis results in persistent cognitive impairment even after cessation of use (Rey et al., 2004). Further, smoking cannabis increases the risk of cancer.

Relapse

One of the greatest problems in the treatment of substance-use disorders is preventing a relapse after abstinence or controlled substance use has been achieved.

Marlat and Gordon (1980) have reported that for alcoholics, 23% of relapses were related to social pressure, such as being offered a drink, and another 29% of relapses were related to frustration and situations in which the individual was unable to express anger. The prevalence of specific relapse precipitants has been found to be fairly consistent across different addictive behaviors, including drinking, smoking, and heroin use (Marlatt & Gordon, 1985). Among alcoholics, there is considerable evidence that relapse is related to high levels of stress, lack of coping resources (Moser & Annis, 1995), and low self-efficacy (see, e.g., Miller, Westerberg, Harris, & Tonigan, 1996; Noone, Dua, & Markham, 1999). Furthermore, even minor stressors and lack of social support were found to be related to craving in substance-abuse patients (Ames & Roitzsch, 2000). Exposure to a heavy drinking model is likely to increase the risk of relapse and continuation of heavy drinking.

Mortality

Alcohol use and drug consumption increase the likelihood of injury and/ or death. About one-third of suicides and cases of accidental death (e.g., car accidents, falls, drownings, and burns) are alcohol related (Hingson, Heeren, Jamanka, Howland, 2000). The life expectancy of alcohol dependent individuals is about 12 years shorter than the average life expectancy. Individuals who drink heavily are more than twice (male) or three times (female) as likely to die before the age of 65 as people who abstain or drink moderately.

Opiate addiction is associated with high morbidity and increased risk of premature death. The mortality rate for regular heroin users is 13 times greater than for the general population. Among those who continually use opiates, estimates are that 42.5% will die within 7.5 years (Galai, Safaeian, Vishov, Bolotin, & Celentano, 2003). The risk of premature death is somewhat lower in addicts who succeed in remaining stable and drug free than in those who continue to use opioids intermittently (Galai et al., 2003; Sørensen, Jepsen, Haastrup, & Juel, 2005).

DIAGNOSTIC ISSUES

Clinicians in mental health settings do not always look for the signs of substance abuse and are not always familiar with the easy to administer, reliable, and valid assessment tools that are available. Clinicians in addiction centers, likewise, are not always aware of the added value of using such instruments. As legislation or third-party insurers now increasingly mandate outcome evaluation, this may become more important. Given the number of substance abusers requiring treatment, the emphasis must be on quick, low-cost measures that adequately target the individual patient's need for specific interventions and evaluate outcome. It is important to make a distinction between the type of measurements: some are useful for assessment and treatment planning, some are more suited to evaluate the effects of treatment, and some are useful both for treatment planning and outcome assessment.

Clinicians should facilitate an assessment context that encourages accurate reporting (e.g., disclosure of use of illicit drugs). Assessment of substance abuse must be postponed if the client is incoherent in cases of psychosis, a manic state, or acute intoxication. When the acute symptoms have abated, a detailed case history of substance abuse can be obtained. Further, collateral reports can be useful to confirm frequency and type of substance used and to assess interpersonal difficulties and other psychosocial problems, marital adjustment, child rearing, and violence.

Biological Markers

Breathalyzers are routinely used to assess recent alcohol intake. Analysis of urine specimens for metabolites of alcohol, cocaine, opioids, marijuana, benzodiazepines, and several other drugs can be used to monitor recent drug use. Recently, comparatively inexpensive rapid on-site urinalysis methods have become available, such as the TestCup and Test-Stik systems. These systems can be used in office settings and provide immediate (less than 5-minute) feedback on recent drug use. Although hair-analysis measures to screen for drug use are also available, these provide a long-term substance-abuse history and are therefore less suited for the assessment of recent substance abuse.

Screening Instruments

A number of screening instruments for substance-use problems have been developed that are particularly useful in mental health settings where patients are referred for primary mental rather than substance-use disorders. The following screening measures require 2 to 10 minutes to complete.

For screening for alcohol use, the Michigan Alcoholism Screening Test, or MAST (Skinner & Sheu, 1982), can be used; it is not affected by comorbid psychiatric disorders (Teitelbaum & Mullen, 2000).

As an alternative, the Alcohol Use Disorder Identification Test, or AUDIT (Allen, Litten, Fertig, & Babor, 1997; Babor et al., 1992; Bohn, Babor, & Kranzler, 1995), can be used (Maisto, Carey, Carey, Gleason, & Gordon, 2000). The AUDIT was recently adapted (as AUDIT-ID) to include other drugs as well (Babor, Higgins-Biddle, Saunders, & Monteiro, 2001; Campbell et al., 2004).

Another alternative is the Drug Abuse Screening Test, or DAST (Skinner, 1982), which has been shown to be a valid screener for drug-use disorders (Cocco & Carey, 1998). Scores of 3 or more on the DAST-10 scale optimize sensitivity and specificity.

The CAGE test (Mayfield, McLeod, & Hall, 1974) is a very brief (four-item) screening tool that focuses on subjective negative consequences of alcohol abuse. (The four questions that make up the CAGE acronym are [C] Have you ever thought you should *cut down* on your drinking? [A] Have you ever felt *annoyed* by others' criticism of your drinking? [G] Have you ever felt *guilty* about your drinking? and [E] Do you have a morning *eye opener*?) Although its brevity is an advantage, it is slightly less reliable than the MAST (Teitelbaum & Carey, 2000).

The Dartmouth Assessment of Lifestyle Instrument, or DALI (Rosenberg et al., 1998), was specifically developed to detect substance-use disorder in acute psychiatric care settings. The DALI, derived from other screening questionaires listed above, has excellent inter-rater and test-retest reliabilities. The DALI has higher sensitivity and specificity than the MAST, CAGE, or the DAST.

If a person screens positive on one of these screening measures, a more thorough evaluation is required to examine the extent of the identified problem.

Structured Interviews

Structured interviews are more informative and reliable than the unstructured clinical interviews used by many clinicians. In unstructured interviews, many co-occurring disorders and problems of prognostic significance in cases of substance abuse are likely to be missed.

The semistructured Time-Line Follow-Back interview, or TLFB (Sobell & Sobell, 1996), is a retrospective method for assessing alcohol- and drug-use patterns and related events, and possesses adequate reliability. The TLFB procedure estimates daily alcohol/drug use through the employment of various memory aids, such as a daily calendar, key dates (e.g., birthdays, personal events, clinic appointments, visits from family), anchor points ([un]employment, illnesses, holidays), and other memory aids to facilitate recall. The TLFB method assesses substance-abuse patterns (e.g., type of drug, quantity, frequency) in greater detail than most other measures. Although the individual can fill in the TLFB, it is more reliable when "administered" by a clinician. The TLFB provides useful information of antecedents and consequences of heavy drinking and illicit drug abuse and of high-risk situations for relapse, which may be of help for treatment planning. For example, clinicians can investigate whether heavy drinking is more likely to occur in certain situations (e.g., at home), under specific conditions (e.g., when the partner is absent), or following certain mood states (e.g., when stressed).

Many clinicians focus on the presenting complaint (e.g., heavy drinking) only and fail to examine other substances that may be used. Therefore, it is essential that a complete overview is obtained of substances used and the problems associated with this use. The Addiction Severity Index, or ASI (McLellan et al., 1992), is a semistructured interview that provides a comprehensive assessment of substance use (history, frequency, and consequences of alcohol and drug use). In addition, it assesses family history, psychological symptoms, health problems, and legal issues as well. ASI scores on the major domains may be used to plan treatments targeting these domains. The ASI is available free of charge, and takes roughly 45 to 60 minutes to administer. In addition to its usefulness as a baseline measure, the ASI may be used as a measure of treatment outcome, particularly when augmented with repeated administrations of the TLFB.

It should be noted that many items on the ASI are less suitable for substance abusers with additional major mental illnesses such as schizophrenia. For example, schizophrenic patients have specific problems that may confound the ASI score (Carey, 2002).

Although the ASI provides a clinically useful measure of psychological distress and history, it does not provide a formal psychiatric diagnosis. For formal diagnoses of substance-abuse disorders and comorbid mental disorders, structured clinical interviews are indispensable. These include the Structured Clinical Interview for DSM-IV, or SCID (First, Spitzer, Gibbon, & Williams, 1995); the Diagnostic Interview Schedule, or DIS (Robins, Helzer, Croughan, & Ratcliff, 1981); the Composite International Diagnostic Interview, or CIDI (Robins, Wing, & Helzer,

1983); and the Psychiatric Research Interview for Substance and Mental Disorders (PRISM; Hasin et al., 1996). We recommend the CIDI, given its reliability and short length: the substance-abuse module takes about 20 to 30 minutes to administer.

Assessment of personality disorders may be important in treatment planning, given the high prevalence of antisocial and borderline personality disorders in substance-abusing individuals, and the worse outcome in comorbid substance abusers (Marlowe, Kirby, Festinger, Husband, & Platt, 1997; Carroll & Rounsaville, 2002). The gold standard to assess personality disorders is a structured clinical interview such as the SCID II, but these interviews are very time-consuming. Therefore, we recommend self-report measure, such as the Personality Disorder Questionnaire–4+ (Hyler, 1994), for screening substance abusers for personality disorders. A positive screen on one or more personality disorders may be followed by administration of the SCID-II to confirm the diagnosis.

Questionnaires

In addition to the measures described above, a number of paper-and-pencil tests may be used for specific purposes. For example, measures have been devised to assess the degree of alcohol dependence, the readiness to change, high-risk situations, coping skills, and expectancies with respect to outcome of substance abuse.

To evaluate the degree of alcohol dependence, the Severity of Alcohol Dependence Questionnaire, or SADQ (Stockwell, Hodgson, Edwards, Taylor, & Rankin, 1979), may be used. A score of 31 or higher on the 20-item SADQ correlates with a clinician's rating of severe dependence, while a score of 30 or less correlated with ratings of mild to moderate dependence.

Related to the degree of alcohol dependence is impaired control over drinking, which can be assessed with the Impaired Control Scale, or ICS (Heather, Tebbutt, Mattick, & Zamir, 1993). This instrument has shown good evidence of reliability, concurrent validity (Heather, Booth, & Luce, 1998; Marsh, Smith, Saunders, & Piek, 2002), and predictive validity (Heather et al., 1998). The clinical value of the ICS and the SADQ include their use in deciding the recommended drinking goal of treatment: moderate drinking versus abstinence.

Stages of Change

Motivation for change is an important concept in treating addiction. Substance abusers are notorious for poor treatment engagement and adherence. A major development in the conceptualization of substance abuse has been the transtheoretical model (to be discussed in chapter 2), which suggests that individuals attempting to change addictive behavior go through a predictable series of stages of change, from precontemplation, to contemplation, to determination, to action and maintenance (Prochaska & DiClemente, 1992). A number of measures have been developed to assign a person to one of the stages of change as articulated by the transtheoretical model, the most important being the University of Rhode Island Change Assessment Scale (URICA; 28 items), with precontemplation, contemplation, action, and maintenance subscales (DiClemente & Hughes, 1990); and the Stages of Change Readiness and Treatment Eagerness Scale (SOCRATES; 19 items), with readiness, taking steps, and ambivalence subscales (Miller & Tonigan, 1996).

These measures of motivation have consistently yielded high indices of internal consistency and test-retest reliability (Carey, Purnine, Maisto, & Carey, 2002). Motivation measures can be highly informative in providing insight into a patient's ambivalence about changing substance-use behavior. Knowing whether a patient is in a precontemplation, contemplation, or action phase may have consequences for the selection of treatment approaches that—ideally—match the patients' motivational state.

Measures to Assess High-Risk Situations, Motives, and Coping

In addition to the TLFB method, a number of paper-and-pencil measures are particularly useful for the purpose of conducting functional analyses and understanding patterns of substance use. These instruments offer the clinician a profile of high-risk situations and motives or reasons patients may give for substance abuse. This information can provide guidelines, tailored to each individual patient, for how to manage high-risk situations. These include the Inventory of Drinking Situations, or IDS (Annis, 1982), and the Inventory of Drug-Taking Situations, or IDTS (Annis & Martin, 1985; Turner, Annis, & Sklar, 1997), which assess specific antecedents of alcohol and drug use. An array of emotional (e.g., "unpleasant emotions") and social situations (e.g., "social pressure to use") are represented in these questionnaires.

Motives or reasons for drinking may also provide important information for treatment planning. Measures include the 14-item Reasons for Drinking Scale (Farber, Khavari, & Douglass, 1980), and the 15-item Drinking Motives Measure (Cooper, Russell, Skinner, & Windle, 1992), which contains subscales for social, coping, and positive-affect-enhancement motives.

Certain measures can be helpful in detecting inadequate specific coping skills, which may be targeted in treatment; among these are the Situational Confidence Questionnaire for alcohol abusers (Breslin, Sobell, Sobell, & Agrawal, 2000), and for substance abusers (Barber, Cooper, & Heather, 1991), which were developed to assess substance abusers, confidence in their ability to resist urges to use; and the Drug-Taking Confidence Questionnaire, or DTCQ (Sklar, Annis, & Turner, 1997), which assesses coping self-efficacy for a number of different types of drug and alcohol use.

Substance-Use Expectancies

Individuals hold beliefs about the expected effects of alcohol and drugs. Given that these expectancies may mediate drinking and drug use, it may be important to assess these expectancies. The most commonly used instrument is the Alcohol Expectancy Questionnaire, or AEQ (Brown, Christiansen, & Goldman, 1987), which has separate versions for adolescents and adults. While the adult version measures only expectations of positive effects, the adolescent version includes items tapping negative effects. In addition, the scale items for common positive effects are not the same in the two versions. Variations to assess expectancies with respect to marijuana and cocaine use have also been developed (Shafer & Brown, 1991).

Concluding Remarks

Assessment may provide a wealth of information to the clinician, but a standardized assessment battery including most of the measures described here is not recommended. It is important to communicate to the patient what the purpose of the assessment is, and not to overburden the patient with measures. As a general rule, when administering a specific questionnaire or structured interview the clinician should consider in which way the results will facilitate the selection of the most appropriate treatment. How this can be achieved in clinical practice is demonstrated in chapter 4.

CHAPTER 2

Clinical Interventions

In this chapter a number of psychological and pharmacological interventions for substance-use disorders will be described that have been found effective in a number of randomized controlled studies. The empirical status of the various interventions will be reviewed in chapter 3.

MOTIVATIONAL INTERVIEWING

Cognitive-behavior therapists are quite prepared to help patients who are motivated to learn how to change their substance-abusing behavior through an amalgam of more-or-less effective coping strategies. It is well recognized that motivation to change is crucial to successful engagement in therapy. Unfortunately, a substantial number of patients who come for treatment of substance abuse do not have sufficient motivation for change. Actually, most patients seeking treatment are ambivalent about it; only few come already convinced that something has to change. Others come reluctantly, pressed by loved ones or the courts.

Unfortunately, patients' deficits are often used to explain unfavorable treatment outcomes, especially in the area of addictive behavior. Lack of motivation for change or motivational ambivalence is widely regarded as a primary obstacle in treating substance abuse and dependence and is related to the high rate of early treatment dropout. The substance abuser experiences insufficient instigation to change, and makes little or no correction in changing his or her substance-abusing behavior despite adverse consequences of continued substance abuse.

The Transtheoretical Model of Change

A useful model for understanding motivation and, specifically, how behavior change occurs is Prochaska and DiClemente's (1982) stages-of-change model, which has become known as the transtheoretical model of change. This stages-of-change model postulates that people progress through five stages when changing behaviors: precontemplation, contemplation, preparation/determination, action, and maintenance (see Prochaska, DiClemente, & Norcross, 1992, for a review):

> *Precontemplation.* This first stage is characterized by lack of problem recognition and no intention to change the behavior.
>
> *Contemplation.* The next stage in this model is characterized by a period of ambivalence and inaction. Contemplation is the stage in which individuals are aware that a problem exists and they weigh equally the positive and negative aspects of the behavior.
>
> *Preparation/Determination.* In this stage a substance-abusing individual perceives a significant discrepancy between current status and desired state. When the balance of pros and cons begins to tip in the direction of change, there ensues a period of preparation in which change options are explored. Preparation is characterized by a decision to take action within the next month, and persons at this stage may already make immediate, small behavior changes.
>
> *Action.* This stage is characterized by more definite changes in behavior, environment, or experiences in order to overcome the problem.
>
> *Maintenance.* In this stage, individuals work to prevent relapse and to continue the previous changes.

Substance abusers can relapse or regress to earlier stages according to this model.

The stages-of-change model is an extremely popular concept in addiction research and has been widely adapted in clinical settings as a heuristic for understanding motivation and, more specifically, readiness for change. If the model is correct, then behavior-change strategies—as, for example, coping-skills training—may not be optimal strategies, at least initially, for many persons needing change in substance abuse. In terms of the stages of change, many patients who are referred to addiction centers are likely to be precontemplators or contemplators, given that they often seek treatment under some form of coercion (DiClemente & Hughes, 1990; Edens & Willoughby, 1999, 2000).

A Description of Motivational Interviewing

Until the 1980s, the usual therapeutic way of dealing with "unmotivated" patients was a confrontational approach, which was thought to be necessary to overcome the resistance of the patient, the "pathological denial" of substance abuse, and the perceived inherent lack of motivation about changing substance abuse. These characteristics were often seen as inherent qualities of the patients themselves. Around 1980, a new style of interviewing substance-abusing people who were ambivalent about change emerged (Miller, 1983). In Miller's view, the interaction between the patient and the therapist is critical in changing the ambivalence of changing substance abuse: The way patients are addressed by their therapists can either enhance or reduce motivation to change.

The clinical method of motivational interviewing was developed specifically to work through this ambivalence and to enhance intrinsic motivation for change. This treatment does not attempt to train the patient through recovery, but instead employs motivational strategies to mobilize the patient's own resources. Motivational interviewing aims to elicit concerns about the problems associated with substance abuse and reasons for change from the patient, rather than directly confronting the patient as needing to change. Direct confrontation is not an effective method for resolving ambivalence. Thus, the therapist seeks to evoke the client's own motivation to change or not change his or her substance abuse. In motivational interviewing, responsibility for change is left with the patient.

Motivational interviewing combines a supportive and empathic counseling style with a directive method for resolving ambivalence in the direction of change. Thus, this therapeutic approach integrates relationship-building principles of nondirective therapy (Rogers, 1961) with active behavioral strategies directly related to the patient's stage of change according to the model of Prochaska and DiClemente (1982). In line with the humanistic tradition in psychotherapy, therapists using motivational interviewing seek to evoke the patient's intrinsic motivation, with confidence in the human desire and capacity to grow in a positive direction. However, although inspired by the humanistic movement in psychotherapy, motivational interviewing is more directive than Rogerian nondirective therapy (as discussed below) and has been defined as a person-centered, directive communication style (Miller & Rollnick, 2002).

In motivational interviewing, readiness to change is not seen as a trait, but as a function of the interaction between patient and therapist. In exploring the client's own arguments for change, the role of the therapist is to elicit self-verbalizations of the patient, reflecting intentions to change his abuse and to offer periodic summaries of change talk that the client has uttered (Miller & Rollnick, 2002). In contrast to other therapies for substance abuse, where therapist and patient often fulfill expert versus passive roles, in motivational interviewing the relationship

TABLE 2.1   Differences between Motivational Interviewing and Confrontational Approaches

Motivational Interviewing	Confrontational Approach
Deemphasis on labels; acceptance of "addiction" label seen as unnecessary for change to occur	Heavy emphasis on acceptance of self as "addict"; acceptance of diagnosis seen as essential for change
Emphasis on personal choice regarding future use of alcohol and other drugs	Emphasis on disease of substance abuse that reduces personal choice and control
Therapist conducts objective evaluation but focuses on eliciting the patient's own concerns	Therapist presents perceived evidence of substance abuse in an attempt to convince the patient of the diagnosis
Resistance seen as an interpersonal behavior pattern influenced by the therapist's behavior	Resistance seen as 'denial', a trait characteristic of substance abusers requiring confrontation
Resistance is met with reflection	Resistance is met with argumentation and correction

Source: Adapted from Miller & Rollnick (1991). Reprinted with permission from Guildford Press, New York.

between therapist and patient is one of partnership: the therapist uses a collaborative method for helping people to explore their own values and motivations by using Socratic dialogue. Finally, as emphasized by Miller and Rollnick (2002), motivational interviewing is a method of communication rather than a set of techniques: "It is not a bag of tricks for getting people to do what they don't want to do . . ." (p. 25). The main differences between motivational interviewing and more confrontational approaches are listed in table 2.1.

As a treatment, motivational interviewing is typically implemented as a brief approach, occurring over the course of one to four sessions. In the first sessions the focus is on building the patient's motivation for change, followed by strengthening the patient's commitment to change later on. However, the empathic, nonjudgmental interviewing style discussed below can be used throughout treatment and even be incorporated into other therapeutic approaches. The following clinical guidelines will enable a set of conditions that will enhance the patient's intrinsic motivation (Miller & Rollnick, 2002).

Expressing Empathy   Empathy is a therapeutic technique of reflective listening, thus helping the therapist to understand and accept the patient's perspective without denigrating or judging the patient. Therapeutic empathy creates a safe environment and thus reduces defensiveness.

The therapist listens carefully to the patient, summarizes the patient's meaning from verbal and nonverbal communication in his own words, and gives it back to the patient often in a slightly reframed form, thus enabling him to explore the topic further. The main purpose of reflective listening is that the patient feels understood and accepted. Giving the patient the feeling that he is understood, however, does not imply that the therapist agrees with everything that the patient reports or that he endorses it:

> Patient: It was awful, you know, I had to get drunk, but I was out of money, so I took two bottles from the shop.

> Therapist: I understand that you felt so terrible, that you saw no other solution than stealing alcohol. Tell me what other concerns you have about your drinking.

Expressing empathy is the dominant technique in motivational interviewing. By using this technique, the therapist builds on a productive therapeutic relationship and reduces resistance on the part of the patient. Although this technique looks rather simple, it requires a lot of training and experience to conduct it properly and to adjust it to the level of complexity the patient can deal with. In its simplest form, expressing empathy boils down to summary statements. Key techniques associated with this style are summarized by the acronym OARS (open questions, affirming, reflecting, and summarizing). However, more complex statements are needed to get the patient in touch with her ambivalence. It is therapeutically wise to start with more simple reflective statements early on in the session and to proceed to more complex statements only when sufficient rapport between patient and therapist has developed. By using these more complex reflections, certain issues can be highlighted:

> Therapist: If I understand you correctly, on the one hand, alcohol helps you not to have to think about your relationship problems and to feel less miserable, but on the other hand I hear you say that you feel that drinking does not solve your problems and even may enhance them.

Used in this way, the therapist is directive in determining which issues he would like to have further explored by the patient. In the statement above the therapist tried to intensify the ambivalence felt by the patient. More generally, reflective listening is far from a passive process. Actually, the therapist may be highly directive in what statements to emphasize and give back to the patient or ignore, thus shaping talk of change.

Finally, it is important to note that when using reflective listening to understand the patient's perspective and giving her room to reflect, the therapist should set aside the wish to ask questions to elicit further information from the patient. The priority should be on building the therapeutic relationship in order to encourage personal exploration on the part of the patient instead of gathering additional information.

Developing Discrepancy   Most substance-abusing patients know that "somewhere down the line" substance abuse may eventually be self-destructive, even if they do not discuss this issue as their main concern in the session. One of the aims of motivational interviewing is to develop the discrepancy between the positive effects of substance abuse and the eventual self-destructive nature of it, and enhancing the discomfort associated with this discrepancy. The therapist may increase this discrepancy in order to help the patient to realize her personal goals and values. This is usually done by an exploration of the personal values of the patient and her aspirations for the future. Further, the patient is encouraged to explore what is negative to the current substance abuse and how it is harming her (and others), thus making the patient more aware of the negative consequences of her behavior. Actually, discomfort resulting from this discrepancy might be a powerful catalyst for changing the substance abuse. As a result, the patient may be more willing to consider behavior change:

> In the first session, Gail, a young student, did not seem to worry very much about the possible negative consequences for her health, career, and social relationships of her continuing heavily drinking alcohol and sniffing cocaine on a nearly daily basis. In the second session, when asked for her future aspirations, she came to realize that continuing the substance abuse did not make her future dreams very realistic: being a happily married women with a professional career as a family doctor, taking care of two small children.

Although at times developing discrepancy might lead to considerable discomfort, it often helps patients to see that their current use of substances is at odds with their own personal values and future aspirations. The confrontation with this "unpleasant reality" helps many patients to move toward positive behavior change in order to reduce the perceived discrepancy. When a behavior is seen as conflicting with important personal goals, change is more likely to occur than when the patient feels coerced by the goals or values of others (e.g., the therapist, a partner).

Avoiding Argument and Rolling with Resistance   As noted above, the conventional way of dealing with resistance was a confrontational approach. Unfortunately, when therapists do the utmost to change the behavior of the patient, many substance abusers will try even harder not to change. Trying to persuade the patient is usually of no avail and may even push her in the opposite direction. Arguing about diagnostic labels such as being or not being an addict is also to be avoided at all costs.

From the perspective of motivational interviewing, patient resistance is not seen as acting out or negative behavior, but is conceptualized as a sign of patient's ambivalence, and in this way provides feedback to the therapist that the patient is not yet ready for change. Often, therapists assume greater readiness to change than felt by the patient. Therapists should be aware that motivation might fluctuate during treatment.

Since direct argumentation tends to evoke defensiveness, in motivational interviewing argumentation is to be avoided. Rather than focusing on resistance and oppositional behavior, in motivational interviewing the therapist "rolls with resistance," thus avoiding a power struggle. Using a metaphor, the pilot of a boat on a rapidly moving river would do wise not to try to steer against the force of the water, but to move the boat to take the best advantage of the river's energy (Moyers & Waldorf, 2004). Phrased in system-theoretic terms, the therapist needs to "go down" when the patient offers resistance. As originally proposed by Haley (1973), when "attacked" by the patient, the therapist should use judo techniques, characterized by complying with the patient's movement and thus using it to good advantage:

> After five weeks of abstinence, Paula told her therapist she wanted to change her treatment goal. Abstinence did not suit her and controlled drinking seemed a reasonable alternative. Rather than focusing on why Paula no longer wanted to strive for abstinence and reminding her about all the reasons why she should remain abstinent, her therapist explored her thoughts on controlled drinking. After thoroughly exploring the pros and cons of controlled drinking and gathering information on what had made her change her mind, Paula rephrased her ambivalence about abstinence; it was not so much that she wanted to drink in a controlled fashion, but that she was fearful about not being able to maintain abstinence, to fail and to disappoint herself and her family.

Supporting Self-Efficacy   Throughout motivational interviewing, the therapist transmits optimism about possible behavioral change. When only changing the patient's perception that she has a serious problem, but not creating hope and confidence that she will be able to do something about it, therapy is deemed to fail. Many patients with substance-abuse problems have the feeling that they cannot change their behavior, even if they try very hard. This is not surprising, given the many unsuccessful attempts some patients have already made before they are referred to treatment for their addiction, resulting in a lack of self-efficacy. *Self-efficacy* can be defined as the specific belief that one is able to perform a particular task or behavior (Bandura, 1997). One of the tasks of therapists in motivational interviewing is to support the patient's belief that she is capable of changing. Often, patients express a rather negative and pessimistic view on being able to cope with their substance abuse by uttering statements such as, "That won't work for me; I tried to stop before, but I am too weak." It is of little avail to have patients replace these statements with statements such as, "I am quite capable of stopping drinking." Rather, the therapist will try to elicit this conviction from the patient herself:

> Therapist: You have the feeling that you never will be able to control your drinking?
>
> Dianne: Yes, I simply am not that kind of person.
>
> Therapist: On the other hand, you said that you did not drink when you were pregnant. So perhaps there are circumstances in which you are less powerless and are able to control your drinking? Does this make sense to you?

By using these kinds of interventions the patient's confidence in her capability to succeed in behavior change might be increased. Helping patients to see their own ability to make positive changes is crucial.

For Whom Is Motivational Interviewing Suited?

It is a misconception that motivational interviewing can also be applied when there is no desire for (some) change of substance abuse. If patients have no concern whatsoever about their substance abuse, motivational interviewing will be of no avail. Even highly skilled therapists are unlikely to elicit motivation in individuals who come to their first contact with no intrinsic motivation at all. In terms of the transtheoretical model, individuals in the *contemplation* and *preparation* stages are most likely to benefit from motivational interviewing. When patients are already in the *action* stage, motivation is less of a problem and other, more directive methods (e.g., cognitive-behavioral methods) are presumably more appropriate. However, motivation is not stable, and ambivalence about changing the substance abuse may reoccur. It then might be therapeutically wise to conduct a few sessions of motivational interviewing.

Having said that motivational interviewing is not appropriate for every patient, unfortunately, the same applies to therapists. Some therapists—even after extensive training—will still feel uncomfortable when applying motivational interview techniques. Presumably, motivational interviewing will only work well when the therapist is transparent and authentic and accepts the fact that many patients are ambivalent about changing their addictive behavior and that motivation is a shifting state. In therapists who are more confident in using a confrontational style, who know what works well for the patient, who try to steer patients in the "right direction," and who endorse the 12-step approach, motivational interviewing is probably doomed to fail.

COPING-SKILLS TRAINING

Traditionally, behavioral models postulated substance abuse as behavior learned and maintained through classical and operant conditioning. Contemporary cognitive-behavioral models (incorporating social learning perspectives) have stressed—although acknowledging that substance abuse may have some genetic component—the importance of cognitions and feelings preceding and directing drinking and drug taking behavior (Carroll, 1999). From a cognitive-behavioral perspective, substance abuse/dependence is defined as a habitual, maladaptive method for attempting to cope with the stresses of daily living. This maladaptive way of coping is triggered by internal and external cues and reinforced by positive rewards and/or avoidance of punishment (Monti, Abrams, Kadden, & Cooney, 1989).

In the treatment of substance-use disorders, cognitive-behavior therapy emphasizes overcoming skill deficits. Different techniques are used to increase the patient's ability to detect and cope with high-risk situations that commonly precipitate relapse. These include interpersonal difficulties as well as intrapersonal discomfort, such as anger, (social) anxiety, and depression. Cognitive-behavioral approaches focus on teaching new strategies and skills for dealing with and reducing problem behaviors and cognitions through modeling, behavioral practice, and homework assignments. Cognitive-behavioral therapy helps patients identify the patterns associated with the perpetuation and maintenance of substance use (i.e., functional analysis) and implement new strategies for more effectively coping with antecedents of substance use (i.e., relapse prevention skills training). As will be discussed in chapter 3, cognitive-behavior therapy has been shown to be effective across a wide range of substance-use disorders, including alcohol, cannabis, and cocaine dependence.

There are a number of important differences between coping-skills training and motivational interviewing. Implicitly, in cognitive-behavior therapy it is assumed that the patient is motivated; there are no direct strategies for building motivation. Where in motivational interviewing the responsibility for change is left with the patient, in cognitive-behavioral approaches the therapist seeks to identify and modify maladaptive cognitions and teaches specific coping behaviors (Miller & Rollnick, 2002). The following techniques are often included in cognitive-behavioral treatment of substance abuse and dependence (Carroll, 1998; Monti, Abrams, Kadden, & Cooney, 1989).

Functional Analyses

Functional or behavioral analysis is a structured way of organizing antecedents and consequences of problem behavior (in this case, alcohol or drug use), and it helps patient and therapist to assess the determinants of the individual's substance abuse. If the patient abuses more then one substance, it is advisable to make a functional analysis per substance as antecedents and consequences of, for example, drinking alcohol may differ from the antecedents and consequences of using cocaine. The functional analysis is a hypothetical model about the problem behavior. It is used to set goals for treatment and to select the type and sequence of interventions to be used. It is not a puzzle to be solved at the beginning of therapy, used to prioritize treatment interventions, and then to be put aside and forgotten. Rather, it is a flexible working model that can be altered during treatment when new information concerning new important antecedents or consequences emerges—for example, in case of a (re)lapse. In addition, renewed attention to the functional analyses is also warranted when treatment interventions continue to have little impact on the problem behavior. So instead of blaming the patient for being difficult and treatment resistant, behavior therapists should remain alert, incorporating new information into their working models and as a result may need to rearrange their plans for treatment when necessary:

> Joe referred himself to therapy because of problematic alcohol and cocaine use. Being under influence of alcohol and cocaine, he had engaged in high-risk behavior (unprotected sex) and, shocked about his behavior, this had increased his motivation to seek treatment for his drinking and cocaine abuse. Exploring the determinants of his alcohol use, alcohol intake during weekdays was especially cued by time and situation (6:00 P.M., coming home after work) and the thoughts "I really need to

unwind" and "Alcohol will help me relax." During weekends drinking was mainly cued by being in a bar, seeing other people drinking, and the thoughts "I want to have fun," "I want to fit in," and "If I don't have a drink people will notice and think bad of me." Exploring the determinants of cocaine use, cocaine craving was in fact primarily triggered by being under the influence of alcohol.

Avoiding Cues Versus Learning to Cope Differently

Overall, there are two main strategies that target the antecedents of the problem behavior. Patients can try to avoid cues that trigger substance use or they can learn to deal differently with high-risk situations. Avoidance strategies are in general more easily applied when compared to learning new coping skills, but although avoidance is an effective short-term solution, not all high-risk situations can be avoided and some are so strongly intertwined with the patient's living condition that avoiding them permanently is in fact unrealistic:

Therapist: We have identified several internal as well as external cues that trigger craving, and among others, feeling angry or mistreated cues alcohol and cocaine craving. What do you think would be a good way to tackle these high-risk situations?

Patient: Well, I need to learn to handle my emotions better. You are going to teach me that, isn't that right?

Therapist: I think learning to handle your emotions more effectively and preventing acting-out behaviors will be extremely important. However, depending on the severity, it may be necessary to refer you to some specialized aggression-management training.

Patient: That's okay with me.

Therapist: Besides learning to handle anger more effectively, what are you planning to do about all those external cues, such as being in certain bars and nightclubs and seeing your friends use alcohol and cocaine?

Patient: Do you want me to give all that up?

Therapist: These people are very important to you?

Patients: No, not at all, but more in general, life would become such a bore without the parties, without the nightlife.

Therapist: You know, I can imagine that becoming a problem for you in the long run; how to on the one hand keep life exciting but on the other hand prevent relapse in alcohol and cocaine use. We definitely need to address this issue further on in treatment. However, for now it is essential to break though this pattern of alcohol and cocaine use and the most effective way of doing so is by avoiding as many external cues as possible.

Patient: So, no more going to bars, no wild parties, no alcohol- and cocaine-abusing friends.

Therapist: I think this would be the most effective way of going about it, yes.

Handling Craving

Almost all patients experience craving in response to changing their drinking or drug-taking habits, although its intensity and frequency differ greatly among individual patients (and different substances). Because craving is closely linked to (re)lapse and sometimes highly disturbing to patients, it is important to target craving early on in treatment by (1) educating patients about the phenomenon; (2) addressing distorted beliefs about craving (e.g., "If you experience craving, this is a sign of weakness and lack of motivation"); and (3) teaching new coping skills. In general, five main strategies of coping with craving can be distinguished:

1. One way to cope is by *distraction*, doing things that may make the patient forget about the cravings. Examples are taking a shower, going for a walk, or watching a scary movie.
2. Another strategy is *talking about the craving* with supportive friends or relatives. Sometimes it's necessary to prepare this strategy with friends or family members because they might become anxious or feel pressured when the patient starts talking about the urge to use.
3. A more cognitive intervention is *recalling the negative consequences of substance use*. This strategy is helpful in order to counter craving-induced fantasies about use.
4. Another, related, strategy is *self-talk*, in which the patient challenges positive beliefs about substance use and replaces them with more realistic thoughts: "I'll go crazy if I don't use now" is replaced by "Craving won't make me go crazy, the feeling will peak and then decrease within a reasonable time."

5. A somewhat different strategy is *going with the craving*. Instead of trying to avoid craving by distraction or changing its impact thru self-talk, this strategy stresses gaining control by avoiding resistance and going with the flow, as, for example, surfers do when riding a wave.

Changing the Consequences of Use

In addition to addressing the antecedents of substance use, one should also try to address the consequences of use. Alcohol or drug use is reinforced because of the physiological characteristics of the substance, but often there are other factors that reinforce use. One example is the so-called enabling behavior of friends or relatives. In order to cope with the substance abuse, or in order to help the patient, the environment may have adopted strategies that, instead of being effective in decreasing use, in fact reinforce substance abuse. Examples of such coping strategies may be lending the patient money, nursing a patient through a hangover, or making up excuses to others for the patient's impaired behavior when under the influence of alcohol or drugs. One of the advantages of involvement of significant others in treatment is that the above issues can be addressed and alternative coping strategies can be discussed. In addition, reinforcement of abstinence or controlled use can be addressed. Examples would be the patient buying himself a present after a period of abstinence, or saving (part of) the money he used to spend on alcohol or drugs and using it for enhancing his own or his familiy's living condition.

Refusal Skills: Learning to Say No and to Act Accordingly

It is essential to prepare patients for situations in which they are offered alcohol or drugs in order to increase the likelihood that they will withstand temptation or social pressure. Rehearsal using role-play is an effective way of learning new refusal skills. During role-play it is important not only to rehearse the verbal component of refusing but also to pay attention to body language and the behavioral expression of refusal by, for example, walking away. In addition to skill enhancement, it is important to scan for possible dysfunctional beliefs that may interfere with practicing refusal skills:

Laura, a 45-year-old architect, was used to drinking a bottle of wine every evening. She entered a drinking-reduction program and decided she was to stop drinking from Sunday through Thursday and on Friday and Saturday she was going to have three units of alcohol, one glass of wine during dinner and two units during the evening. Problems arose when Laura was confronted with her weekly tennis engagement on Wednesday. Although not craving a drink, Laura found it difficult to order a soft drink instead of alcohol in the presence of her friends. It was not so much a lack of behavioral skills that hindered Laura but much more her thoughts about attracting attention by ordering a nonalcoholic drink. We used the technique of "worst-case scenario" to explore Laura's fears about what could happen if indeed, by ordering a soft drink, she would attract her friends' attention.

Questioning Cognitions Related to Substance Use

Patients often hold strong beliefs about how alcohol or drug use may help them cope with specific high-risk situations (anticipatory beliefs: "Drinking alcohol will make me enjoy the party even more"); how substance use will decrease discomfort (relief-orientated beliefs: "Smoking heroin will help me forget all my troubles"); and why substance use is acceptable (permissive beliefs: "After this long time of abstinence I deserve one little sniff of cocaine"). These cognitions are sometimes realistic, but most often have distorted qualities to them. Besides teaching patients to use different coping skills to deal effectively with high-risk situations, it is also advisory to address these dominant positive beliefs about alcohol or drug use and to test their validity using Socratic dialogue.

Lapsing and Preventing Relapse

Following initial abstinence or controlled use, patients will encounter high-risk situations and in some cases they will lapse or relapse. In fact, most patients lapse during the course of treatment and many experience relapses during or after finishing treatment.

In 1985 Marlatt and Gordon presented their very influential cognitive-behavioral model of the relapse process. The model gives a detailed classification of factors or situations that can precipitate or contribute to relapse episodes. The key elements of this model are seemingly irrelevant decisions, coping skills, self-efficacy, and the abstinence violation effect. The model postulates that entering a high-risk situation is often preceded by seemingly irrelevant decisions. These small decisions or rationalizations apparently have no direct link with direct alcohol or drug use, but they enhance the likelihood of entering high-risk situations. In response to entering a high-risk situation, a patient may effectively use coping skills that will increase self-efficacy and thus decrease the likelihood of relapse. If coping skills are not used or not used effectively, self-efficacy will decrease, and the positive-outcome expectancies for the effects of alcohol or drugs will increase. This will enhance the likelihood of lapse, which will trigger the abstinence violation effect. The *abstinence violation effect* refers to feelings of guilt, shame, and failure in reaction to a lapse, which instead of strengthening the patient to remain abstinent triggers thoughts of the perceived positive effects of alcohol or drug use and thus enhances the likelihood of renewed alcohol or drug use in order to cope with these negative thoughts and emotions.

Using information about previous lapses and relapses, the patient is encouraged to make a *relapse prevention plan*, to be used in the case of a lapse in order to prevent it from becoming a full relapse:

Therapist: Albert, I know you find it difficult to even talk about the possibility of a future lapse and as you stated earlier, it is something you want to prevent any way you can.

Albert: Yes, that's right. I lost too many good things as a result of my drinking. It must stop for once and for all!

Therapist: Yes, I'm aware of that, and that's just why I want to address this relapse prevention plan. Not so much because I expect you to relapse, but rather as a way of being on the safe side. To ensure that, if you lapse into alcohol use, you have the tools to prevent it from becoming a relapse.

Albert: You mean, like that example of taking out an insurance, you were talking about just earlier?

Therapist: Correct.

Albert: Okay, but what should such a prevention plan look like?

Therapist: Well, that depends. Imagine lapsing into alcohol use; what would that situation look like?

Albert: Well, I guess it would be due to some negative things happening to me. I would probably go out to buy my usual two bottles of wine at that local store, return home, and just start drinking. But I'm sure I would stop after one or two glasses.

Therapist: Okay, but let's—for argument's sake—imagine a worse scenario. Imagine you finish those two bottles of wine and, as usual, fall asleep on the couch. The next morning you wake up, probably with quite a hangover. What could you do in order to prevent this lapse from becoming a relapse? In other words, what are you going to do in order to prevent yourself from going to the store to buy even more wine?

Albert: I don't know, I guess I have to pay the price of having failed and stay in bed till I feel better.

Therapist: Well that's an option, but somehow I don't think staying in bed will actually make you feel better, it may even make you feel worse, and thus increase the likelihood of you needing additional alcohol to cope with the situation.

Albert: That sounds familiar, but what else can I do?

Therapist: Well, this is an emergency situation and in the case of an emergency one sometimes needs to take extreme measures in order to ensure safety. Patients come up with all kind of safety measures. The most common being contacting friends or family and looking for social support, not staying at home alone, but going out to seek distraction or ask somebody to come over. In addition, some patients use flash cards in order to counter self-defying thoughts.

Albert: I could phone Peter and ask him to come over, he is very supportive and we could rent a movie or something to get me through the day.

Therapist: That sounds like an effective strategy, but what if Peter isn't at home or is unable to visit? What else could you plan?

Other Techniques for Coping

In addition to the standard techniques used in the treatment of substance abuse discussed above, there are many other coping skills that can be added on to treatment, depending on the function of abuse and the patient's skills deficits. The most common coping skills addressed in substance abuse are social-skills training, problem-solving skills training, and handling negative moods.

Enhancing Social Skills In social-skills training, patients learn to be more effective in expressing their emotions and to assert themselves. According to Liberman (1988), the following skills are necessary to display socially competent behavior: (1) accurate perception of the social situation; (2) translation of the perception into a plan of action; and (3) the execution of the social behavior, combining the necessary verbal and nonverbal components of the behavior. Social-skills training can be conducted in individual and group formats. In addition to verbal assertiveness, this training covers nonverbal aspects of assertiveness such as voice pitch, posture, and eye contact. Social-skills training may target (change in) the following behaviors: making a request, refusing a request, expressing a personal opinion, expressing criticism, responding to criticism, and asserting oneself. Over the course of repeated role-play the patient learns to perform these behaviors in a more adequate fashion. Key techniques used by the therapist include modeling, feedback, and behavioral rehearsal. The patient is gradually shaped into effective execution of the required skills. Homework assignments include the registration of (naturally occurring) difficult social situations and, later in therapy, the deliberate practice of the instructed skills in selected difficult social situations. Social-skills training now is a central component of various relapse prevention programs (Emmelkamp, 2004; Monti & Rohsenow, 1999).

Problem-Solving Skills Training Problem-solving skills training (D'Zurilla, Sanna, & Chang, 2004) has a heavy psychoeducational emphasis and is executed according to a fixed number of steps and applicable across a wide array of problems. These steps are:

Problem orientation, during which the patient explores his personal attitude toward problems. The most important aspects are that the patient learns to recognize his negative feelings as signals of problems and learns to distinguish between problems over which one can exert personal control (e.g., arguments) versus those where one cannot (e.g., cancer).

Problem definition, during which the patient and therapist clarify ambiguous references to the problem and define a goal.

Brainstorming, during which the patient and therapist generate as many different solutions as possible, without critical appraisal or censure.

Choice, during which, for each solution, a systematic appraisal of pros and cons are discussed. The patient selects the most effective option.

Execution, during which the patient executes the selected solution and evaluates its effect.

Besides teaching patients about these steps, it is important to teach patients to apply this technique to their personal problems—preferably in a hierarchical fashion, starting off with less severe and relatively uncomplicated problems and continuing into more profound dilemmas.

Dealing with Negative Moods Negative thoughts and dysphoric moods are common triggers for relapse in substance abuse (Marlatt & Gordon, 1985). However, not all patients seem to recognize the link between experiencing negative feelings and subsequent substance abuse. Thus, an important part of therapy is to help patients to recognize and identify negative feelings and to explore how these feelings may affect substance use. In addition, alternative, more productive ways of coping with negative feelings are taught. The behavior therapy for depression is based on the assumption that depressive symptoms originate from a deficit of reinforcement for constructive and pleasant behaviors, and that depression will remit to the extent the reinforcement of those behaviors increases (Lewinsohn, 1975). Behavioral approaches attempt to change behavior in order to secure an increase in positive reinforcement. According to this view, depressive cognitions are the result of depressed mood, and these cognitions change as a result of behavioral change, which increases reinforcement. Treatments derived from Lewinsohn's theory encourage the patient to participate in constructive and pleasurable activities. Activities patients used to enjoy but have ceased doing are now scheduled as homework assignments. Activities are ordered in a hierarchical fashion. Less-challenging activities are scheduled first, and more-challenging activities follow later on in treatment. A number of studies have investigated whether this reinforcement of pleasant and constructive activities would, by itself, lead to a decrease in negative affect. The evidence has demonstrated that the increase in pleasant activities indeed gives rise to mood improvement (Emmelkamp, 1994). Another way to achieve reinforcement from social interactions is social-skills training.

CUE-EXPOSURE

Cravings in response to alcohol and drug-related cues are presumed to play a role in the continuation of substance-use disorders, particularly in relation to lapses and relapses after treatment. In some cognitive-behavioral protocols, patients are treated with cue exposure, consisting of repeated exposure to the sights or smells of substances (e.g., the sight and smell of a glass of beer, or the sight of white powder on a mirror) until the cravings elicited by these cues substantially weaken.

After successful reductions in the strength of experienced craving, substance-abusing patients are assumed to be more able to resist alcohol and drug use when confronted with these cues in daily life. Theoretically, it is assumed that subjective craving and its physiological symptoms are extinguished.

In order to be able to expose the patient to relevant stimuli, a thorough assessment of cues and stimuli that elicit craving must be undertaken, resulting in a hierarchy of situations. Starting with the situation that evokes the least craving, the therapist will expose the patient to situations from the hierarchy. The emphasis in cue-exposure is on external cues such as sights or smells, drug paraphernalia, or the locations (e.g., the pub) where substances are used. In some instances, when the substance abuse takes place at home, home-based exposure sessions are recommended. Cue-exposure treatment is preferably done in vivo (that is, through exposure to the real situation), but can also be accomplished by watching video (e.g., of drug-related neighborhoods), or through imagery. In all cases, response prevention—as in exposure treatment of obsessive-compulsive patients—is essential. That is, patients should be prevented from being able to get access to alcohol or drugs in order to reduce the craving. Patients' subjective feelings are assessed throughout the exposure sessions by having them rate the subjective experience of craving on a scale from 0 (no craving) to 10 (extremely intense craving):

Alan: I can smell the beer from here. Ooh, I need a drink; just let me taste it. I know, I should not, but I am afraid I'll want to run to the bar after we are finished here to get some beer. Oh, god, I want it. I can't take it.

Therapist: What about your rating?

Alan: It was absolutely 10, but it is slightly less now, say 7. I feel like it is going away somehow. I'll say it is about 5 now. The urge to have a beer in the bar is less. I don't want to run to the bar now. It's going slowly down.

Therapist: Concentrate on your feelings.

Alan: It goes up and down, but it is less than a few minutes ago. I have more control now, it's about 3. Great, I don't have this urge to have a beer any more.

The more realistic the exposure, the more craving will be elicited, and—if successfully resisted—the better the outcome will be. In addition to the sight and smell of the substance cues, specific thoughts, images, and physical sensations usually elicited by the cue might be incorporated into treatment by means of imaginal exposure to help individuals induce their cravings.

In contrast to patients with phobias and obsessive-compulsive disorders, where (part of the) treatment can be performed as a homework assignment without supervision by the therapist, such self-controlled exposure in vivo in substance-abusing patients is not recommended. There is a great risk that the patient will feel overwhelmed by the craving and will give in to the urge to take drugs and/or drink alcohol. Exposure during treatment in a clinical setting will often not generalize to everyday life. Even if cue-exposure therapy in the safe clinical setting has resulted in reduced craving, there is a substantial risk that patients—after discharge, when they are confronted with relevant drug-use cues in their everyday life (e.g., walking past the local bar, seeing cocaine or heroin paraphernalia, meeting friends from "the scene")—will feel helpless against the urge to use and will lapse.

It has been suggested (Otto & Pollack, 2004) that to help patients best build resilience to cues and contexts for drug or alcohol use, treatment should consider both external and internal cues for use. Mood states and somatic manifestations of withdrawal may provide specific internal cues for craving. In patients whose craving and substance abuse is typically elicited by internal states, it is recommended to repeatedly expose patients to those emotional states, (e.g., sadness, guilt, grief, anxiety) by negative-mood induction and to somatic sensations that serve as cues for substance abuse. This can be done by imagery (e.g., imaging a sad event for sadness), but moods can also be induced by mood induction procedures (e.g., listening to music).

Cue-exposure treatment is useful in weakening the link between external and internal (emotional and somatic) cues and substance abuse, but, at present, should be considered as an add-on rather than as a stand-alone treatment. By weakening the link between cues and craving, patients might be enabled to consider more adaptive alternatives. It should be stressed, however, that in most patients the necessary, more productive coping skills have still to be trained. Thus, when conducted properly, cue-exposure treatment should be placed in the context of other strategies to ensure that patients are able to deal with stressful situations and problems of living in a more adaptive way than by substance abuse.

Finally, it should be noted that, especially in illicit drug users, this type of treatment could even be harmful. There is a risk that cue-exposure therapy leads to overestimation by the patient of his ability to cope with drug-related situations, subsequently not using avoiding strategies but exposing himself to high-risk situations. Marissen, Franken, Blanken, Van den Brink, and Hendriks (2005) found that a number of opiate-dependent patients reported that they had tested themselves in drug situations after "successful" cue-exposure therapy.

CONTINGENCY MANAGEMENT AND COMMUNITY REINFORCEMENT

Contingency Management

The basic underlying principle of operant techniques is quite simple: to reinforce desired behavior while undesired behavior is extinguished or punished. A prime example of a treatment based on operant principles is contingency management, in which the environment is arranged in such a fashion that reinforcement or punishment occurs contingent to substance use or other behaviors such as medication compliance or attendance at treatment sessions. Typically, "vouchers" are distributed for occurrences of desired behavior (abstinence from substances) with the aim to reinforce this behavior. For example, biochemical verified abstinence from recent drug use is rewarded with vouchers exchangeable for retail items meeting a predetermined therapeutic goal. The patient can exchange these vouchers for various objects (e.g., money or sweets) and services (e.g., for inpatients, a walk outside the clinic or watching TV; for outpatients, access to a rent-free furnished house, an employment program, or methadone take-home privileges). The main advantage of vouchers is that they can be handed out immediately following the desired behavior. Undesired behaviors do not generate vouchers, which causes these behaviors—according to the principle of extinction—to be extinguished. A number of programs also use punishment following positive drug tests. Punishing consequences may include suspension of employment, removal from house facilities, and transportation to a shelter. This voucher-based incentive is often combined with an intensive behavioral treatment know as the community reinforcement approach (CRA) developed by Hunt and Azrin (1973).

Here is an example of how contingency management is introduced to a cocaine-dependent patient:

> In addition to receiving counseling, you will be requested to provide urine samples three times per week during the first half of treatment and twice weekly during the second half of treatment. During the next 3 months, you also will have the opportunity to earn what we call "vouchers." Vouchers have a monetary value and you earn them every time you provide a urine sample that tests negative for recent cocaine use. In fact you can earn

almost $1000 worth of vouchers during the next 3 months. The vouchers can be used in whatever way you and I agree would support the lifestyle changes that we discuss in our counseling sessions. For example, many people use their vouchers to buy skilift passes, fishing licenses, gift certificates to local restaurants, bicycle equipment, educational materials, and other positive things. In other words, anything that you think will help you remain cocaine-abstinent can be considered. You won't receive cash directly, but all you do is decide with me what items you'd like to spend your vouchers on, and the staff will make the purchase and have whatever you select waiting here for you. (Budney, Sigmon, & Higgins, 2004, p. 265)

As shown in the example above, the goal of contingency management is not only to reinforce drug abstinence but also to increase patients' involvement in drug-free activities, thus preventing relapse. In contingency programs for substance abuse, abstinence from substances is reinforced. In a number of programs patients may earn vouchers for completing activities that are incompatible with substance use. For example, in the contingence management program of Petry, Tedford, and Martin (2001), patients had to choose two to four goals from the following areas: family, recovery, education, social/recreation, legal, health, personal improvement, occupation, transportation, and housing. Participants had to identify three specific goal-related activities to complete each week. They received reinforcement for each completed activity. An escalating reinforcement schedule was used: reinforcement escalated weekly when all three activities were completed.

Job-Skills Training

Most individuals with chronic drug abuse are unemployed, and unemployment among drug abusers is often associated with continued drug use and criminal activity. Unfortunately, many chronically unemployed individuals have difficulty in maintaining employment, given that they often lack adequate job skills. Job performance of many of these individuals is often poor (Silverman, Chutuape, Bigelow, & Stitzer, 1996), so there is a clear need of job skills training. Most chronic drug abusers, however, will not participate in a job-skills training program without special reinforcement contingencies for attendance. Contingency management strategies have been used as an intensive employment intervention for such chronic abusers. In contrast to quick entrance interventions, in which substance-abuse patients are offered jobs, in the therapeutic workplace (Silverman, Svikis, Robles, Stitzer, & Bigelow, 2001) an intensive intervention is offered that trains chronic drug abusers in needed job skills in order to promote and maintain optimal job performance. In addition to promoting employment, the therapeutic workplace intervention is designed to promote drug abstinence by using operant conditioning principles. In this program individuals can earn vouchers that have monetary values that are exchangeable for goods and services. The voucher reinforcement contingencies are arranged primarily to promote abstinence and to maintain workplace attendance.

In the therapeutic workplace, individuals in drug-abuse treatment are offered an intensive job-skills training program (e.g., computer data-entry operator) for three to four hours every weekday. Prior to the start of each workday, participants are required to provide a urine sample under observation by staff. If the sample tests positive for drugs (e.g., opiates and/or cocaine), a participant is not allowed to work that day, and thus cannot earn monetary vouchers. Participants are first offered training in typing and numeric keypad operating; after acquiring modest typing and keypad skills, participants are trained in data entry. If the training is successfully accomplished, participants can progress to a second phase of the treatment in which they are hired as data-entry operators in an income-producing therapeutic workplace business. Vouchers can be earned following strict rules. Here are a few examples of how the voucher system is used in the therapeutic workplace:

A participant receives a voucher worth $7 on the 1st day that a drug-free urine sample is provided.

According to an escalating reinforcement schedule, vouchers are increased by $0.50 for each consecutive successful day, to a maximum of $27 per day.

In case of drug-positive urine, the value of the voucher is reset back to $7.

If a participant arrives late, or fails to work a complete work shift, the value of the next day's voucher is reset back to $7.

Participants earn vouchers for productivity while participating in typing and keypad training programs.

Participants also earn vouchers for data-entry productivity. (Silverman, Svikis, Robles, Stitzer, & Bigelow, 2001.)

Although intensive interventions such as the one described above may be needed to keep chronic drug abusers abstinent and employed, there are a number of disadvantages associated with the implementation of such programs in the community, the most obvious being the high costs involved. It is unlikely that health insurance or third-party payers (managed care) will provide the necessary financial means to individual chronic drug abusers.

Implementation of Contingency Management in the Community

Although the results of contingency management are highly encouraging, implementation to clinical practice is often impeded by the high cost of vouchers. In research studies by Higgins and colleagues, patients could earn up to $1,200 over a 12-week treatment period (e.g., Higgins, Budney, Bickel, & Badger, 1994; Higgins, Wong, Badger, Ogden, & Dantona, 2000). Unfortunately, simply lowering voucher amounts has reduced efficacy (Dallery, Silverman, Chutuape, Bigelow, & Stitzer, 2001; Silverman, Chutuape, Bigelow, & Stitzer, 1999). However, Petry and colleagues have developed another contingency management procedure in which patients earned *a chance* to draw from an urn and win prizes ranging from $1 to $100 in value. In studies conducted in community-based clinics (Petry, Martin, Cooney, & Kranzler, 2000; Petry & Martin, 2002; Petry et al., 2004), average expected earnings were arranged at about $250. This so-called fishbowl lottery is much more feasible to be implemented in clinical practice in community settings. This prize-based contingency management procedure is less expensive, yet beneficial effects are achieved. It should be noted, however, that costs related to staff time for prize purchases and urine testing also need to be taken into account. Another promising alternative to voucher-based contingency management that may be more feasible in community treatment settings is the use of abstinence-contingent housing (Jones, Wong, Tuten, & Stitzer, 2005; Milby et al., 2000; Schumacher, Usdan, Milby, Wallace, & McNamara, 2000). The houses provide a structured and supportive drug-free environment. If patients test positive for drug use, they are removed and placed at a community shelter (or with their families). When a patient tests negative for illicit drugs, she may reenter the free housing program.

Contingency Management with Adolescents

A major risk factor for adolescent substance abuse is the presence of childhood conduct disorder, and conduct problems are strong predictors of poor outcome during treatment for substance abuse. Conduct problems often precede adolescent substance abuse, suggesting that targeting conduct problems might enhance outcomes in treatment for such abuse. Kamon, Budney, & Stanger (2005) describe a multicomponent, contingency management–based treatment that specifically targets conduct problems in addition to substance abuse. An abstinence-based reinforcement intervention (voucher program) is used to enhance motivation to engage in treatment and engender marijuana and other drug abstinence. Given that adolescents are rarely motivated to quit use and rarely seek treatment on their own but instead are brought to treatment by their parents, who are usually motivated to take action, the contingency-management procedure used also reinforces appropriate goal-specific parent behavior. Parents were offered training in basic behavioral principles and skills to decrease conduct problems and increase prosocial behavior. Contingency management procedures were used to motivate parent participation. Here, parents earn chances to win prizes for actively participating in each treatment component. Thus, the combination of voucher programs for the adolescent and the parent was designed to increase adolescents' motivation to achieve and maintain abstinence, and enhance parents' skills to use effective parenting to decrease substance use and conduct problems.

Community Reinforcement

In clinical practice, community reinforcement is often used in combination with contingency management and may contribute to persistence of abstinence after discontinuation of contingency management. The community reinforcement approach encourages involvement in rewarding, non-drug-related alternatives to illicit drug use and is directed to change a lifestyle of substance abuse into a lifestyle that is more rewarding. Thus, the emphasis is not only on promoting abstinence of substance abuse using voucher-based incentive programs as described above but also on social activities that are incompatible with substance use.

Jones et al. (2005) describe a community reinforcement approach that they use with heroin-dependent patients exiting brief residential detoxification programs. In the context of a day-treatment program, the therapy provides individual counseling supplemented by abstinence-contingent support for housing, food, and recreational activities as well as skills training for securing employment. The program consists of the following elements: Patients are offered living in a recovery house, as long as they test negative for illicit drugs. Each time a participant attends the clinic, he provides a urine sample that is tested for heroin and cocaine—seven days per week during the first three weeks, and four days per week the following nine weeks. Patients who test positive for illicit drugs only meet with their counselor for an individual one-hour session and are not allowed to take part in the rest of the program. Further, they are removed from the recovery house and placed in a temporary shelter.

Those participants testing negative are allowed to participate in the full range of counseling activities described below. The following abstinent contingent benefits are in effect during the first three months of the program.

Individual counseling two to three times per week.
Group counseling focusing on skill building (Budney & Higgins, 1998; Carroll, 1998).
Vocational counseling (Azrin & Besalel, 1980). Patients participate in vocational counseling until they secure employment.
Recreational activities include outings in the community, such as attending movies and going to a fitness center.
A social club. Patients are served lunch and given the opportunity to interact with non-drug-using peers.

When a patient provides a urine sample that tests positive for opioids and/or cocaine, a "time out" from reinforcer availability, group contact, and living in the recovery house is initiated.

Clinical Guidelines

Contingency management programs must employ an effective monitoring system, providing precise information on the occurrence of the target response. Reliance on self-report is notoriously unreliable (Budney, Sigmon, & Higgins, 2004).
Contingency management is only feasible in clinical settings with positive staff attitudes toward operant conditioning, and with regular urine screens, and in settings that can provide the costs of incentives.
Use an escalating reinforcement schedule. The monetary value of vouchers should increase with each consecutive drug-free test, and reset to lower value if a drug test is positive.
In polydrug users, abstinence from both cocaine and illicit opioids is an important goal, but setting too high a threshold initially for earning a reward may reduce the effectiveness of contingency management and many patients will drop out of treatment. It should be stressed that in research studies with severe drug dependence, many patients never provided a single drug-free urine test (Schottenfield et al., 2005), and thus never had an opportunity to receive the voucher reward.

In combination drug users, it might be clinically wise to start contingency management with one drug only and then include other illicit drugs in the reinforcement schedule if progress is made with the one drug.

Lowering the threshold for earning vouchers (e.g., reinforcing reductions in use rather than abstinence) may enhance the effectiveness of contingency management (Schottenfeld et al., 2005).

Strategies to improve sustained maintenance of abstinence after discontinuation of contingency management are also needed. Rather than abruptly withdrawing the reward procedure, gradual fading of rewards may help with abstinence persistence.

Detailed treatment manuals for community reinforcement approaches are available. A detailed manual for the community reinforcement treatment of alcohol abuse has been written by Meyers and Smith (1995). A treatment manual describing a combination of contingency management and community reinforcement in the treatment of cocaine dependence has been published by the National Institute of Health (Budney & Higgins, 1998).

BEHAVIORAL COUPLE THERAPY

In general, couples in which one or both partners abuse alcohol and/or drugs report low marital satisfaction. Moreover, substance abuse has been associated with other marital issues such as domestic violence and sexual dysfunction, and has been found to affect communication between partners. Effectiveness of individual cognitive-behavior therapy might be impeded by relationship problems, although results of these studies are inconclusive (Emmelkamp & Vedel, 2002). In general, behavioral couple treatment for substance-use disorders focuses on self-control and coping skills to facilitate and maintain abstinence, improve a spouse's coping with drinking-related situations, improve relationship functioning in general, and improve functioning within other social systems the couple is currently involved in. The degree of emphasis on each of these four domains and the techniques used to target these domains vary across different treatment protocols. Two well-known protocols used in the treatment of alcohol-use disorders are the ones used in Harvard University's Counseling for Alcoholics' Marriages (CALM) project by O'Farrell (1993) and the Alcohol Behavioral Couple Treatment (ABCT) protocol used by McCrady (see McCrady, Stout, Noel, Abrams, & Nelson, 1991). The main differences between these two protocols are that O'Farrell's treatment is designed to be used conjointly or subsequent to a treatment focusing on cessation of drinking, whereas the treatment developed by McCrady is designed as a stand-alone treatment. As well, part of the CALM treatment is delivered in a group format while the ABCT is delivered during individual couple sessions (see, e.g., Noel & McCrady, 1993; O'Farrel, 1993). The main components of behavioral couple therapy for substance abuse are listed below:

> In some programs the couple has to engage in a *daily sobriety trust contract*; each day at a specific time the substance-abusing patient has to initiate a brief discussion with his partner and to reiterate the intention not to drink or use drugs. The couple has to agree to refrain from any discussing of substance abuse at any other time, to keep the daily trust discussion very brief, and to end with a positive statement to each other. The Antabuse contract adds on daily Antabuse ingestion in the presence of the partner.
>
> Prior to formulating the treatment plan, the therapist will, in close collaboration with the couple, make a *functional analysis* of the substance abuse problems, with special emphasis on potential relationship factors functioning as an antecedent or consequence of substance abuse.
>
> The therapist will try to address *attention bias* between the couple. Thus rather than focusing only on each other's negative behaviors, the couple are asked to record positive behaviors of each other. As a homework assignment both partners are asked to write down pleasant or positive behaviors they have observed in each other (e.g., asking how the other's day was, getting up to make some coffee) and are asked to acknowledge these behaviors during the next treatment sessions.
>
> Besides shifting attentions toward the more positive aspects of their relationship, partners are prompted to actually *increase positive interaction* by increasing caring behaviors and planning pleasant activities. Positive interaction has often disappeared as a result of substance abuse and marital discord. Having entered treatment, couples sometimes find it difficult to reinstate positive behaviors, because of feelings of resentment and distrust. Although acknowledgment of these feelings is very important, it remains essential that abstinence is reinforced though an increase of positive interaction between the couple in order to decrease the likelihood of relapse.
>
> *Communication training.* The main objective of communication training is to teach couples how to improve their communication. Partners receive training in skills that enable them to talk

to one another more effectively. Modeling, feedback, shaping, and role-playing are specific techniques used in communication training. The following skills are instructed in a structured fashion:
- active listening
- expression of empathy
- expression of emotion
- assertiveness

When the partners have adequately mastered these skills they can apply them when discussing their *specific relationship issues* in the session and as a homework assignment.

Problem-solving training is also an important part of communication training among substance-abusing couples.

Talking through the possibility of lapses and relapse and coming up with a *relapse prevention plan* consisting of effective helping strategies to be carried out by patient and spouse in the case of a lapse, in order to prevent relapse.

Clinical Guidelines

If the partner is unsupportive toward change or is actively abusing substances herself, standard behavioral couple therapy is not advisable.

It is good practice to schedule some pretreatment sessions in order to inform partners about what is to be expected of behavioral couple therapy and in order to assess (and possibly enhance) the treatment motivation of both partners.

Although not customary in marital treatment, in substance abuse it is often necessary to interview partners separately, in order to assess possible secrets regarding substance abuse and/or to be informed about the presence and severity of domestic violence.

If the patient is ambivalent about behavioral change, the presence of a partner during the first part of treatment may hinder the patient in exploring the pros and cons of change freely, pressuring him to comply to the demands of the spouse.

Sometimes partners have difficulty controlling feelings of resentment and distrust during treatment sessions. If this continues to be the case, and partners seem unable or unwilling to shape into a more productive way of addressing problems, continuing a stand-alone substance-focused behavioral couple therapy

TABLE 2.2   Major Tenets about Alcoholism

- Alcoholism is a physical, mental, and spiritual disease
- The disease is progressive and has a biological or genetic basis
- Psychological problems are the result, not the cause of drinking
- Alcoholics are self-centered
- Loss of spirituality is central to the cause of alcoholism

---

treatment will most often be of little avail, and changing behavioral couple therapy into individual cognitive-behavior therapy is advisable.

12-STEP APPROACHES

Treatment and recovery for substance abuse often involves multifaceted approaches, not only including treatment of the addiction by a professional, but in a number of cases participation in Alcoholics Anonymous (AA) and Narcotics Anonymous (NA) as well.

Alcoholics Anonymous was founded in the United States in 1935 and since the mid-1940s has spread around the world. AA is based on major tenets about the nature of addiction; the most important are shown in table 2.2. The basic philosophy is summarized in the 12 steps listed in table 2.3. According to Alcoholics Anonymous (Alcoholics Anonymous World Services, 1986) the 12 steps are "a group of principles, spiritual in their nature, which, if practiced as a way of life, can expel the obsession to drink and enable the sufferer to become happily and usefully whole" (p. 15).

Narcotics Anonymous (NA) and Cocaine Anonymous (CA) are the primary self-help groups available in many countries for the assistance of recovery from illicit drug-use problems. These self-support groups are international fellowships based on the program and organizational traditions first espoused by AA (Kelly, 2003). Self-help groups based on the NA and CA framework offer a 12-step program, regular group meetings, and other assistance for people recovering from substance-abuse problems.

Enthusiasm for the 12-step approach is high among clinicians in the United States (Forman, Bovasso, & Woody, 2001). In 1988, 95% of U.S.-surveyed inpatient alcohol treatment programs incorporated AA and NA into their programs of recovery (Brown, Peterson, & Cunningham, 1988). Further, it is estimated that 30% of patients meeting the criteria for substance abuse or dependence in general hospitals attend AA or NA meetings (Johnson, Phelps, & McCuen, 1990). Because managed

TABLE 2.3 The 12 Steps

Step 1	We admitted we were powerless over alcohol—that our lives had become unmanageable.
Step 2	Came to believe that a Power greater than ourselves could restore us to sanity.
Step 3	Made a decision to turn our will and lives over to the care of God as we understood Him.
Step 4	Made a searching and moral inventory of ourselves.
Step 5	Admitted to God, to ourselves, and to another human being the exact nature of our wrongs.
Step 6	Were entirely ready to have God remove all these defects of character.
Step 7	Humbly asked Him to remove our shortcomings.
Step 8	Made a list of all persons we had harmed, and became willing to make amends to them all.
Step 9	Made direct amends to such people wherever possible, except when to do so would injure them or others.
Step 10	Continued to take personal inventory and when we were wrong promptly admitted it.
Step 11	Sought through prayer and meditation to improve our conscious contact with God as we understood Him, praying only for knowledge of His will for us and the power to carry that out.
Step 12	Having had a spiritual awakening as the result of these Steps, we tried to carry this message to alcoholics, and to practice these principles in all our affairs.

care has reduced the amount of time available for practitioners to work with patients, substance-abuse workers in the United States are increasingly interested in facilitating patient involvement in self-help groups as an inexpensive way of achieving and maintaining treatment gains. In societies outside the United States, there appears to be much less interest in this approach by substance-abuse workers (Day, Lopez Gaston, Furlong, Murali, & Copello, 2005; Luty, 2004). There are nearly twice as many AA/NA fellowships in the United States as in all other countries combined (Alcoholics Anonymous UK, 2005).

Since many patients attend 12-step meetings, and there is some support of the effectiveness of the 12-step approaches (as will be discussed in chapter 3), professionals in the field of mental health need to have a thorough understanding of the principles of 12-step anonymous programs.

First of all, it is important to note that self-support groups such as AA do not provide formal treatment. AA does not conduct assessments, write treatment plans, provide case management, or provide therapy (Wallace, 2004). It is best conceptualized as a social movement or fellowship. AA's philosophy is rooted in a Christian evangelical movement, but one does not need to be Christian to become a member of AA. However, many meetings will begin and end with prayer, although this is in less usage in other countries than in the United States. Nevertheless, patients who are modest in religious practice, or even nonpracticing, may profit from the 12-steps approach (Winzelberg & Humphreys, 1999). According to the second and third steps of AA, individuals have to believe in a power greater than themselves. Currently, increasing emphasis is on the experience of a more general spirituality (a "higher power") than on an all-powerful God or some other supernatural source. Many substance-abusing individuals are assumed to be characterized by a lack of purpose in life, inner emptiness, meaninglessness, feelings of alienation, and despair, and a sense of spirituality might give meaning to life. Spirituality is a highly individualized experience, and for areligious people, the higher power can be conceptualized as AA itself, the therapist, or the support group (Sheehan & Owen, 1999; Wallace, 2004).

From participants in AA and NA, commitment to the philosophy is expected, including endorsement of the sobriety principle, acceptance of the importance of spirituality, abstinence-oriented social networks, and regular attendance at the meeting. The 12 steps cannot be taken individually, as the program is a unified process. Initially, one does go through these 12 steps one after the other, but soon learns that recovery is a continual cycling through the various steps. AA is a lifelong program of recovery. Sponsorship is an important element of 12-step support groups. Senior members serve as mentors and teachers for newcomers and provide one-to-one guidance and encouragement to stay sober. Sponsors play a pivotal role in members' working through their program of recovery. AA sponsors will tell newcomers to avoid former substance-abusing friends and situations associated with substance abuse. For newcomers, sponsors may offer the opportunity for day-to-day contact, either face-to-face or by telephone. Over time, members can increase their involvement with AA by becoming a sponsor or leading meetings.

More recently, alternative organizations have been founded that also adhere to abstinence as the goal of recovery from substance abuse, but do not rely on belief in God or a supernatural source to get rid of the addiction (one example is Save Our Selves). For an overview of available self-help groups for substance abuse, the reader is referred to Nowinsky (1999).

The Minnesota Model

The disease model of substance abuse contends that substance abuse is not the result of lack of willpower, personality traits, or learned maladaptive behavior, but a progressive chronic illness, eventually affecting all facets of the person's life. The Minnesota Model was developed, incorporating many components of the Alcoholics Anonymous philosophy, emphasizing total abstinence as the only realistic goal for substance abuse. Although originally developed in a residential setting, it is also widely applied in outpatient settings. Treatment usually consists of bibliotherapy, psychoeducation, and individual and group sessions, and addresses the 12 steps of AA systematically to promote therapeutic change and to resolve risk factors for relapse.

In the early stage of treatment the emphasis is on acceptance that the substance-abusing individual suffers from a chronic, progressive illness, recognition that substance abuse is a disease beyond the control of willpower, and acceptance that the only viable option is complete abstinence from alcohol and drugs. The powerlessness of the individual has to be recognized by the addict before any progress with the other steps can be expected. In the initial stage therapists work hard on recognition by the patient of self-defeating consequences, and recognition of denial, rationalization, and minimization. The person must become aware of the role these defenses play in her life. Further, in doing so, therapists will enhance motivation for change and recognition of the need for help from others to achieve effective and enduring behavior change.

Later on, the concept of spirituality is introduced: patients need to trust in a power greater than their own willpower. Another aspect dealt with in the Minnesota Model is to work toward increasing the individual's awareness of inadequate coping styles with problems of living, stress, anger, and anxiety. Cognitive-behavioral techniques are integrated in the program to deal with stressful events and to enable behavior change. In the Minnesota Model, patients are highly encouraged to participate in 12-step self-help groups at the posttreatment stage, thus providing support from peers (former substance abusers) to continue on with sobriety.

Therapeutic Processes

Twelve-steps approaches such as AA and NA may encompass some key active ingredients that are comparable to cognitive and behavioral coping skills. Thus, although cognitive-behavior therapy and 12-step approaches speak different languages and endorse different philosophies, both approaches facilitate the development of behavioral and cognitive change processes. In 12-step approaches, active behavioral coping is encouraged (McCrady, 1994), including engaging in incompatible behaviors when experiencing urges to drink or take drugs, avoiding drinking individuals and situations. In the Minnesota Model, behavioral changes are encouraged. Further, behavioral techniques such as relaxation training, problem solving to deal more adequately with stress and negative emotions, and assertive training and social-skills training are frequently applied in treatments based on the Minnesota Model (Sheehan & Owen, 1999).

It has been suggested that AA and NA meetings are particularly suited to change maladaptive cognition of substance-abusing individuals (see, e.g., Bean-Bayog, 1993; DiClemente, 1993; Khantzian & Mack, 1994), such as denial that they cannot control drinking, that they drink because of pain and drinking relieves pain, and that they are unable to solve this problem. In 12-step groups substance abusers are encouraged to explore self-centered thinking. First, when patients recognize the maladaptive thinking style of fellow group members, they might start to realize that they themselves do not think straight, either ("stinking thinking"), and that something is basically wrong with their own cognitions and that this underlies their substance abuse. When experiencing craving, the substance abuser is encouraged to think of the negative consequences of drinking rather than the immediate relief. The frequent use of typical AA slogans such as "Let go and let God"; "Live and let live"; "Easy does it"; "In order to win, one has to lose"; "One day at a time"; "Keep it simple"; and "In order to give, one has to receive" are actually not so much different from self-statements used in cognitive restructuring therapy along the lines of Meichenbaum (1977). Similarly, the Serenity Prayer—"God grant me the serenity to accept the things I cannot change, courage to change the things I can, and wisdom to know the difference"—can be conceptualized as a spiritually oriented way of cognitive restructuring. In the Minnesota Model, these slogans are taught and reinforced to modulate emotionality and increase awareness of behavioral coping options (Sheehan & Owen, 1999). There are, however, important differences with cognitive restructuring as practiced by cognitive-behavior therapists when compared to practice in self-help groups. In 12-step approaches, the strategy is to try to break through denial and faulty belief systems rather than assist patients to recognize their own faulty beliefs associated with substance abuse at their own pace and replace those faulty beliefs with more productive ones.

Clinical Guidelines

Many psychotherapists want to integrate 12-step self-help groups into a comprehensive treatment program. However, just recommending that a patient attend the meetings of such support groups is often not enough. In the context of the Project MATCH (Matching Alcoholism Treatments to Client Heterogeneity) study a protocol was developed (Nowinsky, 2004; Nowinsky, Baker, & Carroll, 1992) that provides a number of clinical guidelines to facilitate participation in 12-step support groups.

Presentation of goals. Professionals who would like to facilitate 12-step adherence and meeting attendance should themselves endorse the disease model of addiction at least to some extent, in order to come across as authentic. Thus, consistent with AA philosophy, substance abuse should be presented as a disease that cannot be cured but only arrested by abstinence.

Being knowledgeable about mutual help groups. It is recommended that therapists be familiar with the mutual help groups available in the region. These groups often differ in important aspects, such as how the steps and concepts of AA are applied. Having some knowledge about specific groups may be helpful in recommending particular groups that more closely match the patient's beliefs and "culture."

Suggest bibliotherapy. Specific recommendations should be made regarding reading 12-steps publications (e.g., *Alcoholics Anonymous*, the "Big Book").

Recommend attendance. The therapist should recommend specific meetings in the region at convenient locations, and provide a current schedule. Further, goals should be set for meeting attendance. Initially, daily sessions are recommended.

Work through resistance to attendance. Some resistance is due to stereotypes the patient may have about people attending AA/NA meetings (e.g., that they are dogmatic religious people). In these cases it is often useful to invite patients to attend an open meeting to check whether their beliefs and attitudes about AA members are in need of some change. In contrast to motivational interviewing, adherents of the Minnesota Model recommend a firm stand on the part of the therapist to deal with resistance of the patient. The therapist might, for instance, say, " I think that part of your unwillingness to go to meetings is denial. I think there is a part of you that does not want to accept this limitation—that you are an alcoholic and that you have to give up drinking. That part of you wants to avoid going to an AA meeting" (Nowinsky et al., 1999, p. 42).

Active facilitation. The therapist may need to pay attention to underlying beliefs of the patient (e.g., "I am too shy to benefit from such a group") or to actively rehearse through role-play the adequate social behavior expected in self-support groups (e.g., self-disclosure, speaking in front of others), in order to enhance the self-efficacy of the patient—that he will be able to cope with the group meetings.

Monitor attendance. The therapist should be informed at every session as to whether the patient has gone to any meeting, and if so, how he reacted to it.

Facilitate identification. The therapist should ask the patient if there has been someone at the meeting(s) that he can identify with.

Acceptance of personal limitation. The therapist should assist the patient in accepting that he is powerless over alcohol or drug use, helping the patient to acknowledge that earlier attempts at stopping substance abuse have failed.

Encourage commitment. The therapist should encourage patients to choose a sponsor and to follow the 12 steps.

Reinforce attendance. If the therapist ignores the fact that the patient participates in a self-support group, the attendance of group meetings is likely to wane or be extinguished.

Reinforce sober days. Similarly, it is import to reinforce any attempt to stay sober; for instance, saying, "It's great that you succeeded in calling the AA emergency line when you had this feeling of sadness and the urge to drink; I am happy to hear that the support offered helped you to keep off the bottle."

Support change in friends. The therapist should support patients in reconstructing their social network; encourage and reinforce contacts with sober friends.

Invite significant others. If patients are living with family, the therapist and/or patient should invite a partner or significant others (e.g., parent) to a few sessions to enable them to understand the facilitation program and the basic tenets of the 12-step approach.

Termination. Appraise how much progress has been made and, if treatment has been successful, terminate therapy and encourage lifelong commitment to the 12 steps.

PHARMACOTHERAPY

Detoxification

In many patients who are dependent on alcohol and/or drugs, the first stage of treatment consists of detoxification: the patient is tapered off the drug on which she has become dependent. Detoxification to alcohol takes about a week, but in opioid-dependent patients it will usually take longer. Medically assisted tapering services may be offered either as an inpatient or outpatient service under close supervision. In many patients, the detoxification process is rather difficult, since patients will experience marked withdrawal symptoms. In alcoholic patients, detoxification is often assisted with medication (e.g., benzodiazepines, which reliably block alcohol withdrawal symptoms) to prevent withdrawal symptoms, seizures, and delirium. Stimulant withdrawal often needs no medication.

During detoxification of opioid-dependent patients they are taken off opioids and withdrawal signs and symptoms are controlled under medical supervision, preferably as inpatients. Unfortunately, if this is the only treatment, in many cases it hardly contributes to reducing the likelihood of relapse. Relapse rates are rather high following the tapering off of opioids. One month after inpatient opioid detoxification, relapse rates around 75% have been reported (Broers, Giner, Dumont, & Mino, 2000; Chutuape, Jasinski, Fingerhood, & Stitzer, 2001). The relapse does not come as a surprise. One can hardly expect that the changes in brain pathways created by years of drug use will automatically revert to normal when the body is cleansed of the drug. Currently, detoxification in opioid-dependent persons is preferably done by first substituting heroin with methadone, followed by slowly tapering off the substitution medication.

Maintenance treatment is not the panacea for opioid addiction, but it helps patients to normalize their lives and provides them the opportunity to solve other problems associated with the chronic use of illicit drugs (e.g., financial, housing, social, employment, and legal problems). Moreover, stabilization by maintenance medication may set the stage for additional psychotherapy.

An Aversive Deterrent in Alcohol Use: Disulfiram

Disulfiram (Antabuse) is widely used in alcohol dependence in patients who are trying to refrain from drinking alcohol, and blocks the chemical breakdown of alcohol. Disulfiram blocks the enzyme alcohol dehydrogenase so that if the patient takes a drink, acetaldehyde is produced, causing a very unpleasant flushing reaction, manifesting itself in extremely unpleasant symptoms such as increased respiration rate, heavy sweating, nausea, vomiting, headache, dizziness, and palpitations (increased heart rate). The goal of disulfiram treatment is to create an aversion to alcohol rather than to modulate its neurochemical effects. Disulfiram produces nausea only after the ingestion of alcohol but not after the ingestion of drugs, which limits its use in polydrug users.

Most patients (but not all) who are taking disulfiram will refrain from drinking alcohol to prevent the negative effects described above. In clinical practice the success of disulfiram use is mixed. A number of patients decide not to take the medication when experiencing a high craving for alcohol. Others stop taking the drug because they believe they can stay sober without it. Preferably, it is prescribed when daily monitoring of ingestion is feasible (e.g., in the presence of a partner). In patients with liver disease, which is unfortunately highly prevalent among alcohol-dependent patients, disulfiram has toxic effects. Aversive therapy with disulfiram is not without risk for certain patients, and should be closely supervised. For this reason disulfiram is not really suitable for long-term outpatient use in the community without regular monitoring by a medical doctor (Mann, 2004). Disulfiram can be combined with anticraving medication. Besides using disulfiram on a daily or near daily basis, patients can also use it in single high-risk situations, as illustrated by the following example:

> Fred had tried cutting down on alcohol several times on his own (with little avail) before he was referred to us. During the first phase of treatment, treatment goals were assessed, and Fred made daily recordings of cravings, and skills to cope with craving were rehearsed. He was able to remain sober in many craving-eliciting situations, but Sunday's football match remained lapse prone. Not going to these matches was an option, but only a short-term one because Fred did not want to part with his favorite leisure activity. After trying several other techniques, which turned out to be unsuccessful (role-playing—e.g., how to refuse a drink offered by his friends), Fred and this therapist decided he was going to take disulfiram every Sunday morning before going of to the football match.

Anticraving Medication in Alcohol Use

In contrast to an aversive deterrent such as disulfiram, which produces illness as a person drinks, anticraving medication reduces the urge to drink. Naltrexone (Revia), an antagonist of endogenous opioids, reduces the person's craving by blocking alcohol's ability to stimulate the opioid system. Although naltrexone was developed for the treatment of opiate addiction, it was also found to reduce cravings for alcohol (by reducing the rewarding effect of alcohol), which led the U.S. Food and Drug Administration (FDA) to add alcoholism to the indications for naltrexone. Although there is no need for daily dosing, with one dose lasting up to two days, adherence is often a problem. Research on depot medication of naltrexone is currently being conducted, and it is expected that this will become available to clinical practice in 2007 (Kranzler, Wesson, & Billot, 2004).

An alternative anticraving medication is acamprosate (Campral). Although already widely used in Europe, it was only recently (in 2004) approved by the FDA for use in the United States. Acamprosate is believed to maintain abstinence by blocking the negative craving that alcohol-dependent patients experience in the absence of alcohol.

Both naltrexone and acamprosate are generally well tolerated; nausea is reported in about 10% of patients treated with naltrexone, while the most frequent adverse effect reported with acamprosate is diarrhea (Mann, 2004). Both naltrexone and acamprosate improve outcome in rehabilitation of alcohol-dependent patients, but seem to act on different aspects of drinking pathology; both drugs are particularly useful as an add-on to psychological treatment.

Opiate Agonist Maintenance Treatment

Among clinicians, there is increasing awareness that people who are dependent on opiates can best be treated as suffering from a chronic disease, with continuing care and monitoring over time. Earlier reluctance to prescribe maintenance therapies in opiate-addiction treatment has waned. Much of the damage caused by heroin addiction results from using unsterile needles, overdoses, and drug-related criminality. The emphasis in treatment of chronic opiate-dependent patients is now on reducing intensity, frequency, and length of relapse, thus preventing overdose risk and HIV seroconversion (Leshner, 1998). In doing so, treatment providers may help heroin addicts to get their lives back on track, to hold jobs, and to reduce criminal activity.

Opioid-dependent individuals have a variety of treatment options available to them. This is in part because opioids are the one class of addictive drugs for which highly efficacious substitution therapies have been developed, including methadone, levo-alpha-acetylmethadol, and buprenorphine. The patient is prescribed a medication in the same category as the drug of dependence, and withdrawal symptoms are blocked. Then the medication can be gradually reduced. Substitutive treatments have consistently been shown to enable dependent heroin users to achieve a sustained reduction in their heroin use. The rationale of maintenance treatments is that by substituting medication (e.g., methadone) for an opioid (typically heroin), users will be more able to regain control over their heroin use. There will be less need to spend time on drug-related activities because the craving for heroin has been relieved.

Opiate agonist treatment has relied almost exclusively on methadone since the mid-1960s, generally in a maintenance regimen requiring daily dosing. Methadone is a synthetic opiate that can be taken orally and prevents withdrawal symptoms for 24 hours. When patients continue to take heroin when they are on active methadone, the euphoric effects ("rushes") do not occur. Patients are still physically dependent on methadone, but the withdrawal effects are less intense. Although methadone maintenance is the most widely used treatment for opioid addiction, its effects are variable. Another disadvantage is the need for daily dosing. Given the variation in effects, and the inconvenience of daily dosing, alternative maintenance medication has been investigated.

One strategy for improving the treatment of opioid dependence has been the development of a longer-acting opiate agonist maintenance medication, levo-alpha-acetylmethadol (LAAM). Like methadone, LAAM in a maintenance regimen suppresses withdrawal symptoms and blocks the intoxication effects of illicit opiates. The main clinical advantage of LAAM over methadone is the duration of stable effect: LAAM can be taken three times per week instead of daily. Despite promising findings, LAAM has not widely been used due to some concern about the possibility of cardiac arrhythmia. Because of the possible side effects, the manufacturer recently discontinued the distribution of LAAM.

Since 2002 buprenorphine, a schedule III partial opiate agonist, can be prescribed by physicians trained in its use in the United States for treating opiate dependence outside the specialized setting of narcotic treatment programs. Advantages of buprenorphine over methadone are fewer sedative effects and a lower risk of overdose (Schottenfeld et al., 2005). It can be taken in pill form only three times a week. Further, less frequent dosing schedules reduce the need for patients to attend a treatment program on a daily basis, thus enhancing treatment compliance, and eliminate the risk of diversion from take-home medication, since—unlike with methadone—no take-home doses of buprenorphine are necessary (see, e.g., Bickel and Amass, Crean, & Badger, 1999).

Maintenance medication can be taken indefinitely, but eventually a number of opioid addicts succeed in withdrawing from the maintenance treatment and in leading an opiate-free life. Although maintenance medication has been shown to be effective in a substantial proportion of opioid addicts, it is not without its critics. It has been argued that maintenance medication does not really cure substance abuse but merely transfers the dependence from one drug to another. Some still subscribe to the adage, "You can't treat a drug problem with a drug." Further, since the maintenance medication in normal doses does not produce a "rush," some patients may turn to other drugs as supplement to the maintenance medication to get high (e.g., cocaine).

Opiate Antagonist Medication

Naltrexone (discussed above for alcohol dependence), although not widely utilized in opioid-dependent patients, is a medication that blocks the effects of opioids, thus making it impossible to experience its usual euphoric effect. Thus, if a former addict takes heroin while taking naltrexone, the effects will be neutralized. Pharmacologically related is naloxon; both drugs may be of some use in helping opioid addicts avoid relapsing following detoxification. Given severe withdrawal reactions, naltrexone is not very popular among opioid addicts and careful prescription is needed. Many patients drop out, especially in the first months of treatment.

Cocaine Dependence

Several randomized, controlled clinical trials have shown that disulfiram, acting as an indirect dopamine agonist, decreases cocaine use more then either a placebo or naltrexone. Besides disulfiram, other medications currently marketed for other indications show good promise for cocaine abuse including modafinil, which is a glutamate agonist, and tiagabine, topiramate, gabapentin, and baclofen, which are gamma-aminobutyric acid enhancers (e.g., Bisaga et al., 2006). A possible new development for cocaine dependence includes a vaccine that prevents cocaine from leaving the bloodstream and entering the brain. A large placebo-controlled clinical trial testing its efficacy is currently being conducted (Koster, 2005).

Concluding Remarks

In our view, none of the psychological treatments discussed in this book conflicts in any way with the use of medication to further reduce the probability of relapse. Some clinicians, especially psychologists, are opposed to using medication in addition to psychotherapy, since they feel that patients are not helped by replacing one drug with another. Given the recent evidence for medication for substance abuse, as discussed later on in Chapter 3, this reluctance and opposition against pharmacotherapy is unjustified. In cases where patients have been prescribed medication, such therapists may, often unwittingly, actually have been reinforcing non-compliance with the medication regime. Better, therapists should use their skills to provide objective information about the pros and cons of medication, bolster motivation for taking prescribed medication, and reinforce adherence.

It should be acknowledged that pharmacotherapy on its own is usually of little avail to prevent relapse. Generally, it is widely recognized that pharmacotherapies (apart from detoxification) have a place as adjunctive strategies to psychological interventions and are often prescribed as psychological treatment delivered alone has proven insufficient to reduce the substance abuse. Pharmacotherapy as stand-alone treatment without any psychosocial intervention is generally insufficient to prevent relapse. Further, for most types of illicit drugs such as amphetamines, cannabis, and hallucinogens, currently no effective pharmacotherapies are available. Thus psychological treatments, most notably different types of cognitive-behavioral therapy, will be needed in nearly all cases.

CHAPTER 3

Research Basis of Treatments

Although a large number of controlled studies have investigated the effectiveness of a variety of psychological interventions and medications, few of this evidence is currently used in the treatment of substance-abusing patients (Fals-Stewart & Birchler, 2002a; Foreman, Bovasso, & Woody, 2001; McGovern, Fox, Xie, & Drake, 2004). In this chapter the research into the effects of treatments for substance abuse and dependence will be discussed. The emphasis will be on those psychological interventions and pharmacotherapies that have shown to be evidence-based in a series of controlled clinical trials. For that reason, a number of psychological interventions that are still used in the treatment of substance abuse, including psychodynamic therapy, experientially oriented therapies, and system-theoretically based approaches, will not be discussed here, given that the effectiveness of these interventions has not been established in a number of controlled clinical trials. On the whole, successful interventions that appear to be targeted at substance abuse and testable psychodynamic or experientially oriented protocols of this kind have not yet been developed.

MOTIVATIONAL ENHANCEMENT THERAPY

Motivational interviewing is one of the most popular treatment methods in the addiction field. Some claim that motivational interviewing is a behavioral method, although one might wonder what is exactly behavioral in this procedure: actually, the method is primarily nondirective. Motivational interviewing was developed by Miller (1983, 1996) and tries to influence the expectations and behavior of the substance abuser. An empathetic therapist who tries to help the patients to reach their own decisions with respect to the pros and cons of substance abuse, by giving advice, clarification, and feedback, achieves this. Thus, rather than being coercive or confrontational, the therapist facilitates the patient to become aware of the necessity for behavioral change, and to convey the patient's responsibility in choosing whether and how to make changes.

Alcohol-Use Disorders

In alcohol abuse, motivational interviewing was found to be more effective than directive confrontational counseling (Miller, Benefield, & Tonigan, 1993). The degree to which a therapist engaged in direct confrontation as contrasted to an empathic style was predictive of continued drinking one year after treatment. Similarly, Karno and Longabaugh (2005) found that the interaction between resistance of patients and therapist's directiveness predicted alcohol use during the year after the treatment. Among highly resistant patients, increasing levels of therapists' directiveness were associated with worse drinking outcomes, whereas less directiveness was associated with less posttreatment alcohol use. Although motivational interviewing originally was intended to be a prelude to treatment, it might also be used as a stand-alone treatment. Motivational interviewing has now been evaluated in a number of controlled studies with alcoholic patients either as "appetizer" or as a stand-alone treatment. As far as enhancement of motivation and prevention of dropout is concerned, this procedure is more effective than other treatments, but only in less severely dependent drinkers (Noonan & Moyers, 1997). Although motivational interviewing was found to be as effective as cognitive-behavior therapy and the 12-step approach (Project MATCH Research Group, 1997a), in a recent meta-analysis by Andréasson and Öjehagen (2003), comparing the effects of specific treatments for alcohol dependence with treatment as usual, the effect size of motivational interviewing was less (d = 0.26) as compared to cognitive-behavior therapy (d = 0.73) and contingency reinforcement (d = 0.59).

Few studies investigated for which patients motivational interviewing is particularly suited. In a randomized clinical trial with problem drinkers, motivational interviewing was significantly more effective than coping-skills training for precontemplators (those not currently considering change) and contemplators (those ambivalent about changing), whereas at later stages of change the two treatments were equally effective (Heather, Rollnick, Bell, & Richmond, 1996). This matching hypothesis was not supported in one study with alcoholics (Project MATCH Research Group, 1998), nor with hazardous drinkers in primary care (Maisto et al., 2001). There is some support that motivational interviewing is particularly suited for oppositional and resistant patients. In the Matching

Alcoholism Treatments to Client Heterogeneity (MATCH) study, alcohol-dependent patients who were angry (high on hostility) at the start of treatment profited more from motivational enhancement therapy than from the 12-step approach. Apparently, encouraging angry patients to attend Alcoholics Anonymous meetings elicits resistance, thus lowering the likelihood of successful outcome (Project MATCH Research Group, 1998).

Drug-Use Disorders

In the last decade, a number of studies have involved drug users. Motivational interviewing was found to be a useful adjunct to methadone treatment in opiate abusers (Saunders, Wilkinson, & Phillips, 1995). Drug abusers (N = 122) received either motivational interviewing or psychoeducation. At the six months follow-up, the patients who had received motivational interviewing showed less relapse than the patients in the control condition. Since then, another 15 randomized controlled trials demonstrated the feasibility of motivational interviewing for drug-dependent populations, including cannabis-dependent adults, opiate-dependent adults, cocaine-dependent adults, amphetamine users, and polydrug users (see, e.g., Dennis et al., 2004; Miller, Yahne, & Tonigan, 2003; Rohsenow et al., 2004; Secades-Villa, Fernande-Hermida, & Arnaez-Montaraz, 2004; Stephens, Roffman, & Curtin, 2000). Most studies found that motivational interviewing led to better adherence and increased motivation, but only a few studies found that motivational interviewing led to decreased drug use or abstinence. Two studies found that four group sessions of motivational interviewing significantly reduced HIV risk behavior in women, including substance use before sex, and decreased rates of unprotected intercourse (Carey et al., 1997, 2000). However, not all studies supported the incremental value of motivational interviewing. In four studies the addition of motivational interviewing did not enhance treatment effectiveness in polydrug users (Booth, Kwiatkowski, Iguchi, Pinto, & John, 1998; Miller et al., 2003; Schneider et al., 2000) and in cocaine-dependent patients (Donovan, Rosengren, Downey, Cox, & Sloan, 2001). Further, negative effects were reported for motivational interviewing in mixed psychiatric inpatients with substance-use disorders (Baker et al., 2002). Motivational interviewing did not enhance engagement in a specialist substance misuse service after discharge. These negative results of motivational interviews warrant a different approach. Alternatives for this severe dual-diagnosis group might be to start the substance-abuse treatment during the stay in the hospital rather than refer these patients after discharge.

In drug users, there is some evidence that motivational interviewing is more effective for those who are ambivalent or not yet motivated to change substance use than for those already motivated. In a pilot study (Stotts, Schmitz, Rhoades, & Grabowski, 2001), patients in cocaine detoxification with low motivation were more likely to complete detoxification if given motivational interviewing than no motivational interviewing, but the reverse was true for patients with high initial motivation. Similarly, motivational interviewing as an "appetizer" to an intensive treatment program led to less relapse for cocaine and alcohol use at the one-year follow-up, but only in less-motivated patients (Rohsenow et al., 2004). In patients with higher pretreatment motivation to change, results were rather negative. Higher-motivated patients at the start of treatment who did receive motivational interviewing reported a higher frequency of cocaine use and more severe alcohol problems during the following year than higher-motivated individuals who did not receive motivational interviewing. As noted by the authors, "It might be that the more permissive message used in Motivational Enhancement Therapy is maladaptive for the more motivated who may be impatient for a more directive approach" (Rohsenow et al., 2004, p. 872).

Meta-Analyses

Two recent meta-analyses (Burke, Arkowitz, & Menchola, 2002; Hettema, Steele, & Miller, 2005) analyzed the data of clinical trials into the effects of motivational interviewing not only on substance abuse but also on health behavior. Motivational interviewing was equivalent to other active treatments and superior to no-treatment or placebo controls for problems involving alcohol and drug abuse and overeating, but not for smoking cessation. Motivational interviewing resulted in a medium effect size in studies with drug addicts and in small to medium effect size in the area of alcohol addiction. Surprisingly, Hettema et al. (2005) found that manual-guided motivational interviewing was associated with smaller effect sizes as compared to nonmanual guided interviewing. Further, Burke et al. (2002) found an investigator allegiance: studies by the founder of motivational interviewing, W. R. Miller, resulted in better outcome than studies conducted elsewhere. Whether this effect is due to differences in training and supervision is unclear, but it shows that results of motivational interviewing by Miller's group may not be generalizable in other settings. In a study conducted in the Netherlands (De Wildt et al., 2002) in which a large number of treatment centers were involved, a significant effect for individual treatment centers was found, indicating that motivational enhancement therapy was differentially effective in different treatment centers. Taken together, the results of these studies suggest that not all clinicians are equally effective in motivational interviewing, and that training and supervision is mandatory. Studies by Miller, Yahne, Moyers, Martinez, and Pirritano (2004) and Schoener, Madeja, Henderson, Ondersma, and Janisse (2006) underscore the value of training and supervision to achieve skill proficiency in motivational interviewing.

Therapeutic Processes

Studies into the processes that moderate the effects of motivational interviewing are inconclusive. Taking together the results of studies that addressed this issue, there is strong support for the assumption underlying motivational interviewing that therapists who practice it elicit increased levels of "change talk" and decreased levels of resistance from clients, as compared to more confrontational therapeutic styles. Further, the extent to which clients show verbal resistance during motivational interviewing is found to be inversely related to the degree of subsequent behavior change (Miller et al., 1993). There is hardly any evidence, however, that the extent to which clients verbalize arguments for behavioral change in a motivational interviewing setting is associated with the degree of subsequent change in substance abuse (Hettema et al., 2005). Verbalizing that one wants to change the substance abuse by itself is insufficient. In psycholinguistic analyses of motivational interviewing sessions, only commitment or stating the intention to change during the *final minutes of a session* directly predicted behavior change (Amrhein, Miller, Yahne, Palmer, & Fulcher, 2003). Results indicate that the clinician should attend to the commitment language of the patient during a session. Thus, a patient's verbalizing that she "needs to change," "wants to change," will "think about changing," or "will try to change" is just not enough to elicit behavior change. Using such terms as "I promise" and "I will change my behavior" reflect much stronger commitment, and only the latter verbalizations are associated with subsequent change of substance abuse. Further, results of this study indicate that midsession or late-session drops in the strength of commitment language should be seen as renewed resistance and reflect the need for additional motivational sessions.

COPING-SKILLS TRAINING

In the 1960s and '70s, behavior therapy for substance abuse consisted primarily of aversive methods, based on aversive conditioning. Aversion therapy includes a variety of specific techniques based on both classical and operant conditioning paradigms. Aversion therapy used to be widely employed in the treatment of alcohol abuse/dependence, but is currently more of historical interest.

With aversive conditioning in alcohol-dependent subjects a noxious stimulus is paired with actual drinking or with visual or olfactory cues related to drinking, with the aim to establish a conditioned aversion for drinking. A variety of aversive stimuli have been used, the most popular of which were electric shocks and nausea- or apnea-inducing substances. Covert sensitization is a variant of aversive conditioning, wherein images (e.g., of drinking situations) are paired with imaginal aversive stimuli (e.g., a scene in which the patient vomits all over himself or herself). It is called *covert* because neither the undesirable stimulus nor the aversive stimulus is actually presented; they are presented in the imagination only. *Sensitization* refers to the intention to build up an avoidance response to the undesirable stimulus. Aversion therapy has been ethically controversial, and research has not supported its efficacy (Emmelkamp & Kamphuis, 2002). Many studies into electrical aversion therapy, chemical aversion therapy, and covert sensitization were conducted, but taken together, results were meager (Emmelkamp, 1986, 1994).

Interest into aversive conditioning has waned in the last decades. In recent years the interest of clinicians and researchers has moved away from aversive conditioning methods to alternative methods. Based on cognitive-social learning theory a number of cognitive-behavioral treatments have been devised, including self-management programs involving self-monitoring of drinking and training in drinking-rate control; functional analysis of drinking behavior including identifying high-risk situations; social-skills training; cognitive restructuring; relapse prevention; and problem solving. A central feature of these various methods is the development of coping skills to enable the patient to stop substance abuse or control his use. These approaches are based on the assumption that substance abuse is a habitual, maladaptive way of coping with stress. A clear advantage of cognitive-behavioral programs is that they attempt to teach coping skills to deal with stressful events that occur after the end of treatment, although the emphasis placed on relapse prevention varies across the various programs.

Alcohol-Use Disorders

Exposure to a heavy drinking model is likely to increase the risk of relapse and maintenance of heavy drinking. Marlat and Gordon (1980) reported that for alcoholics, 23% of relapses involved social-pressure situations such as being offered a drink, and in another 29% of the cases, frustrating situations in which the individual was unable to express anger preceded drinking behavior. These findings suggest that social-skills training may be a useful treatment procedure. Previous controlled studies on the effects of social-skills training with alcoholics have been reviewed elsewhere (Emmelkamp, 1986, 1994). The controlled studies in this area clearly showed beneficial effects of social-skills training with previous drinkers (abstinent patients). It was concluded that social-skills training might be an important ingredient in multimodal treatment programs for socially anxious alcoholics who lack necessary social skills.

Other techniques that are directed at relapse prevention include self-monitoring of craving and substance (ab)use, the identification of high-risk situations for relapse, strategies for coping with craving, and training in problem solving to deal with future lapses. Such multimodal relapse prevention programs were found to be more effective than no treatment at all (Chaney, O'Leary, & Marlatt, 1978; O'Farrell, Choquette, Cutter, Brown, & McCourt, 1993). In the MATCH study, coping-skills training was compared with 12-step facilitation and motivational enhancement therapy. Results of the MATCH study found that all three treatment approaches were more or less equally effective (Project MATCH Research Group, 1997a, 1997b, 1998). The results of comparative evaluations with other interventions—that is, interactional group therapy (Ito, Donovan, & Hall, 1988; Kadden, Cooney, Getter, & Litt, 1989; Litt, Kadden, Cooney, & Kabela, 2003) and supportive therapy (O'Malley et al., 1996)—are inconclusive. Cooney, Kadden, Litt, and Getter (1991) showed that cognitive-behavioral aftercare treatment was better for alcoholic patients with high psychiatric severity scores than was interpersonally focused after-care treatment.

Drug-Use Disorders

Coping-skills training has also been used for patients with drug abuse, primarily in order to prevent relapse. Several coping skills–based treatments designed specifically for cocaine abusers (i.e., with abuse or dependence diagnoses) have resulted in significant improvements in cocaine-use outcomes. In cocaine-dependent patients, relapse prevention based on cognitive-behavioral principles was found to be more effective than interpersonal psychotherapy and clinical management (Carroll, Rounsaville, & Gawin, 1991; Carroll, Rounsaville, Gordon et al., 1994a; Carroll et al., 2004). For depressed cocaine abusers, cognitive-behavioral response prevention produced better drug-use outcomes and retention, as compared to supportive clinical management (Carroll,

Nich, & Rounsaville, 1995). Brief, individual, cocaine-specific coping-skills training based on functional analysis of high-risk situations was added to full treatment programs and found to result in significantly less frequent cocaine use when compared to a control procedure during the first six months following discharge (Monti, Rohsenow, Michalec, Martin, & Abrams, 1997; Rohsenow et al., 2000).

Results in drug disorders other than cocaine are inconclusive. In amphetamine users, Hawkins, Catalano, Gillmore, and Wells (1989) found coping-skills training slightly more effective than a therapeutic community one year after treatment. Baker et al. (2005) found that there was a significant increase in the likelihood of abstinence from amphetamines among those receiving two or more treatment sessions of motivational interviewing and coping-skills training. However, apart from abstinence rate, the group who did not receive motivational interviewing and coping-skills training improved equally well. Reduction in amphetamine use was accompanied by significant improvements in stage of change, polydrug use, risk-taking injection behavior, criminal activity level, and psychiatric distress and depression level. In a study on heroin and methaphetamine users (Yen, Wu, Yen, & Ko, 2004), five sessions of coping-skills training resulted in enhanced confidence in managing risk situations, but results on (reduced) drug use were not reported. In marijuana users, relapse prevention led to rather disappointing results. In a study by Stephens, Roffman, and Curtin (2000), a relapse prevention support group resulted in 37% abstinence rate at the 16-month follow-up. In an earlier study only 15% of the patients were abstinent at the one-year follow-up (Stephens, Roffman, & Simpson, 1994).

A number of studies compared coping-skills training with the 12-step approach. In a study on cocaine abusers who were also alcohol dependent, cognitive-behavioral relapse prevention was found to be superior to clinical management, but not to a 12-step enhancement program. There were no differences found between relapse prevention and the 12-step enhancement program for either alcohol abuse or cocaine abuse (Carroll, Nich, Ball, McCance, & Rounsaville, 1998). In a study of cocaine abusers by Wells, Peterson, Gainey, Hawkins, and Catalano (1994), relapse prevention was not found to be more effective than a 12-step recovery support group: both treatments led to a considerable reduction in cocaine use at the six-month follow-up. However, the 12-step patients showed significantly greater increases than the relapse prevention patients in alcohol use from 12 weeks to the six-month follow-up. Further, in a study by McKay et al. (1997), group counseling based on the 12-step enhancement program proved to be superior in terms of total abstinence. Relapse prevention resulted in less relapse than in the 12-step facilitating counseling group. Further, relapse prevention fared better in limiting the extent of cocaine use in the patients still using. In a large study, the effectiveness of cognitive-behavior therapy and 12-step approaches was compared in over two thousand male veterans treated as inpatients for their substance abuse (36% for alcohol, 13% for drugs, 51% for both alcohol and drugs). Both treatments were found to be more-or-less equally effective at the one-year follow-up after discharge (Moos, Finney, Ouimette, & Suchinsky, 1999). However, as in the McKay et al. (1997) study, 12-step enhancement proved to be superior in terms of total abstinence. Given that this is the explicit goal in the 12-step approach, this does not come as a surprise.

Meta-Analysis

In a meta-analysis by Irvin, Bowers, Dunn, and Wang (1999), relapse prevention in substance-abuse disorders resulted in a rather modest effect size ($d = 0.25$) that tended to decrease over time. Relapse prevention was most effective in alcohol-use disorders in contrast to drug use and smoking. Further, relapse prevention was found to have more effect on psychosocial functioning than on alcohol use. Andréasson & Öjehagen (2003) reported an effect size of $d = 0.73$ for cognitive-behavior therapy.

Therapeutic Processes

Although it is generally assumed that the results of coping-skills training are mediated by a change in coping skills, this has hardly been investigated. In a review by Morgenstern and Longabaugh (2000) in which they investigated whether the use of coping skills predicts better treatment outcomes, the results were inconclusive. Further, Morgenstern and Longabaugh found support for a mediational role of coping in only one study. More recently, a direct effect of coping skills on drinking outcome one year after treatment was established in patients with alcohol use (Maisto, Zywiak, & Connors, 2005), but given that the specific treatment received is not described it is unclear whether this should be accounted for by coping-skills training.

A recent study (Litt, Kadden, Cooney, & Kabela, 2003) with alcohol-dependent patients investigated whether specific coping-skills training was essential for increasing the use of coping skills. Patients received either coping-skills training or interactional group treatment, and coping skills were measured at multiple time points. It was hypothesized that those in the cognitive-behavior therapy group would report greater use of coping skills than would those in the interactional group treatment and that higher levels of coping would predict better treatment outcome. Both treatments yielded very good drinking outcomes throughout the follow-up period. Increased coping skills were a significant predictor of outcome. So far, so good. But in contrast to what one would expect, coping-skills training did not effect greater increases in coping than interactional group treatment. Similarly, in the Marijuana Treatment Project, coping skills–oriented treatment did not result in greater use of coping skills than motivational enhancement therapy (Litt, Kadden, Stephens, & the Marijuana Treatment Project Research Group, 2005). One of the reasons that studies so far failed to find more support for coping skills as mediator of outcome may be that in most programs coping skills are trained irrespective of whether patients lacked a specific skill.

Thus, although coping-skills training has been found to be effective in a number of studies, it is unclear which components in the treatment package are responsible for the results achieved. Further studies are needed to determine which of the various components included in the treatment package (e.g., self-monitoring, the identification of high-risk situations, strategies for coping with craving, and training in problem solving) are the necessary ingredients for successful therapeutic outcome and prevention of relapse, and which components are redundant.

CUE-EXPOSURE

Many addiction theories assume that craving plays a central role in the acquisition and maintenance of drug dependence, and in relapse (Tiffany & Conklin, 2000). Based on these theories, cue-exposure programs have been developed.

Alcohol-Use Disorders

After the pioneering work of Rankin, Hodgson, and Stockwell (1983), which looked into the effects of cue-exposure in alcoholics, there is now substantial evidence in favor of cue-exposure as (part of) a cognitive-behavioral intervention for alcohol problems. Studies that have used in vivo exposure to alcohol cues typically find that a majority of individuals report an increase in alcohol craving following relatively brief (e.g., three-minute) exposure durations. In addition, several studies have found that exposure to alcohol and drug cues produces an increase in self-reported negative mood as well (Franken, De Haan, Van Der Meer,

Haffmans, and Hendriks, 1999; Sinha, Fuse, Aubin, and O'Malley, 2000; Stasiewicz & Maisto, 1993).

Cue-exposure treatment, involving exposing patients to the sight and smell of alcohol during the treatment sessions and response prevention of drinking afterward, has resulted in changes in drinking behavior in problem drinkers. For example, Monti et al. (1993) compared a group exposed to the sights and smells of alcohol combined with imaginal exposure with a daily-contact control condition. The cue-exposure treatment group, as compared with the control group, demonstrated more days abstinent as well as lower use on drinking days. Positive effects on alcohol consumption were also reported by Drummond and Glautier (1994), McCusker and Brown (1990), Monti et al. (2001), and Rohsenow et al. (2001). Increased physiological reactivity in the presence of alcohol cues has been associated with decreased time to relapse following cue-exposure treatment (Drummond & Glautier, 1994; Rohsenow et al., 1994).

It is questionable whether exposure to the sight and smell of alcohol alone provides functional exposure. McCusker and Brown (1990) found that urges for and tolerance to alcohol were greater when alcohol was used in a typical situation (e.g., a bar) as compared to a setting that was not previously linked to regular use. Laberg & Ellertsen (1987) showed that exposure to alcohol per se did not elicit craving. Increased autonomic arousal and craving were found only in subjects given alcohol and exposed to more available alcohol. Similarly, Sitharthan, Sitharthan, Hough, and Kavanaugh (1997) found an exposure program consisting of sight-and-smell cues and small priming doses of alcohol in a supervised setting to be effective in problem drinkers. Further studies directly comparing alcohol-related cues with priming doses of alcohol as cues in the cue-exposure program are needed.

Drug-Use Disorders

Treatments using these approaches have also yielded promising results in illicit drug users (e.g., Childress et al., 1993; Litman et al., 1990; O'Brien, Childress, McLellan, & Ehrman, 1990; Powell, Bradley, & Gray, 1993). Dawe et al. (1993), however, did not find any difference in cue reactivity and prevention of relapse in opiate addicts treated with either cue-exposure therapy or routine treatment. In a recent, large controlled study (Marissen, Franken, Blanken, Van den Brink, & Hendriks, 2005) of 127 abstinent opiate-dependent patients, results were rather negative. Although cue-exposure therapy led to reduced physiological reactivity, neither subjective craving nor mood improved more after cue-exposure therapy than after a credible placebo psychotherapy. In addition, cue-exposure therapy led to more dropouts and more relapse than the control condition.

Therapeutic Processes

There is some evidence that the effects of cue-exposure are context specific. Collins and Brandon (2002) exposed moderate-to-heavy drinkers to the sight and smell of alcohol. Such cue-exposure was successful in terms of reduced urges to drink. However, drinkers who were later tested in a novel context had a greater return of these urges compared to those who were retested in the original cue-exposure context.

Cue-exposure can be understood in terms of both classical and operant conditioning. Although cue-exposure is usually explained in terms of habituation and extinction, it is likely that cognitive factors (e.g., self-efficacy and outcome expectancies) are also involved. Cue-exposure makes the patient aware that an urge to continue drinking can be weakened and may enhance self-efficacy in naturally occurring risk situations (Staiger, Greeley, & Wallace, 1999). However, cue-exposure may be less effective when the risk situation is dissimilar to the exposure situation (Monti & Rohsenow, 1999).

Concluding Remarks

The studies discussed above show that cue-exposure results in statistically significant decreases in (subjective) craving in alcohol abusers, but results of studies in illicit drug abusers are inconclusive. It should be noted that in most studies of alcohol abusers cue-exposure was combined with other treatments (coping and communication skills training), rendering the *clinical* relevance of cue-exposure as a treatment difficult to evaluate.

CONTINGENCY MANAGEMENT AND THE COMMUNITY REINFORCEMENT APPROACH

Contingency Management

There is now considerable evidence that contingency management is particularly useful for drug abusers. Contingency management, which is based on principles of operant conditioning, typically provides incentives or rewards to patients for demonstrating observable target behaviors, such as abstinence verified by drug-free urine specimens or other treatment goals. In contingency management programs, tangible reinforcers (vouchers) are provided when the desired behavior is shown, or withheld when the desired behavior does not occur. These vouchers are redeemable for goods and services, the value of the vouchers escalating with each successive drug-free specimen. Some studies have used take-home methadone doses as reinforcers in polydrug-abusing methadone patients (Stitzer, Iguchi, & Felch, 1992), but methadone licensing laws in various countries strictly regulate the use of take-home methadone doses in clinical practice.

In these programs various target behaviors have been used (e.g., drug abstinence, medication compliance, or attendance at therapy sessions). Contingency management procedures have been found to be effective in cocaine-dependent patients (Higgins & Wong, 1998; Kirby, Marlowe, Festinger, Lamb, & Platt, 1998; Silverman et al., 1998, 2002), opiate-dependent patients (i.e., methadone maintenance; see, e.g., Bickel, Amass, Higgins, Badger, & Esch, 1997; Gruber, Chutuape, & Stitzer, 2000; Iguchi et al., 1996; Jones, Haug, Silverman, Stitzer, & Svikis, 2001; Petry & Martin , 2002; Stitzer et al., 1992) and also led to a reduced use of marijuana (Petry, 2000). There is also some evidence that contingency management is efficacious for cocaine-dependent methadone patients (Preston, Umbricht, Wong, & Epstein, 2001; Rawson et al., 2002; Silverman, Chutuape, Bigelow, & Stitzer, 1996). Positive results of contingency management procedures have also been reported in adolescent substance users (Azrin et al., 1994; Corby, Roll, Ledgerwood, & Schuster, 2000; Kamon, Budney, & Stanger, 2005).

In contrast to most other treatments in cocaine and opiate dependence, generally high rates of retention and slightly higher rates of abstinence are reported. There is also some evidence that in a number of patients, treatment effects continue after cessation of the contingencies (Higgins, Wong, Badger, Ogden, & Dantona, 2000). Contingency management interventions appear to affect the behaviors they target, and they do not readily extend to other areas. For example, in a study by Petry, Martin, and Simcic (2005) of cocaine-dependent methadone patients, no changes in other psychosocial problems or other drug use were noted. Although the targeted cocaine use was reduced, concurrent opiate use remained fairly constant.

It is important to note that it is not the delivery of the reinforcer per se, but the *contingent* delivery of the reinforcer that is effective. Stitzer et al. (1992) evaluated methadone take-home privileges as a reward for decreased illicit drug use and found that take-home privileges that were contingent on drug-free urine samples were more beneficial than noncontingent take-home privileges. Similarly, Silverman, Higgins et al. (1996)

found in cocaine-abusing patients that contingent delivery of reinforcers based on drug-free urine screens resulted in a 42% abstinence rate (at least 10 weeks), whereas that was only the case for 17% of the yoked control patients, who received the reinforcers noncontingently.

Reinforcement is usually contingent upon abstinence but contingency management techniques that reinforce completion of nondrug-related activities that are incompatible with drug use may be efficacious in treating substance dependence as well (Iguchi, Belding, Morral, & Lamb, 1997; Petry, Martin, Cooney, & Kranzler, 2000; Petry, Tedford, & Martin, 2001). According to Petry et al. (2001), working toward improving family relationships is an important goal for some substance abusers. Engagement in family activities may improve outcomes because family members may provide social reinforcement for abstinence, thus preventing relapse. Lewis and Petry (2005) investigated whether participants who selected to engage in family related activities during contingency management treatment would have better outcomes than participants who did not select family activities. Family activities included accompanying a relative (e.g., to a movie), attending a child's school play, visiting a relative in the hospital, or writing letters to a relative. Results revealed that engaging in only three family activities was associated with some benefits in family functioning and drug-abuse treatment outcomes. Cocaine-abusing adults who engaged in family activities remained in treatment longer, and were abstinent for more weeks. Moreover, engaging in family activities was associated with reductions in days of family conflict when compared to participants who did not engage in family activities.

Community Reinforcement

Contingency management is usually imbedded in the community reinforcement approach (Azrin, 1976). In this individualized treatment, the therapist systematically alters the drug user's environment so that reinforcement density from nondrug sources is relatively high during sobriety and low during drug use (Higgins & Wong, 1998). The community reinforcement approach involves an amalgam of techniques, including training in social skills and/or drug refusal skills, cognitive behavioral marital therapy, procedures to support medication compliance, and vocational counseling for the unemployed. Higgins et al. (1995) found the community reinforcement approach along with contingent vouchers treatment to result in slightly better results at follow-up than the community reinforcement approach alone, but this was not corroborated in the urinalysis results.

Community reinforcement has also shown promise in opioid-dependent patients exiting a brief residential detoxification. In the context of a day treatment program, the therapy provides individual counseling supplemented by abstinence-contingent support for housing, food, and recreational activities alongside skills training for securing employment. Rates of treatment retention were about 60% at the one-month postdetoxification point. Retention over six months was approximately 40%. Approximately 40% of patients entered recovery housing at some point, and about 30% of patients obtained employment at some point during treatment (Jones et al., 2005; Katz et al., 2001). The results of these randomized studies suggest that an intensive reinforcement-based therapy that includes abstinence-based recovery housing is a promising approach.

A comprehensive behavioral program was evaluated by Azrin et al. (1994). This extensive behavioral treatment was an extension of the community reinforcement approach and consisted of (1) stimulus control procedures to eliminate stimuli that were predecessors of drug use and to increase activities incompatible with drug use; (2) urge-control procedures to interrupt internal stimuli associated with drug use; and (3) social-control procedures, wherein abstinence was assisted through significant others. In addition, a number of other procedures could be used, including specific social-skills training, relationship enhancement, problem-solving training, and vocational counseling, if needed. The effects of this behavioral program were compared with those of a nonbehavioral group program. The behavioral program was clearly superior to the nonbehavioral treatment, both in terms of reduction of cocaine use (assessed with urinalysis) and in terms of depressed mood.

Community reinforcement approaches with or without incentives (vouchers) have been found effective in a number of studies, but are these approaches equally effective with regard to the various substances? Roozen et al. (2004) critically reviewed the controlled outcome studies in this area and found 11 studies of high methodological quality. The results of community reinforcement approaches in alcohol dependence are rather positive. Community reinforcement was found to be more effective than care as usual in terms of reduction in drinking days; results with respect to continuous abstinence were equivocal. As far as illicit drugs are concerned, there is strong evidence that community reinforcement approaches with vouchers are more effective than care as usual with regard to cocaine abstinence, but less so in opioid detoxification and methadone maintenance programs. Similarly, in their overview of research on the voucher-incentive approach, Higgins, Alessi, & Dantona (2002) conclude it to be effective in the treatment of cocaine dependence and a promising treatment intervention regarding other disorders (alcohol, marijuana, nicotine, and opiod dependence). However, the authors note that the effectiveness of this type of intervention has been tested mainly in specialized research clinics and that its usefulness in everyday drug-abuse treatment practice remains to be seen.

Meta-Analysis

In a recent meta-analysis (Lussier, Heil, Mongeon, Badger, & Higgins, 2006), studies that utilized voucher-based reinforcement therapy to treat substance-use disorders were statistically analyzed. Voucher-based reinforcement therapy generated significantly better outcomes than did control treatments, the average effect size being 0.32 (r). More immediate voucher delivery and greater monetary value of the voucher were associated with larger effect sizes. This meta-analysis also offers support for the efficacy of voucher-based contingency management for facilitating other therapeutic changes (e.g., medication compliance).

BEHAVIORAL COUPLE THERAPY

Formerly, spouse-aided interventions with alcohol-dependent patients were regarded as most appropriate for only a subset of clients with severe marital or family problems. These patients were presumed to be in an "alcoholic relationship" with a specific pathological marital structure, and in need of distinct treatment interventions. There is, however, little in the way of empirical research to support this notion. Moreover, family members (or other significant others) often play an important part in getting substance-abusing patients into some kind of formal treatment (Meyers, Miller, Smith, & Tonigan, 2002). Several studies have shown the drinking of unmotivated (treatment-reluctant) alcoholics to be positively influenced by teaching concerned family members appropriate reinforcement procedures (see, e.g., Sisson & Azrin, 1986).Given the reciprocal relationship that often exists among couples of whom one is a substance abuser, it is of clinical interest to know whether involvement of the partner in the treatment might be beneficial.

Alcohol-Use Disorders

Most work in this area has been conducted by the groups of O'Farrell and McCrady. O'Farrell, Cutter, and Floyd (1985) found behavioral couple therapy significantly more effective than an interactional couples therapy group and no-treatment control, particularly on marital adjustment. These results were supported by McCrady, Noel, and Abrams (1986), who compared three stand-alone outpatient treatment conditions, minimal spouse involvement, alcohol-focused spouse involvement, and alcohol-focused spouse involvement in combination with behavioral marital therapy. Overall alcohol consumption decreased and life satisfaction increased in all three treatment conditions. However, couples receiving behavioral couple therapy were more compliant with homework assignments, decreased drinking more quickly during treatment, postponed relapsing longer after treatment, and maintained marital satisfaction better when compared to couples receiving alcohol-focused spouse involvement. Comparing alcohol-focused spouse involvement with the minimal spouse involvement condition, they found couples from the alcohol-focused spouse involvement condition to stay in treatment longer and maintain their marital satisfaction better after treatment.

Further research into the effectiveness of behavioral couple therapy over individual therapy was provided by the follow-up data of the above-mentioned randomized trails. O'Farrell, Cutter, Choquette, Floyd, and Bayog (1992) found the advantages of behavioral couple therapy over individual treatment in terms of drinking outcomes to disappear over time, and they were no longer apparent at two-year follow-up. The positive effects on marital adjustment of behavioral couple therapy and interactional therapy when compared to individual treatment disappeared over time. Couples receiving either behavioral couple therapy or interactional therapy spent fewer days separated, suggesting that both marital interventions promoted relationship stability. In an 18-month follow-up on their original study from 1986, McCrady, Stout, Noel, Abrams, and Nelson (1991) found behavioral couple therapy to remain more effective when compared to alcohol-focused spouse involvement or minimal spouse involvement, both in terms of drinking behavior and marital satisfaction.

More recently, the clinical efficacy and cost effectiveness was tested of adding brief relationship therapy (six sessions) or a shortened version of the standard behavioral couple treatment (12 sessions) to a 12-step-orientated group counseling program (Fals-Stewart, Klostermann, O'Farrell, Yates, & Birchler, 2005). Results showed brief relationship therapy to be as effective as shortened behavioral couple therapy and having superior drinking and dyadic adjustment outcomes when compared to only group counseling or group counseling in combination with psychoeducation. In addition to being effective, brief relationship therapy was shown to be more cost-effective when compared with shortened behavioral couple therapy, psychoeducation, or group counseling sessions. Contrarily, in a recently conducted Dutch randomized clinical trail comparing individual cognitive-behavior therapy (10 sessions) with stand-alone behavioral couple therapy (10 sessions), behavior couple therapy had no superior outcomes compared to individual therapy (Vedel, Emmelkamp, & Schippers, 2006).

Testing the effects of alcohol-focused spouse involvement and behavioral couples therapy in treatment for male problem drinkers using a group drinking-reduction program, Walitzer and Dermen (2004) found that including the partner in treatment resulted in fewer heavy drinking days and more abstinent/light drinking days in the year following treatment when compared to patients of whom the partner was not involved in treatment. However, the combination of alcohol-focused spouse involvement with behavioral couple therapy yielded no better outcomes when compared to the alcohol-focused spouse-involvement treatment alone.

Besides being effective in the reduction of drinking problems and enhancing overall relationship satisfaction, behavioral couple therapy is hypothesized to target specific relationship problems, especially sexual functioning and intimate partner violence. O'Farrell, Kleinke, and Cutter (1998) proposed that sexual impotence is caused both by prolonged heavy drinking and by relationship conflict, and expected that behavioral couple therapy would restore sexual functioning more than individual counseling would. This was, however, not supported by the results of their study. Although behavioral couple therapy produced some slight gains in sexual adjustment, it was not superior in impotence rates. Overall, independent of treatment condition, alcoholism treatment improved impotence rates. However, after treatment, patients still experienced over twice the rate of impotence problems compared to the impotence rate of demographically matched nonalcoholics. In the case of domestic violence and marital violence, O'Farrell & Murphy (1995) found that although treatment did not specifically focus on violence, behavioral couple therapy reduced the occurrence of domestic violence considerably. In successfully treated couples, in which the patient was no longer dependent on alcohol, the risk of domestic violence was not greater than that in the community at large. This finding was further supported by O'Farrell, Murphy, Hoover, Fals-Stewart, and Murphy (2004), who examined partner violence before and after behavioral couple therapy in married or cohabiting male alcoholic patients and compared these findings with a sample of demographically matched nonalcoholic men. In the year before behavioral couple therapy, 60% of the patients had been violent toward their female partner. This is five times higher than the matched sample rate of 12%. In the one to two years after behavioral couple therapy, intimate partner violence decreased significantly.

Drug-Use Disorders

Fals-Stewart, Birchler, and O'Farrell (1996) investigated the value of adding behavioral couple therapy to an individual cognitive-behavior treatment package in male drug abusers. Results showed that couples who received additional behavioral couple therapy had more positive dyadic adjustment and less time separated when compared to couples in which the patient received individual-based treatment only. Further, patients in the behavioral couple treatment condition used less drugs and had longer periods of abstinence through the 12-month follow-up period. However, some of the differences in drug use and relationship adjustment between treatment conditions dissolved over the course of the follow-up period (Fals-Stewart et al., 1996, 2000). Overall, similar results were found in the treatment of female drug-abusing patients (Winters, Fals-Stewart, O'Farrell, Birchler, & Kelly, 2002). Comparing behavioral couples therapy (consisting of group, individual, and behavioral couples therapy sessions) with an equally intensive individual-based treatment condition, those couples receiving behavioral couple therapy reported less substance use, longer periods of abstinence, and higher relationship satisfaction. However, differences disappeared during follow-up and were no longer significant one year after treatment.

In the treatment of substance-abusing patients entering methadone maintenance treatment, patients either received individual-based methadone maintenance or an equally intensive behavioral couples therapy treatment condition, including couples therapy as well as individual counseling. Patients in the behavioral couple treatment condition had fewer opiate- and cocaine-positive urine samples during treatment when compared to patients in the standard treatment condition and at posttreatment reported higher levels of dyadic adjustment and a greater reduction in drug-use severity (Fals-Stewart, O'Farrell, & Birchler, 2001).

Therapeutic Processes

Although behavioral couple therapy is a valuable asset to substance-use treatment, effective in reducing alcohol and drug use and enhancing relationship functioning, it is questionable whether the focus should be on the relationship in all incidences. Walitzer and Dermen (2004) demonstrate, in the treatment of problem drinkers (who were relatively satisfied with their relationship), that adding behavioral couple interventions has no advantage over alcohol-focused spouse involvement. This findings support the notion that the severity of marital problems may be an important indicator for allocating patients to treatments that actively involve the partner versus a treatment package including behavioral couple therapy. Investigating the relationship between patient characteristics and differential emphasis on relationship enhancement, Longabaugh, Wirtz, Beattie, Noel, and Stout (1995) found a brief exposure to relationship enhancement with an emphasis on increasing the patient's own coping skills to be the treatment of choice both in the least maritally distressed couples as well as in highly problematic relationships. On the other hand, extended relationship-enhancement therapy was found to be most effective with patients who were either highly invested in unsupportive relationships or less invested in highly supportive relationships. When there were no relationship difficulties, relationship enhancement was probably ineffective since it focused on a nonexisting problem; when the relationship is too problematic, relationship enhancement would be futile.

A possible disadvantage of behavioral couple therapy is that it is best applied by a relatively highly skilled clinician who not only has a clear understanding of the cognitive behavioral conceptualization of substance abuse but also has skills in dealing with a couple and is able to move partners toward productive behavioral change. Comparing master's-level counselors versus bachelor's-level counselors in the treatment of behavioral couple therapy, Fals-Stewart and Birchler (2002) found adherence ratings among counselors to be similar, but competence of treatment delivery to be superior from master's-level counselors. Similarly, Raytek, McCrady, Epstein, and Hirsch (1999) found more-experienced therapists to develop a better therapeutic alliance with their couples when compared to less-experienced therapists, and the quality of the therapeutic relationship was significantly related to treatment sessions attended and treatment completion.

12-STEP APPROACHES

The 12-step model is one of the most widely used treatment philosophies for substance-use problems around the world, and the dominant approach in the United States. The model has a number of important therapeutic elements, including social support enhancement through group attendance, strategies for coping with dependence, and promoting the development of spirituality.

Few randomized controlled studies have directly compared treatment based on the 12-step approach with other therapeutic approaches, the MATCH study being a landmark study. In the MATCH study a 12-step facilitation (TSF) approach was compared with motivational enhancement therapy and cognitive-behavior therapy. Results of the MATCH study found that treatment based on the 12-step model was more-or-less equally effective as motivational enhancement and cognitive-behavior therapy (Project MATCH Research Group, 1997a, 1997, 1998). Not surprisingly, TSF was significantly more effective than the other approaches in increasing involvement in Alcoholics Anonymous (AA) and following the 12 steps. At the three-year follow-up point, 36% of the TSF outpatients reported being abstinent in the three months preceding the assessment, a percentage only slightly higher than the percentage of abstinence in motivational enhancement therapy and cognitive-behavior therapy (25%; Tonigan, Connors, & Miller, 2002). It should be noted, however, that the latter two approaches neither explicitly motivated patients to attend AA meetings nor had abstinence as a treatment goal; moderate drinking was viewed as an acceptable goal as well. Seen in this perspective, the results of TSF are slightly disappointing, with only one-third of the patients achieving the only acceptable treatment goal from the AA perspective: abstinence. Lifelong abstinence as AA's treatment goal is based on the view that alcoholism is a disease that will progress as long as the individual continues to use alcohol.

Is the 12-step approach better suited for some patients than for others? In patients who are angry and resistant, the 12-step approach appears to be less effective than motivational interviewing (Project MATCH Research Group, 1998). In patients with family and friends who are supportive of drinking, the 12-step approach was found to be superior to motivational enhancement therapy and cognitive-behavior therapy (Longabaugh, Wirtz, Zweben, & Stout, 1998; Project MATCH Research Group, 1998).

Inpatients who are highly dependent on alcohol profit more from the 12-step approach than from cognitive-behavior therapy (Project MATCH Research Group, 1997a).

Drug-Use Disorders

While 12-step self-help groups are typically recommended for drug-dependent patients as well, few studies separate individuals dependent on alcohol alone from those with drug dependence as their primary problem. Benefits of 12-step affiliation have been reported among samples of alcohol and/or drug abusers combined (Christo & Franey, 1995; Miller & Hoffman, 1995; Ouimette, Moos, & Finney, 1998; Toumbourou, Hamilton, U'Ren, Stevens-Jones, & Storey, 2002) and drug abusers (see, e.g., Fiorentine and Hillhouse, 2000). In the Collaborative Cocaine Treatment Study (Crits-Christoph et al., 1999), nearly five hundred patients were randomized to 12-step-oriented individual therapy, individual cognitive-behavior therapy, individual emotional-supportive therapy, or group drug counseling. In terms of drug use at one-year follow-up, the 12-step individual therapy was the most effective. In one large study, the effectiveness of cognitive-behavior therapy and 12-step approaches was compared in over two thousand male veterans treated as inpatients for their substance abuse (36% for alcohol, 13% for drugs, 51% for both alcohol and drugs). Both treatments were found to be equally effective at one-year follow-up after discharge (Moos et al., 1999), the only notable exception being percentage of abstinence. At one-year follow-up, 45% of the 12-step patients reported being abstinent from alcohol and drugs, as compared to 36% of patients in the cognitive-behavior therapy program.

Psychiatrically Impaired Patients

It is questionable as to whether 12-step approaches are suited for dual-diagnoses patients. In the MATCH study, the 12-step facilitation was particularly suited for less psychiatrically impaired patients. Generally, in psychiatrically impaired patients cognitive-behavior therapy has been found to be superior to 12-step facilitation. Maude-Griffin et al. (1998) found cognitive-behavior therapy to be superior to the 12-step approach in a study of crack cocaine users with high rates of concomitant psychopathology. In other studies with dual-diagnoses patients, cognitive-behavior therapy was found to be more effective than 12-step approaches (Fisher & Bentley, 1996; Jerrell & Ridgely, 1995). Another study (Penn & Brooks, 2000) suggests that cognitive-behavior therapy is more effective with respect to psychiatric symptoms, whereas the 12-step approach is slightly more effective in terms of substance abuse.

Meta-Analyses

In three meta-analyses the effectiveness of AA approaches was systematically evaluated. In Emrick, Tonigan, Montgomery, and Little's meta-analysis (1993), only studies with primary alcoholics were included. They concluded that 12-step facilitation was moderately effective in terms of drinking reduction and enhanced social functioning. In the meta-analyses of Tonigan, Toscova, and Miller (1996) and Kownacki and Shadish (1999), special emphasis was given to the methodological quality of the studies reviewed, which was often poor. Methodologically better-controlled studies found less support for the effectiveness of AA approaches with respect to abstinence after treatment than the methodologically poor studies. The meta-analysis of Kownacki and Shadish (1999) revealed that inpatient treatment based on the AA principles (the Minnesota Model) was not better than alternative approaches. Attending AA meetings was even worse than no treatment.

Therapeutic Processes

One would expect that the attendance of sessions, participation, and endorsement of the 12-step philosophy would all be related to succesful outcome, but results of studies into these processes have led to conflicting results.

Endorsement of 12-step philosophy. Among patients who relapse after treatment based on the 12-step model, those with greater commitment to AA and a stronger belief in a higher power had less severe relapse than those who did not hold these beliefs (Morgenstern, Labouvie, McCrady, Kahler, & Frey, 1997). Research by Finney, Noyes, Coutts, and Moos (1998) has indicated that patients in 12-step programs improve more than those in cognitive-behavioral therapy on measures of beliefs and behaviors important to 12-step treatment. However, endorsement of 12-step beliefs and engagement in recommended AA activities did not precede changes in drug use in a study on cocaine-dependent patients (Crits-Christoph et al., 2003); as stated by the authors, an alternative hypothesis needs to be considered in which changes in 12-step philosophy and related behaviors are concomitant with or occur after improvements in drug use.

Attendance and Participation. Patients who attend AA and NA regularly experience better short-term alcohol- and drug-related outcomes than do patients who attend AA and NA infrequently or irregularly (Christo & Franey, 1995; Fiorentine, 1999; McKellar, Stewart, & Humphreys, 2003; Tonigan et al., 2002).

Studies of 12-step groups for substance-dependent patients have rarely differentiated attendance at 12-step groups from active participation, such as speaking at meetings, working on one or more of the 12 steps, or having a sponsor. Some studies reported a linear relationship between AA group attendance and duration of participation in AA and outcome: higher frequency of attendance (Ouimette et al., 1998; Ritsher, Moos, & Finney, 2002) and a longer duration of participation (Moos and Moos, 2004) being associated with better outcomes. Results of other studies do not support these findings. Montgomery, Miller, and Tonigan (1995) found that only greater participation predicted better drinking outcomes but attendance did not, while neither was correlated with alcohol use in the Tonigan, Miller, Juarez, and Villanueva (2002) study.

In drug users, attendance and participation in NA meetings had no impact on drug use (see, e.g., Toumbourou et al., 2002; Weiss et al., 2005). However, in the Weiss et al. study, patients with consistent participation in 12-step activities in a given month reported fewer days of cocaine use when compared to patients with inconsistent participation. Moreover, patients with increased participation during the first half of treatment reported fewer days of cocaine use during the second half of treatment when compared to patients with low participation.

Sponsorship is an important element of 12-step approaches, with sponsors serving as mentors and teachers for newcomers to assist in the support of keeping sober. Sponsorship also serves a dual purpose. Sheeren (1988) found that the most important predictor of stable sobriety was being a sponsor yourself.

CONTROLLED SUBSTANCE USE VERSUS ABSTINENCE

Controlled Drinking

While 25 years ago there was almost unanimous consensus that total abstinence was the only viable treatment goal, more recent results of a number of studies have suggested that a substantial number of problem drinkers can learn and maintain a pattern of moderate and nonproblem drinking. Proponents of the abstinence goal for alcoholics hold that alcoholism is more or less an irreversible disease, as illustrated by the AA's insistence that its members are but "one drink away from a drunk." In the United States, controlled drinking has been a controversial issue leading to unjustified accusations by supporters of the abstinence-oriented approach (Pendery, Maltzman, & West, 1982) of unscientific conduct of Sobell and Sobell (1984), pioneers of the controlled drinking program. There is now considerable evidence, however, that a substantial number of problem drinkers can drink without problems, even when the treatment is focused on total abstinence.

Controlled-drinking treatment programs typically involve self-monitoring of drinking, training in drinking rate control (e.g., expanding the time frame between drinks), goal setting, functional analysis of drinking behavior (including identifying high-risk situations), and instructions about alternatives to alcohol abuse.

A series of studies have evaluated this particular approach, and there is some evidence that it is at least as effective as more traditional abstinence-oriented programs. Most controlled-drinking clients achieve moderation of alcohol use, and most abstinence-oriented clients fail to completely abstain but nonetheless moderate their drinking

(Emmelkamp, 1994; Marlatt, Larimer, Baer, & Quigley, 1993; Miller, Leckman, Delaney, & Tinkcom, 1992). More recently, Walters (2000) included 17 studies in a meta-analysis and found that behavioral self-control programs were more effective than no treatment, and at least as effective as abstinence-oriented programs, especially at follow-ups of one year or longer. The follow-up findings are rather important because the proponents of the abstinence-oriented approach hold that the effects of controlled drinking programs are temporary. In addition, this meta-analysis does not support claims that abstinence-oriented programs achieve superior results to controlled-drinking programs in alcohol-dependent subjects rather than in problem drinkers. The proponents of the abstinence-oriented approach have further argued that the studies of controlled drinking have been conducted in academic centers, not involving real clinical alcohol abusers. Walters (2000) meta-analyzed the results of eight clinically representative studies, but this did not lead to different conclusions than those based on all 17 studies. Thus, there is considerable evidence that controlled drinking may be a viable alternative for abstinence in a substantial number of patients.

More recently, a few studies have investigated whether cue-exposure therapy could also be used as treatment for individuals, with controlled drinking rather than abstinence as their treatment goal. Studies from the United Kingdom (Heather et al., 2000) and from Australia (Dawe et al., 2002) investigated whether moderation-oriented cue-exposure would be superior in effectiveness to the conventional method of training problem drinkers to moderate their consumption, which is known as behavioral self-control training (Hester & Miller, 1989). Results revealed that moderation-oriented cue-exposure was equally as effective as behavioral self-control training. It should be noted, however, that the generalizability of these findings applies to the population of problem drinkers with a mean level of dependence in the mild to moderate range. Severely dependent patients were not included in these studies.

Further research is needed to investigate for which alcohol-abusing patients abstinence-oriented programs are better suited than controlled-drinking programs, and vice versa. Studies in the United Kingdom and the United States found that clinicians held the following factors important in establishing whether moderation was acceptable as a treatment goal: severity of dependence, drinking history, and results of liver-function tests (Rosenberg & Davis, 1994; Rosenberg, Melville, Levell, & Hodge, 1992). Unfortunately, few studies have investigated the predictive validity of these variables for treatment outcome of moderation-oriented approaches. There is some evidence that impaired control as assessed with the Impaired Control Scale may predict who will benefit from moderation-oriented approaches (Heather & Dawe, 2005), but more studies are needed before firm clinical guidelines can be developed.

Controlled Use of Illicit Drugs

Until recently it was held by most authorities in the field that controlled use of substances other than alcohol and cannabis was impossible. The inevitability of the long-term negative outcome of heroin use (e.g., health and mortality) has been questioned, primarily on theoretical grounds (see, e.g., Davies, 1992). The same discussion has surrounded controlled use of cocaine.

There are, however, indications that some cocaine and heroin users can turn to controlled use of these substances. Studies conducted in the Netherlands (Cohen & Sas, 1994), Scotland (Mugford, 1994), and Australia (Hammersley & Ditton, 1994) have shown that recreational nondeviant cocaine users can revert to less frequent and controlled use of cocaine. But does this also apply to the more deviant heroin users? A 15-month longitudinal study conducted in Scotland has shown that a substantial proportion of the sample of chronic heroin users were able to live a life with unobtrusive heroin use with relatively few negative social and health consequences (Shewman & Dalgarno, 2005). Actually, most negative consequences reported were due to heavy alcohol use rather than to heroin use. In contrast to patients seen in clinical settings, over half of the sample were in a stable relationship (57%) and most heroin users were employed (75%).

From a harm reduction perspective, it is odd to see that the emphasis in the addiction field is on total abstinence for illicit drug use. The other side of the coin of this rigid mental-health approach is that a number of severe illicit drug users, who are not motivated to give up substance abuse, will not apply for treatment or will drop out of treatment early if the only treatment goal is abstinence. There is a clear need to develop and investigate the effectiveness of interventions for this group of patients who have controlled substance abuse rather than total abstinence as a treatment target.

PHARMACOTHERAPY

Maintenance Treatment in Opioid Dependence

Clinical trials have shown that maintenance treatment with methadone leads to a reduction in opiate use. Further, a number of studies have found that methadone treatment is superior to untreated control conditions in terms of retaining patients in treatment and reducing relapse, criminal activity, and mortality (Vocci, Acri, and Elkashef, 2005). Further, in a prospective study (Metzger et al., 1993), methadone maintenance treatment led to a sevenfold reduction in the incidence of HIV as compared to an untreated control group. A recent study showed that rates of abstinence from illicit drugs increased after participation in methadone programs (Gossop, Marsden, Stewart, & Kidd, 2003).

A number of studies have shown that levo-alpha-acetylmethadol (LAAM) is also effective as maintenance treatment for opioid addiction (see, e.g., Eissenberg et al., 1997; Fudala, Vocci, Montgomery, & Trachtenberg, 1997; Jones et al., 1998). Numerous clinical trials have demonstrated that thrice-weekly LAAM maintenance is comparable to, if not superior than, daily methadone maintenance by various outcome criteria (Clark et al., 2004; Longshore, Annon, Anglin, & Rawson, 2005), although some studies found a greater attrition from LAAM as compared to methadone.

Buprenorphine has also shown to be effective, and may be even slightly superior to methadone in terms of discontinuing treatment and decreased illicit opiate use (Barnett, Rodgers, & Bloch, 2001; Kosten & O'Connor, 2003). Van den Brink & van Ree (2003) reviewed the available evidence, including Cochrane Reviews, and concluded that methadone is the first choice maintenance treatment, but buprenorphine might be an alternative for those heroin-dependent patients who do not seem to benefit from methadone in adequate dosages.

Marsch, Bickel, Badger, and Jacobs (2005) evaluated the relative efficacy of dosing schedules with buprenorphine in the treatment of opioid-dependence. Results demonstrated that daily, twice-weekly, and thrice-weekly dosing regimens with buprenorphine were of comparable efficacy in promoting retention in treatment, and in terms of opioid and cocaine abstinence. In co-occurring cocaine and opioid dependence, however, methadone is preferred (Mattick, Kimber, Breen, & Davoli, 2002; West, O'Neal, & Graham, 2000). For example, in a recent study by Schottenfeld et al. (2005), illicit drug use decreased over time both for subjects who received methadone and for those who received buprenorphine, but the subjects who received methadone experienced a faster reduction in opioid and cocaine use, remained in treatment longer, and achieved longer periods of sustained abstinence from illicit drugs.

Alcohol-Use Disorders

A number of controlled studies have evaluated the effects of anticraving medication in alcoholics, usually in combination with some form of counseling or psychotherapy. Most studies examining the effects of naltrexone or placebo found that patients who were randomly assigned to naltrexone had significantly fewer relapses than those in the placebo groups (see, e.g., King, Volpicelli, Frazer, & O'Brien, 1997; O'Malley et al., 1996; Rohsenow et al., 2000; Volpicelli, Clay, Watson, & O'Brien, 1995). Generally, naltrexone reduced heavy drinking and brought an increase in time to first relapse. However, data from other naltrexone clinical trials are somewhat inconsistent, with several large studies being negative (Killeen et al., 2004; Kranzler & Van Kirk, 2001; Krystal, Cramer, Krol, Kirk, & Rosenheck, 2001; Mann, 2004; Streeton & Whelan, 2001). Generally, only subjects who are highly compliant with naltrexone have reduced drinking and reduced risk of relapse. To counter the problem of noncompliance with medication, a naltrexone long-acting depot has become available. Naltrexone depot enhances the effects of motivational interviewing more than placebo does (Kranzler, Wesson, & Billot, 2004).

In a large number of studies the effects of acamprosate have been established. Most studies have shown a beneficial effect of acamprosate in drinking frequency and on increasing abstinence rates—in some studies up to one year (Garbutt, West, Carey, Lohr, & Crews, 1999; Kranzler & Van Kirk, 2001; Mann, Lehert, & Morgan, 2004; Verheul, Lehert, Geerlings, Koeter, & Van Den Brink, 2005). However, this efficacy is relatively modest, with an average effect size of only 0.26 (Berglund, Thelander, & Jonsson, 2003).

The effects of acamprosate and naltrexone relate to different aspects of drinking behavior, with acamprosate decreasing alcohol consumption and naltrexone stabilizing abstinence. Few studies have directly compared the effectiveness of acamprosate and naltrexone. Although the results of these studies (Kiefer et al., 2003; Rubio, Jimenez-Arriero, & Ponce, 2001) are inconclusive, they suggest a superiority of naltrexone. Rubio et al. (2001) found naltrexone more effective than acamprosate. However, the conclusions from this trial should be interpreted cautiously, since the study was not blinded. A placebo-controlled, double-blind study found both naltrexone and acamprosate to increase the time to first drink and time to first relapse into heavy drinking when compared to placebo, without showing a significant differential treatment effect (Kiefer et al., 2003). The combined effect from acamprosate and naltrexone was the strongest. The difference between the medication combination treatment and acamprosate alone was significant, but the combination of acamprosate and naltrexone was not found to be more effective than naltrexone alone. In a meta-analysis, effect sizes for naltrexone and acamprosate were modest: $d = .28$ and $d = 0.26$, respectively (Berglund, 2005). More definite answers on the question of which anticraving agent is the most effective are expected in a few years when the results become available of a large comparative study addressing this issue (the Combined Pharmacotherapies and Behavioral Interventions [COMBINE] study), which is currently underway in the United States.

Disulfiram is an alcohol deterrent that inhibits acetaldehyde dehydrogenase and leads to a sense of uneasiness, flushing, nausea, and vomiting. Although disulfiram continues to be used widely, there is still no unequivocal evidence from randomized, controlled clinical trials that disulfiram improves abstinence rates over the long term. In large randomized, controlled trials, disulfiram has not been effective because many patients did not comply with daily medication adherence (see, e.g., Fuller et al., 1986; Garbutt et al., 1999; Mann, 2004). It does not seem to be sufficiently recognized that disulfiram can only be effective unless it is closely monitored and supervised by clinicians and family members (Fuller & Gordis, 2004).

Few studies have compared anticraving medications and disulfiram. De Sousa and De Sousa (2004) found disulfiram more effective in reducing the frequency and severity of relapse than naltrexone; they also compared disulfiram and acamprosate (DeSousa & DeSousa, 2005). Disulfiram was associated with a significantly greater reduction in relapse and significantly more abstinent days. Both studies, however, were open trials rather than blind ones. The psychiatrist, patient, and family members were aware of the treatment prescribed. Further, these studies were conducted in India, where family support is typically strong. Wives monitored medication in 90% of subjects; in the remainder, parents monitored it (De Sousa & De Sousa, 2005). Weekly group psychotherapy was also available.

Cocaine

Currently, few pharmacotherapies are available to treat cocaine dependence. A few controlled studies support the use of disulfiram, traditionally used to treat alcohol abuse based on the very unpleasant reaction produced by the interaction between it and alcohol. In addition, however, disulfiram inhibits dopamine beta-hydroxylase, resulting in increased dopamine and decreased synthesis of norepinephrine. Disulfiram may diminish cocaine craving or alter the cocaine high because of this effect on dopamine. There is some evidence that disulfiram may be helpful in patients who abuse cocaine, even without concurrent alcohol abuse (Sofuoglu & Kosten, 2005). The results of a randomized controlled trial in cocaine-dependent patients revealed that disulfiram treatment was more effective than placebo in reducing the frequency of cocaine use and the frequency of cocaine-positive urine samples over time, independent of alcohol use (Carroll et al., 2004). Other medications that show some promise for treating cocaine dependence include modafinil, a mild stimulant used to treat narcolepsy, and antiepileptic agents such as tiagabine and topiramate (Kleber, 2005; Kosten, 2005). More clinical trials, however, are needed before these medications will be established as evidence-based treatments for cocaine dependence.

Does Medication Enhance Psychological Treatment Effects in Alcohol-Use Disorders?

Medications are probably most effective in the context of psychotherapy for the prevention of relapse in alcohol-dependent patients, but this evidence is stronger for naltrexone than for acamprosate and disulfiram.

Studies that investigated the effects of naltrexone in combination with cognitive-behavior therapy found this treatment package to be more effective than naltrexone together with supportive therapy or the placebo/supportive-therapy condition (Balldin et al., 2003; Heinälä, Alho, Kiianmaa, Lönnqvist, & Sinclair, 2001; O'Malley et al., 1992). In a study by O'Malley et al. (1992), alcohol-dependent patients receiving naltrexone in combination with supportive psychotherapy showed higher abstinence rates than patients receiving naltrexone in combination with cognitive-behavior therapy (coping-skills training). Patients who had received cognitive-behavior therapy in addition to naltrexone were less likely to relapse into heavy drinking than patients who had received naltrexone alongside supportive psychotherapy. Further, depot naltrexone enhanced the effects of motivational enhancement therapy (Kranzler et al., 2004). Finally, one study reported postive results of a combination of nalmefene (an opiate receptor antagonist with similar pharmacological properties to naltrexone) and cognitive-behavior therapy (Mason, Salvato, Williams, Ritvo, & Cutler, 1999).

Results with respect to the combination of acamprosate and psychotherapy are inconclusive. De Wildt et al. (2002) found that neither three sessions of motivational interviewing nor seven sessions of cognitive-behavior therapy enhanced the effectiveness of acamprosate alone.

There are only a few studies that have investigated whether disulfiram enhanced the effect of psychotherapy in alcoholics. One study compared disulfiram only with community reinforcement in combination with disulfiram and 12-step facilitation therapy (Azrin, Sisson, Meyers, & Godley, 1982). The combined disulfiram community reinforcement approach resulted in better drinking outcome than traditional therapy based on 12-step facilitation or disulfiram only. In a study by Miller,

Meyers, Tonigan, & Hester (1992b), disulfiram together with 12-step facilitation was more effective than 12-step facilitation alone. Disulfiram did not enhance the effects of the community reinforcement approach.

Does Medication Enhance Psychological Treatment Effects in Drug-Use Disorders?

Few studies investigated combined medication treatment and psycho-therapy in drug-use disorders. Carroll et al. (2004) investigated, in cocaine-dependent patients, whether disulfiram enhanced the effects of coping-skills training. Combining the two provided little additional incremental benefit.

In opioid-dependent patients, pharmacological maintenance has been combined with voucher-based contingency management, vouchers being contingent on drug-free urine samples. Results of these studies have shown that maintenance treatment with naltrexone (Carroll et al., 2001; Carroll, Sinha, Nich, Babuscio, & Rounsaville, 2002), methadone (Preston et al., 2000), or bupropion (Poling et al., 2006) may be combined with contingency management. Earlier studies (Woody, McLellan, Luborsky, & O'Brien, 1983, 1995) found emotional expressive therapy in combination with methadone maintenance to be superior to maintenance medication alone, but this has not been replicated by independent groups.

TREATMENT MATCHING

It has been hypothesized that substance-abuse outcomes will be better if patients receive individualized treatment that addresses their specific needs. A number of studies have been conducted regarding treatment matching; most of this work has been done in alcoholics.

Alcohol-Use Disorders

Kadden et al. (1989) randomly assigned alcoholics who had been treated as inpatients to either a coping-skills training or interaction group therapy after-care program. The group-administered coping-skills training included problem solving, interpersonal skills, relaxation, and skills for coping with negative moods and urges to drink. Although both treatment formats were found to be equally effective, coping-skills training was found to be more effective for subjects higher in sociopathy or psychopathology (so-called Type B alcoholics). Interaction group therapy was more effective for subjects lower in sociopathy. Nearly identical results were found at two-year follow-up (Cooney, Kadden, Litt, & Getter, 1991). In a study by Litt, Babor, DelBoca, Kadden, & Cooney (1992), Type B alcoholics also had better outcomes with coping skills than with interactional therapy, whereas the reverse was true for subjects low in sociopathy. Results of this study are consistent with the view that treatment should be matched to the patients' needs, rather than providing uniform treatment to all alcoholics.

In the largest multicenter psychotherapy trial ever conducted, project MATCH investigated which patient characteristics were related to beneficial outcomes in three different treatment programs. Two related randomized clinical trials were conducted, one with outpatients (N = 952), and the other with after-care patients who had received inpatient or day hospital treatment (N = 774). Patients were followed up to three years after treatment (Project MATCH Research Group, 1998). Patients in both trials received either (1) 12 sessions of cognitive-behavior therapy, (2) 12 sessions of 12-step enhancement therapy, or (3) 4 sessions of motivational enhancement therapy. All three conditions resulted in significant and sustained improvement on a range of alcohol-related outcome variables. All three types of interventions were equally effective. Unfortunately, very few significant matching predictors were found. The major results of the MATCH project are summarized in two publications (Project MATCH Research Group, 1997a, 1998). The predictor variables with the most compelling theoretical justification and strongest empirical support were designated "primary a priori matching variables." Less supported but promising matching variables were designated "secondary a priori matching variables." Only one out of ten primary variables (severity of psychiatric problem) was consistently related to outcome across the various time periods related to matching, but not at the three-year follow-up. Patients with low psychiatric severity as measured by the Addiction Severity Index had less abstinent days after cognitive-behavior therapy than after 12-step enhancement therapy, but only in the outpatient sample. Contrary to prediction, no significant differences were found among the three treatments for patients with moderate to severe psychological problems.

As for the secondary hypotheses (Project MATCH Research Group, 1997b), in the outpatient sample but not in the after-care sample, hostility predicted better drinking outcome in the motivational enhancement therapy than in the cognitive-behavior therapy condition. Furthermore, 12-step enhancement therapy led to superior results in high-alcohol-dependent patients; low-dependent patients did better in cognitive-behavior therapy, but only in the after-care sample.

Finally, Thevos, Roberts, Thomas, and Randall (2000) investigated social phobia and outcome in the MATCH study. It was hypothesized that social phobic alcoholics treated with cognitive-behavior therapy would have better drinking outcomes than social phobic alcoholics treated with 12-step facilitation (TSF) therapy. This hypothesis was partly supported. Cognitive-behavior therapy was superior to TSF only in female social-phobic alcoholics and only in the outpatient arm. No matching effects were noted in the after-care arm.

In sum, despite the millions of dollars invested in the largest multi-center study ever, we still know little if anything with respect to treatment matching. It should be noted that no matching effect was observed in one arm of the study that was also present in the other arm. The major value of this mammoth project (which some have compared to the building of the Titanic!) is not the finding on matching it was designed for, but the fact that a four-session motivational enhancement therapy was as effective as 12 sessions of cognitive-behavior therapy or 12-step enhancement therapy. Thus, the MATCH study provides us with arguments for a stepped-care model in the treatment of alcohol dependence. Why not start with four sessions of motivational enhancement and provide one of the more intensive treatments only for those patients who did not benefit from the motivational enhancement treatment?

Drug-Use Disorders

Matching has received relatively little attention in the area of illicit drug abuse. However, a few studies have investigated the influence of prognostic variables on treatment outcome. There is substantial evidence that severity of the cocaine addiction is related to dropout from treatment and less effective treatment outcome (Alterman, McKay, Mulvaney, & McLellan, 1996; Carroll et al., 1991; Carroll, Power, Bryant, & Rounsaville, 1993). Bad outcome is further predicted by current alcohol dependence (Carroll et al., 1993, 1994b) and higher psychiatric symptom severity at intake as assessed with the Addiction Severity Index (Carroll et al., 1991, 1993). Good outcome is predicted by self-efficacy and commitment to abstinence (McKay et al., 1997).

In a mixed substance-abuse sample (Rosenblum et al., 2005) two treatments were compared: cognitive-behavior therapy versus a combination of motivational interviewing and cognitive-behavior therapy. Both treatments were conducted in group format. Three out of six variables moderated treatment outcome: alexithymia, a network that supports alcohol use, and antisocial personality disorder. Results indicate that patients who are high in alexithymia (i.e., have difficulty in expressing their feelings), have a network that supports their alcohol use, or have an antisocial personality disorder are better off with standard cognitive-behavior therapy. Patients low in alexithymia are better of with the combined motivational/cognitive-behavior therapy approach. Surprisingly, low motivation at pretest did not moderate treatment effects; neither did hostility.

Clinical Significance of Matching

To date, research hardly provides robust guidelines with respect to the matching of treatment to specific patient characteristics. This finding is not specific for research in the addiction field, but is also generally found in other mental health areas (Vervaeke & Emmelkamp, 1998). The few significant findings reported in the studies conducted so far have hardly any clinical significance. In the MATCH study, only a few matching effects were found but these tended to account for rather small degrees of variance in the outcome achieved. The few significant differences found in the MATCH study can hardly influence treatment decisions in individual cases, given the large number of individuals involved and the many predictor variables tested in this project. With such a large number it does not come as a surprise that some—rather small—differences among groups become statistically significant. In individual cases, treatment decisions could better be based on a functional behavior analysis, a topic that will be addressed in the next chapter.

CHAPTER 4

Clinical Cases

As already mentioned in chapter 2, it is imperative to conduct a thorough analysis of the different problem areas of the patient. This is critical in arriving at a clear definition of the problem behavior and in evaluating the effects of treatment. Several modalities of assessment can be distinguished. In addition to interviewing the patient, the most important methods are self-report using questionnaires, self-monitoring of behavior, and, in a number of cases, information provided by significant others (e.g., a partner). Questionnaires are often useful to generate a first impression of the problem behavior. In regard to substance-use disorders, the Time-Line Follow-Back method gives a good impression of the quantity and frequency of drinking/drug taking during the past months, as well as more detailed information on pattern of substance use (Sobell & Sobell, 1992; Sobell, Toneatto, & Sobell, 1994). When additional problems are present in addition to the substance abuse (e.g., anxiety, depression, personality disorder, marital distress) the therapist can select from a number of questionnaires that collect domain specific information. When the domain is depression, the therapist can administer the Beck Depression Inventory, or BDI (Beck, Steer, & Brown, 1996), which was developed to assess the behavioral manifestations of depression, as well as, for example, the Pleasant Events Schedule (MacPhillamy & Lewinsohn, 1982), which aims to assess to what extent the patient still initiates pleasant activities that may serve as reinforcers. The use of other questionnaires is illustrated in a number of case studies described in this chapter. In the case of interpersonal problems, role-playing can provide useful information that may supplement the information gathered through interviews, diaries, and questionnaires. An example may clarify this point:

> Bill is a patient who regularly relapses into binge drinking after interpersonal conflicts. Although Bill reports feeling anxious in response to conflict and arguments, he claims not to avoid these situations and even to cope adequately. Bill's therapist suggests using role-play in order to clarify what actually happens during

these situations. The therapist plays Bill's boss, who criticizes Bill for something that is not his, but a colleague's, fault. In trying to counter this criticism, Bill becomes visibly tense and immediately takes back his critical comments, which in return reduces his tension. Role-play of other situations (conflicts with his wife and his oldest son) revealed that Bill was incapable of dealing adequately with criticism. After such conflict situations he was inclined to start drinking heavily.

DETOXIFICATION

In many incidences detoxification will be a necessary prelude to treatment (or even a prelude to intake and clinical assessment) because without detoxification any changing of substance use will be difficult or even dangerous. For example, stopping alcohol use abruptly without medical supervision may in a number of cases lead to serious medical conditions: seizures, delirium, and arrhythmias. Detoxification refers to the process of taking the patient off the drugs or alcohol on which he has become physically dependent. Detoxification can take place in an outpatient, day-hospital, or inpatient setting depending on the severity of dependence, the patient's general medical condition, and living conditions. It may be done in an abrupt or gradual fashion, with or without medication to relieve withdrawal symptoms. Detoxification itself is not considered to be a therapeutic treatment but rather a medical intervention. Many treatment institutions, however, have incorporated psychoeducation or other treatment interventions into the detoxification program to motivate patients to maintain change and/or to seek additional substance-abuse treatment.

CLINICAL ASSESSMENT AND TREATMENT PLANNING

In the research discussed in chapter 3, most studies made use of manualized treatment protocols. Manual-based treatments of substance-use disorders are empirically supported, but some have questioned the use of them in clinical practice. Critics of manual-based treatments suggest that the use of manuals precludes idiographic case formulation, and undermines therapists' clinical creativity. Treatment manuals, however, should not be used rigidly without any adjustment to the needs of the individual patient. Most current manuals for substance-use disorders provide the necessary flexibility in applying the techniques prescribed.

In describing a number of cases in this chapter we resort to the hypothesis testing approach that characterizes functional behavior analysis in cognitive-behavior therapy (Emmelkamp, Bouman, & Scholing, 1993). We use macro- and microanalyses as a way of identifying the core processes and variables maintaining problems and pathologies that bring the patient to treatment.

Macro-Analysis

The prelude to good treatment is a thorough problem analysis. Thus, before embarking on a specific treatment technique, the therapist utilizes the collected information from the intake sessions and assessment to conduct an analysis of the problem behavior and associated problems. This is not identical to arriving at a formal diagnosis. Two patients may meet the criteria of a particular diagnosis from the fourth edition of the American Psychiatric Association's *Diagnostic and Statistical Manual of Mental Disorders* (*DSM-IV*) but a careful analysis might reveal that patient A would benefit more from method X while patient B would likely benefit more from method Y. Problem analysis is indispensable for constructing a treatment plan. Patients often present more than one complaint, and in most cases there are functional relationships between these problem areas. Common problems in substance-abusing patients in addition to the substance abuse are anxiety, depressed mood, relationship difficulties, financial problems, and work problems. In a macroanalysis these relationships are delineated in order to establish where treatment should commence in the first place.

Generally, in the case of substance abuse in combination with other problems, a rule of thumb is to target the substance abuse first. Patients sometimes think differently about this prioritization, finding, for example, the depression, anxiety disorder, or marital discord of a higher priority than the substance-use disorder. In that case, the macroanalysis is not only a tool for the therapist but should also be used to inform the patient about the relationship between the different problem areas and substance abuse, and in line with this information, motivate the patient for changing substance use first. At the same time, treating substance abuse first does not mean that other problems areas should be neglected, or that treatment of co-occurring problem must be postponed until substance-abuse treatment has finished. Rather, the co-occurring problem must be monitored during substance-abuse treatment and, if still prevalent after a period of abstinence or controlled use, must be addressed in treatment, and in some cases referral to specialized treatment centers may be called for.

Microanalysis or Functional Analysis

A microanalysis or functional analysis is a hypothetical working model of the problem behavior (e.g., drinking) and from it specific treatment interventions are derived. The key questions that the therapist attempts to answer in the functional analysis are the following:

What are the situations in which the behavior occurs?
Which responses (emotional, physiological, cognitive, overt behavior) occur?
What are the consequences of the behavior that reinforce the behavior?

When the therapist and patient have determined what behavior (e.g., drinking) needs changed, it can be useful to have the patient complete a self-monitoring diary to elucidate the conditions under which the behavior occurs. Such diary registrations can illuminate crucial associations between problem behavior and critical events (antecedents and consequences of the problem behavior). In the treatment of substance-use disorders, a patient's self-monitoring of daily craving and substance use enables the patient and the therapist to identify specific recurring situations, thoughts, or feelings that elicit craving and also to identify the positive and negative consequences of the problem behavior. This information can later be used to construct a functional analysis. In general, such diaries address the following questions:

Which *day* and what *time* was it? (External cue.)
What was the *situation* you were in? (External cue.)
What were your *thoughts* while you were in this situation? (Internal cue.)
How did these thoughts make you *feel*? (Internal cue.)
Did you experience any *bodily sensations*? (Internal cue).
What was the intensity of your *craving*, between 0 and 100? (Internal cue.)
What happened next, and how did you *cope*?
What were the *consequences* of this coping behavior?

There are different kinds of consequences that can reinforce problem behavior; the most obvious are positive reward, for example, an increase in self-esteem, and negative reinforcement, for example, a decrease in anxiety or depressed mood. The therapist should, however, also try to identify the more subtle forms of reinforcement. An example of subtle forms of reinforcement are so-called *enabling* behaviors: behaviors by significant others that are often meant to help the patient but in fact reinforce the problem behavior through shielding the patient from the

DATE & TIME	SITUATION	THOUGHTS	FEELING	CRAVING (0–100)	BEHAVIOR	CONSEQUENCES
	WHERE WERE YOU AND WHAT WERE YOU DOING?	WHAT WAS GOING THRU YOUR MIND?	HOW DID THIS MAKE YOU FEEL?	HOW STRONG WAS THE CRAVING?	HOW DID YOU RESPOND?	WHAT HAPPENED NEXT?

FIGURE 4.1   Example of a diary form

negative consequences of the substance use. Although the patient, as well as the significant other, may not be aware that these behaviors influence the occurrence of the problem behavior, it is the clinician's task to find out about their existence and incorporate them into the treatment plan.

Homework Assignments

Often the assignment to record craving is the patient's first encounter with the phenomenon of treatment "homework." In cognitive behavior therapy, homework assignments are assigned on a regular basis in order to gather detailed information about the problem behavior, as well as to enhance skill mastery and generalization of new behaviors outside treatment. However, patients are not always compliant, and motivating patients to do their homework may sometimes take a lot of effort. But is it really necessary to keep reminding patients about the importance of these assignments? Are they related to treatment outcome? The answer is yes, homework is an important ingredient in the process of behavioral change. In their study, Carroll, Nich, and Ball (2005) have found homework compliance, in the treatment of cocaine-dependent patients, to be positively associated with treatment outcome. Homework completion was significantly associated with treatment retention, and patients who completed homework assignments showed significantly better coping responses and were more confident about their ability to withstand high-risk situations when compared to those patients who had done no homework or only had attempted to. Moreover, patients who completed their homework assignments had a significantly higher percentage of days abstinent during treatment, as well as during the one-year follow-up, compared to patients who did not do their homework assignments. Important to note is that homework compliance was not significantly associated with the patient's educational level or level of motivation. However, the time therapists spent on emphasizing the importance of homework and the time spent reviewing the homework were significantly related to homework compliance. From a clinical perspective this research underscores the importance of keeping homework compliance high on the agenda in each treatment session, despite the fact that doing so might sometimes generate feelings of frustration in the patient (as well as the therapist).

Setting the Goals for Treatment

In other conditions, such as anxiety or mood disorders, the treatment goal is often clear from the start; patients want to get rid of their panic attacks or depressed mood and although the treatment interventions to achieve change are often negotiated (as in the case of exposure in vivo), the treatment goal itself is seldom a topic of discussion. In the treatment of substance-use disorders, patients often enter treatment without the wish to get rid of the problem behavior (to stop drinking or drug taking); rather, they desire to moderate their substance use, or reduce the harmful consequences of their use without stopping use altogether. Although many may be willing to obey the abstinence-oriented treatment policy of their therapist or the treatment institution in order to receive treatment, this is fundamentally different from an internal strive for abstinence. Thus, in many cases early interventions are directed at exploring ambivalence and to bolster motivation for change.

In a number of cases, especially in patients with alcohol abuse who are not alcohol dependent, controlled use may be a realistic treatment goal. However, whether this is realistic or possible for a given individual is an empirical question. If patients opt for moderation rather than abstinence we propose to them a "behavioral experiment." Such a supported attempt at moderation is often the best way of discovering from within one's own experience whether moderation is a realistic goal. It is advisory to make clear beforehand, preferably in writing, what is acceptable drinking behavior. In making these arrangements it is important that there are both limits in terms of number of drinks per day and number of alcohol-free days per week. As a general guideline we use the following limits: not more than 3 drinks a day and a minimum of three alcohol-free days per week. In addition, patients are discouraged from drinking in high-risk situations because this will interfere with learning new coping skills, as well as enhancing the likelihood of lapsing:

> Susan, 37 years old, single, and working as a public-relations consultant, sought treatment because of problematic alcohol use. Given the mild severity of the abuse, Susan and her therapist agreed she was going to try controlled drinking over a period of four weeks. After these four weeks Susan and her therapist would evaluate this behavioral experiment and decide whether to continue controlled drinking or to change the treatment goal and opt for a period of complete abstinence. Susan decided she was going to drink one night during weekdays, two nights during the weekend, no more then two units per occasion, and with no drinking before 6:00 P.M. and no drinking after 10:00 P.M. In addition, Susan and her therapist agreed she was not to drink during work-related occasions (e.g., dinner appointments) and during certain family gatherings because both were associated with elevated stress, feeling insecure, and an increase in alcohol craving.

If a patient is unable to keep to the agreed-upon arrangements, the belief endorsed by the patient that she is able to control the drinking is empirically rejected. Difficulties encountered in such a guided attempt at moderation can lead to increased motivation for abstinence. Subsequently, once the treatment goal has been determined (abstinence or controlled use), many patients have difficulty remaining committed to it through the course of treatment. This recurring ambivalence is quite common, and instead of just reminding the patient about the original goals for treatment, without addressing ambivalence further, therapists would do better to use motivational interviewing techniques in order to ensure treatment commitment and prevent treatment attrition.

AN EXPLANATION OF CRAVING

In chapter 2, examples are given of how patients can learn to handle their cravings. It is, however, essential to start off by explaining what craving actually is. Craving, and thus the principals of classical conditioning, can be explained using the example of the famous Pavlovian dog. Patients should be informed about the fact that once craving starts it will not continue until it's countered by the use of alcohol or drugs. Instead, craving is time limited; it will appear, increase, peak, and decline over a limited period of time. Further, if the cues that trigger craving are no longer reinforced by subsequent substance use, their signal potential will diminish, decreasing the amount and frequency of craving. To underscore the power of craving and its highly physiological character (versus "it's all just in your head") we often use the example of Pavlovian overdose to illustrate its magnitude and its relationship to tolerance. In addition, in the case of patients who use alcohol and drugs in high quantities, the information about Pavlovian overdose may be lifesaving.

The human body prefers being in homeostasis; in other words, the body wants to keep all its functions stable over time in order to facilitate optimal functioning. If homeostasis is challenged, for example, because the individual starts jogging and the body temperature rises, the body will respond by activating the sweat glands in order to reduce temperature. It will keep on doing so until the body temperature has returned to within normal parameters. In order to be even more effective in maintaining homeostasis, the body also uses cues that predict upcoming disturbance of homeostasis to anticipate disruption.

Alcohol or drug use is extremely disruptive to homeostasis and over time the body learns to recognize all kinds of different cues that predict upcoming substance use. These cues help the body to prepare, but what does the body actually do to prepare itself? The body prepares by changing those physiological processes that will be affected by alcohol or drug intake but in an opposite direction. For example, alcohol intake increases the body temperature. When upcoming alcohol intake is cued, the body will respond by dropping the body temperature, thus countering the effect of alcohol intake. Larger amounts of alcohol will be needed to achieve the same intoxicating effect. This phenomenon is called situational-specific tolerance. The physiological changes of the body in preparation for oncoming alcohol or drug use are called craving. That this classical, conditioned, anticipating response is a powerful physiological reaction can best be illustrated by the following. There have been many thorough animal studies and several human case reports that have demonstrated a relationship between situation-specific tolerance and drug overdose. It has been shown that rodents who are made dependent on drugs or alcohol under specific living conditions are at least two times as likely to die of an overdose when administered a higher dose after being moved to a different living environment when compared to counterparts who remained in their original surroundings. This is comparable with the high mortality of, for example, "drug tourists." Many of these patients do not die because they make a judgmental error and administer more drugs then they are used to. They die because they administer under different situational conditions, resulting in no or less cued anticipative response by the body.

In the next part of this chapter we will give some case examples of cognitive-behavioral treatments of patients abusing alcohol or drugs. These case examples are abstracts and not complete recordings of all interventions used during treatment. In the appendix you can find some references to some excellent treatment protocols, some of which can be downloaded for free from the Web. We caution the reader, however, that these protocols are not ready-to-use treatment packages. To be able to use these protocols, one needs formal training and supervision from an experienced colleague.

THE CASE OF PETER

Background and History of Substance Use

Peter, a 21-year-old man, referred himself to our clinic because of cannabis abuse. Peter was the older of two siblings; he had one sister and was brought up in a loving but somewhat protective family. At the age of

18, he moved away to college to study history. Together with two boys from high school, he rented a small apartment near the university and found himself a part-time job in a small bookstore. Peter really struggled with these major changes in his life; he found living on his own hard, and aside from his two roommates he had little contact with fellow students. Studying history became a disappointment: it was not what he had expected it to be, and during his second year at the university, after failing a major exam, he quit history and tried switching to philosophy. However, after a few months he quit philosophy as well. He started working at the bookstore on a full-time basis but, after turning up late several times at the bookstore, he was fired. Not able to cover his living expenses, he moved back to his hometown to live with his parents.

Peter had started experimenting with alcohol and cannabis when he was 16, mainly during the weekends. When he went off to college, no longer under the supervision of his parents, he started using cannabis more regularly and a few months later he was smoking on a daily basis (mainly during the evenings). During his second year of college he also started smoking during the daytime. It was moving back in with his parents that confronted Peter with the fact that his cannabis use really had gotten out of control. Peter had never smoked or been stoned in the presence of his parents; in fact, Peter's use of cannabis was completely unknown to them. The first week after moving in with his parents, Peter tried to cut down his cannabis use several times but always relapsed within a few days. After a few months, Peter's parents found out about his use and they commanded him to quit immediately and pressured him to seek help.

Assessment and Macroanalysis

The Time-Line Follow-Back method adapted for drug use was used to assess the past three months' use of cannabis and other substances. Aside from cannabis, Peter did not use any other drugs and nearly never drank alcohol. We interviewed Peter using the Structured Clinical Interview for *DSM-IV* Axis I Disorders, or SCID-I (First, Spitzer, Gibbon, & Williams, 1995a), to confirm our diagnosis: 304.30, cannabis dependence. Peter was screened for other mental disorders but didn't meet any of the criteria that warrant further assessment.

We combined the information that Peter had told us about the development of his cannabis use to draw up a macroanalysis. There were no major current co-occurring problems beside the cannabis, so it was obvious that treatment should be focused on changing Peter's cannabis use (see Figure 4.2).

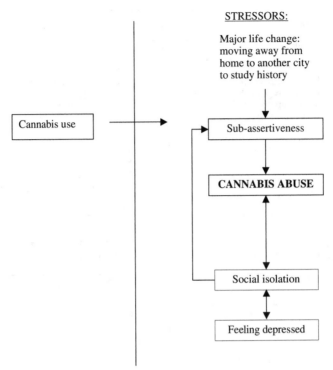

STRESSORS:

Major life change: moving away from home to another city to study history

Cannabis use

Sub-assertiveness

CANNABIS ABUSE

Social isolation

Feeling depressed

FIGURE 4.2   Macroanalysis of Peter's complaints

Building Motivation and Detoxification

His parents pressured Peter into treatment, and although this is a good reason to seek treatment, in our experience these kinds of external motives for change are often not enough to keep a patient motivated during the difficult process of change. During the first two treatment sessions a lot of time was spent exploring other, more internally motivated reasons for change. A helpful way of gathering information about motives to change is by using a balance sheet (see Figure 4.3), a tool often used in motivational interviewing but which can also be used as a way of gathering information to make a functional analysis because of the overlap between pros and cons of the balance sheet with the consequences of the problem behaviors.

At the beginning of treatment Peter was very clear about his treatment goal: he wanted to stop using cannabis for at least a year. Exploring the reasons why this was so important to him, Peter was able to sum up external as well as more internal motives for change. Although he was very determined to stop using cannabis, he felt very insecure about

ADVANTAGES OF USING	DISADVANTAGES OF USING
SHORT TERM:	SHORT TERM:
- Better able to relax - Better able to sleep - Don't have to think about how I messed up my life - Less depressed	- Expensive - Getting into a fight about smoking pot with my parents - Becoming indifferent
LONG TERM:	LONG TERM:
	- Relationship with parents - Poor concentration - Bad for my health - Less contact with non-using friends

ADVANTAGES OF CHANGE	DISADVANTAGES OF CHANGE
SHORT TERM:	SHORT TERM:
- Saves money - Parents will be very happy	- Not able to sleep - Confrontation with negative mood
LONG TERM: - Better for my health - Normal relationship with my parents - Able to pick up my life	LONG TERM:

FIGURE 4.3   Balance sheet

his ability to change (self-efficacy). This made him ambivalent about pursuing change: "If I try and I fail, I will become even more disappointed with myself." We addressed this issue by giving Peter information about the phenomenon of lapse and relapse and normalizing it in the context of behavioral change. Because of this heavy use of cannabis, his previous failed attempts to cut down in combination with his low self-esteem, and his desire to undergo some kind of formal detoxification, we decided to refer Peter to an outpatient detoxification program. This seven-day program, meeting each day from 9:00 A.M. to 5:00 P.M., combines detoxification under medical supervision with psychoeducation and interventions aimed at building motivation for change. In order to enhance the success rate, one treatment session was used to prepare Peter for this detoxification program. We discussed what Peter could do to try to remain clean outside the detoxification program, especially during the evenings. Peter decided to ask his sister to watch his money, his credit cards, and so on. We agreed with Peter that he was not to leave the house during the evenings except under supervision of a supportive significant other (his father, his sister, or an old school friend he had reacquainted with after moving back to his hometown) and made specific plans on how he would spend the evenings.

During the first session after Peter's successful detoxification, we started off with explaining the cognitive behavioral model of addiction (see Figure 4.4), a model that states that alcoholic or drug-taking behavior is learned behavior, which is triggered by external as well as internal cues and is reinforced by the positive consequences of the alcoholic or drug-taking behavior. After this rather formal introduction to cognitive-behavior therapy, we used an example close to Peter's own experience to explain the model further.

> Therapist: Let me try to explain it more clearly using an example. You told me that you tried to cut down your cannabis use several times, the last time being a few months ago—isn't that right?
>
> Peter: Yes, but it didn't work out. I remained clean for two days but on the third day I lapsed.
>
> Therapist: What happened, that made you lapse, do you think?
>
> Peter: Well, it sounds like a stupid excuse, but some guy I knew from college phoned, and talking to him made me feel so down that I just started using again.
>
> Therapist: You label it as an excuse, but explaining it in cognitive-behavior therapy terms it would sound something like: What happened was that you had a phone call and talking to your friend from university triggered certain thoughts that made you feel bad. This negative mood triggered craving. Some people experience craving as primarily physiological, by starting to sweat, for example. Others have specific thoughts like, I really need to smoke now. Do you have any bodily sensations or thoughts that you associate with craving?
>
> Peter: Well, I know my muscles become tense.
>
> Therapist: Okay, so you started feeling depressed and didn't know how to handle that; in addition, your body started craving cannabis, you became tense, and eventually you responded by going out and buying pot. The consequence of that behavior was that for a short while you didn't feel so down anymore.

Peter: That's true; however, after smoking I also started feeling sad again because I failed my attempt of cutting down on the pot.

Therapist: Good, that's a very important adjunct you're making. Smoking cannabis did not only make you feel less upset but it also triggered thoughts about failing, which made you feel sad again and which probably functioned as a trigger in eliciting even more craving.

Peter: Yes, it seems like I'm running around in circles. I use pot to feel less upset and in return I feel guilty and ashamed of smoking, which makes me want to smoke even more.

Therapist: Exactly; your drug use has all kinds of side effects that in cognitive-behavior therapy terms are called the negative consequences of drug using. And often these consequences also become triggers for renewed or continued use. Can you think of another personal example to illustrate this?

Peter: Like having an argument with my father about my drug use? That is, of course, a consequence of my use, but at the same time fighting with him about past use makes me want to use even more.

Therapist: Indeed, that is a good example of how a consequence of use is also a cue or trigger associated with renewed use.

Sometimes using a piece of paper or a chalkboard can help patients (as well as therapists) to better understand the model. In addition, we introduced the diary exercise, explaining that in order to change behavior one first needs to understand why and how the behavior occurs and that keeping a journal is an effective way of gathering information.

Unfortunately, Peter was noncompliant and didn't keep his journal. We addressed the issue immediately during the second treatment session. Common reasons for noncompliance include having no clear understanding of why the homework assignment is relevant for treatment success, not understanding how to do the homework assignments, having negative associations regarding the concept of "homework" (e.g., negative school experiences), or holding myths about the consequences of doing homework. In the case of Peter it was the last reason. He had become ambivalent about doing his homework because he had noticed that completing his diary triggered craving and he had become convinced that doing his homework would increase the likelihood of lapsing into cannabis use. Experiencing craving during homework assignments is a fairly common response and even talking or thinking about issues related to alcohol or

CBT MODEL	CASE EXAMPLE
Situation	Talking to a friend on the phone
⇓	⇓
Thoughts	"I'm just one big failure"
⇓	⇓
Feeling	Sad
⇓	⇓
Craving	Muscle tension
⇓	⇓
Behavior	Going out to buy and smoke pot
⇓	⇓
Consequences	Feeling less sad (primary) Feeling ashamed and even more sad (secondary)

FIGURE 4.4   Illustration of CBT model

drug use during treatment sessions may trigger craving. Both are case examples of classical conditioning: talking or thinking about the situation triggers the full experience of the situation, including the craving response. It is important to explain to patients that to some extent this is inevitable and that avoidance by not doing one's homework or having superficial conversations in treatment sessions in order to prevent craving are ineffective strategies. Using the diary form, we filled out the situation in which Peter was doing his homework and was starting to experience craving. Looking at the circumstances under which Peter had been filling out his craving diary, we found out he had been doing so around 8:00 P.M., after finishing dinner. We discussed with Peter the possibility that the time of day had made filling out the diary extra difficult because it was also an external cue strongly linked to previous use of cannabis. Brainstorming about alternative options for how to do the homework without becoming overwhelmed by craving, Peter decided to write his diary entries in the morning instead of the evening. In addition, he decided he would combine writing in his diary with going jogging afterward as a way of getting rid of any leftover feeling of craving.

During the detoxification program, Peter had to undergo urine controls. Although somewhat embarrassed at first, he noticed it was having a motivating effect on his strive for abstinence. On Peter's instigation we agreed he would continue to do urine analyses once per week for the next two months. The use of urine analyses, breath analyses, or collecting information through a significant other to cross-validate a patient's nonuse has advantages as well as disadvantages, and to some extent it is up to a therapist's personal style, in combination with the guidelines of the affiliated treatment facility, as to whether these measures are taken and, if so, for how long and under which conditions. Advantages of external cross-validation of nonuse are that some patients find it motivates abstinence (as in Peter's case) and it helps the patient to be open about possible lapses or relapse ("I better tell you, because you will find out any way"). A disadvantage, however, is the hidden message this cross-validation might give rise to: "You don't trust me telling you the truth." In the process of deciding whether or not to use measures of external control, here are some clinical considerations that may be of help:

> Overall, the more severely dependent the patient is, the more likely it is that he will find it difficult to be truthful about use, lapses, and relapse. In cognitive-behavior therapy terms this behavior is not moralized but rather viewed as behavior learned and reinforced during the course of the development of the disorder; substance use has repeatedly led to conflict with others, and in order to prevent future conflict and to decrease the likelihood that others will hinder future substance use, the patient has become used to keeping substance use a secret or to minimalizing its impact. The more frequently the patient has lied about use in the past, the more likely he is to do so in the future, and this interferes with treatment.

> The circumstances under which patients enter treatment, if they enter treatment voluntary or, for example, are referred by the criminal justice system, influence honest reporting of use, lapse, and relapse.

> Whether (re)lapsing has negative consequences for continuation of the treatment program—for example, if after two lapses patients would be expelled from the treatment program—should be considered.

> The type of treatment delivered also influences the need for external control. In, for example, outpatient group therapy, the standard use of breath analysis before start of treatment may be warranted. Checking alcohol use in this case is not only a tool in the treatment of the individual but also an instrument to guarantee safe, alcohol-free treatment conditions for the collective.

Using the information gathered at intake and combining this with the information from Peter's diary recordings, we completed Peter's functional analysis. Although Peter wasn't clinically depressed and didn't meet criteria for social phobia, the functional analysis (see Figure 4.5)

EXTERNAL CUES

SITUATION			
	• Sitting in my room doing nothing. • Going out for a walk with no specific plan where I want to go/what I want to do. • Seeing other people having fun together (on the street, movies, etc.). • Interacting with peers.		

SPECIFIC DAYS OR TIMES OF THE DAY	SPECIFIC PLACES	SPECIFIC PEOPLE	OTHER SPECIFICS
• After 20.00 • Weekends around 15.00	• Area where my dealer lives.	• Meeting my dealer. • Seeing other people use cannabis.	• Having money in my pocket.

⇓

INTERNAL CUES

THOUGHTS	FEELINGS	BODILY SENSATIONS
• I failed university • I'm not able to cope with life • I won't amount to anything • I'm all alone • They'll think I'm a failure too	• Sad • Anxious	• None (so far)

⇓

CRAVING

PHYSICAL MANIFESTATIONS	COGNITIVE MANIFESTATIONS	BEHAVIORAL MANIFESTATIONS
• Tense muscles • Sensations in stomach	• I really need to smoke now! • Cannabis will make me feel better!	• Restlessness

⇓

BEHAVIOR

WHAT SUBSTANCE	HOW MUCH	HOW IS IT USED
• Cannabis	• Around 6 joints per day	• Smoked

⇓

CONSEQUENCES

	POSITIVE	NEGATIVE
SHORT-TERM	• Able to relax • Feel less sad • Feel less anxious • Better able to sleep	• Expensive • Becoming indifferent • Arguing with my parents
LONG-TERM	• None (so far)	• Increases low self-esteem • Deterioration in relationship with parents • Isolation • Poor concentration and general health

FIGURE 4.5   Functional analysis of Peter's cannabis use

showed that negative mood, interacting with other people, and feeling lonely were recurring triggers for craving.

We discussed the functional analysis with him and made plans about which interventions were needed for achieving prolonged behavioral change. We made the distinction between the ad-hoc strategy of avoiding high-risk situations and the more time-consuming but essential ingredient of treatment—namely, learning new coping skills. The following situations were classified as ones that could relatively easily be avoided:

> going out in the evenings (to be avoided for a period of three weeks)
>
> going out during the daytime without a clear destination or plan
>
> having large amounts of money in one's pocket
>
> having too much spare time and, more generally, having no day routine

Regarding enhancing Peter's coping skills, we decided to focus on strategies to handle craving (see the more detailed description in chapter 2) in combination with strategies to handle negative thoughts and depressed mood. The most helpful interventions for Peter were handling craving through talking to others about it (especially his sister) or distracting himself through activities (cleaning up his room, going to the gym to work out).

The most effective intervention in regard to his depressed mood was activation. Peter had developed the tendency to withdraw in response to negative thoughts and depressed mood, and this tendency reinforced feelings of loneliness and caused Peter to withdraw even more, creating a high-risk situation for (re)lapse. We prompted Peter to come up with activities he could undertake during the day that could prevent him from withdrawing:

> Therapist: So, besides the fact that you withdraw from interacting with other people and become inactive in response to negative thoughts, this withdrawing in fact causes you to feel even more depressed and creates an increased risk for lapsing.
>
> Peter: Yes, I understand that, but that was in the past. Withdrawing from everything around me and smoking my brains out during those years at college caused me to feel even more depressed, but what about now? I am inactive, but that's mostly because I haven't got anything to do!
>
> Therapist: So that is an additional problem; besides your tendency to withdraw during discomfort, you currently lead an inactive life, which gives you little pleasure and reinforces your negative perception of yourself. But what is holding you back from just changing that; from finding yourself a job, some voluntary work or some other kind of daytime activity?

Prompting Peter to find things to do during the daytime triggered several other of his uncertainties ("Who would want to hire me?" and "What if I'm unable to hold that job, what will my parents and my sister think of me?"). During the last phase of treatment, however, Peter found the courage to start applying for jobs.

Cognitive Restructuring

Peter's thoughts about failing at college often triggered craving, and we used several sessions to explore these dysfunctional beliefs and to question their link with reality using Socratic dialogue. We combined this with addressing Peter's distorted assumptions about how cannabis could be effective in dealing with negative thoughts and feelings ("If I use cannabis I will feel better" and "Without cannabis I won't be able to handle my sadness"). The result of this restructuring was that Peter made a flash card for himself; on it he wrote several helpful alternative thoughts he could prompt himself with when he was feeling down:

Not finishing college does not make me a bad person because a
   bad person is somebody who lies, steals, and willingly hurts
   other people; that is not me.
Feeling down is not a permanent state; rather, like craving, it
   comes and goes.
I will feel different tomorrow.
For years I tried solving my problems using cannabis; well . . . did
   it actually get me anywhere?

Inviting a Significant Other

Because Peter was living with his parents and their concerns had been an important reason for him to seek treatment, the therapist proposed inviting them for a joint session. Peter, however, was not thrilled about this idea. Inviting his parents triggered strong emotions and negative thoughts ("It's bad enough to have to ask your parents if you can move back in with them; I will not ask them to go to therapy because of me as well!"). Motivational techniques and cognitive restructuring were in vain; we decided to postpone the topic and discuss it on a later date. Peter was, however, willing to invite his sister. She had been very supportive during the past few weeks, somewhat to Peter's surprise, and we were able to schedule a joint session within two weeks. In general it is advisory to invite a significant other into treatment. However, deciding who this significant other should be—a partner, another family member, a friend, a colleague from work—is not always so easy. Important is that the significant other is close to the patient and supportive of change and is not abusing alcohol or drugs herself. In order to be most effective we usually prepare the session together with the patient and set out specific goals. As a rule we always ask the patient to invite the significant other to join a treatment session. If the patient finds this difficult, we use role-play in the therapy session to have the patient practice motivating the significant other to join. In addition, we ask the patient to inform the significant other about the specific goals of the session, in order to prevent false hope or unexpected surprises.

Preparing for Relapse

It is important to prepare patients for the possibility of lapses and relapse. Relapse is explained as part of a learning process rather than as a final outcome of treatment. Doing so might cause some friction between therapist and patient (and concerned others) because some will interpret the above as a self-fulfilling prophecy ("Planning for it will make it more likely to occur"), or a disqualification of the ability and determination of the patient to remain abstinent.

Peter was quite reluctant to discuss the matter of relapse. To counter some of his ambivalence we used the comparison of preparing for a lapse with having a first-aid kit in the back of your car: having so does not mean that you expect to have a car accident, but in case of a car accident you will be prepared. Peter combined several strategies including addressing a letter to himself, to be opened in the case of a lapse. In this letter Peter described his past month's struggles but also the good things that had happened to him since he stopped using cannabis.

Evaluation

Peter was successfully treated for his cannabis addiction; during treatment he lapsed once, but effectively recuperated from the lapse. At the end of treatment we referred Peter to an assertiveness group-training program for abstinent patients, in order to enhance his social skills. At the six-month follow-up, Peter was still clean and had experienced no lapses. After unsuccessfully applying for several jobs he had found himself a part-time job at a bookstore across town and was thinking about starting college again the following year. He was still living with his parents.

THE CASE OF JAN

Background and Complaints

Jan, a single 46-year-old construction worker with no children, was referred to our outpatient clinic because of alcohol dependence and anxiety. Jan was the youngest of three children. He reported having had an unhappy childhood, his father being an alcoholic and his mother being rather phobic. Jan's father died when Jan was 20 and his mother died a few years later. After the death of his mother, Jan and his brother and sister lost contact. Jan had started drinking at the age of 17. By the age of 21, he drank large amounts of alcohol a few times a week and when he was 30 he started drinking on a daily basis. When Jan was 34, his partner left him, and shortly after he lost his job due to cutbacks. During these difficult times, Jan started getting panic attacks and starting avoiding public transport, which rapidly generalized into all kinds of agoraphobic avoidance behaviors.

Previous Treatments

When Jan was 25, he had sought help for his drinking at an outpatient addiction treatment center. He had become alarmed by the amount of alcohol he drank during the weekends and was afraid he would end up like his father. Jan was prescribed medication (disulfiram) and had several meetings with a counselor. After three months of abstinence, treatment stopped and Jan discontinued the medication. During the next 12 months he drank in a controlled fashion but in the years to come his drinking increased and at the age of 30 he was drinking heavily on a daily basis. Four years after his first panic attack, at the age of 38, Jan referred himself to treatment for his panic disorder and agoraphobia; the treatment consisted of therapist-guided exposure. During intake Jan kept quiet about his alcohol use because he had learned from a friend that alcohol abuse was an exclusion criterion. Although enthusiastic about the treatment format, Jan had little benefit from it because he was only able to do his homework assignments under the influence of alcohol.

Assessment

When we met Jan he was drinking between 10 and 16 units of alcohol per day, on a nearly daily basis. We used quantity/frequency measures to assess past-year drinking as well as self-monitoring records to assess

Jan's current drinking pattern. In addition we interviewed Jan using the SCID-I to confirm our diagnosis: 303.90, alcohol dependence with physiological dependence. To assess Jan's confidence to control his drinking, the Situational Confidence Questionnaire (SCQ) was used (Annis & Graham, 1988). Jan had little confidence in remaining abstinent in drinking situations (social pressure to drink) and in situations where he would experience bodily sensations.

The screening of Jan's anxiety and depressive symptoms was done at intake, and formal assessment using the SCID-I and questionnaires was conducted after one month of abstinence. The SCID-I was used to confirm our diagnoses: 300.21, panic disorder with agoraphobia, and 300.23, social phobia. Jan didn't meet diagnostic criteria for depression at intake, nor after one month of abstinence. To get a clearer picture of sensations and cognitions associated with panic we used the Bodily Sensation Questionnaire, or BSQ (Chambless, Caputo, Bright, & Gallagher, 1984) and the Agoraphobic Cognitions Questionnaire, or ACQ (Chambless et al., 1984). The BSQ revealed that the following sensations were most alarming to him: palpitations; chest pain; numbness in arms, legs, or other parts of the body; sensation of shortness of breath; blurred vision; sweating; depersonalization; and feeling detached from oneself. On the ACQ, Jan reported the most dominant thoughts during a panic attack as, "I will become paralyzed by fear; I will not be able to control myself; I will get a heart attack; I will faint." We used the Social Phobia and Anxiety Inventory, or SPAI (Beidel, Turner, & Stanley, 1989), in order to get some more detailed information about his social anxiety. His anxiety was mainly triggered in situations in which he had to interact with or was exposed to strangers or authority figures. Although Jan did not fulfill the criteria of any depressive disorder, during the course of treatment we kept track of Jan's mood using the BDI; after four weeks his score was 18 and after six weeks his score was 26, which reflects a moderately depressed mood. We used the Personality Disorder Questionnaire–4, or PDQ–4+ (Hyler, 1994), in order to screen for personality disorders. Jan met all criteria for the diagnosis 301.6, avoidant personality disorders.

MACROANALYSIS

In the case of Jan, there were four current problem areas intertwined. First of all was Jan's drinking; in addition were his panic attacks and related agoraphobic avoidance behavior, his social phobia, and his depressed mood (see Figure 4.6). We hypothesized that Jan's drinking elevated his panic and social-phobic complaints and that the drinking

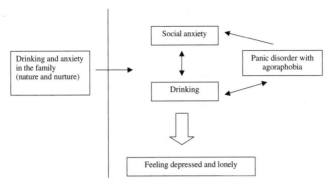

FIGURE 4.6   Macroanalysis of Jan

prevented Jan from learning new strategies for coping more effectively with panic attacks and social anxiety. In addition, we hypothesized that Jan's drinking, his panic attacks and avoidance behavior, and his social phobia were causal to Jan's depressed mood. We expected that if Jan were to stop drinking, and his panic attacks, avoidance behavior, and social phobia were to disappear—either as a result of reduced drinking or as a result of additional treatment—his mood would improve as well. Based on this problem analysis we decided to target drinking first. Choosing between tackling panic attacks and avoidance behavior or social anxiety as a second treatment, we chose the panic attacks and avoidance behavior because in Jan's perception it was the disorder interfering most with normal life. We decided not to treat, but to monitor, Jan's depressed mood during the course of treatment. If the depressed mood would become more severe, our hypothesis would be altered and treatment adapted.

Motivating for Change and Detoxification

Parallel with assessment, we started educating Jan about the relationship between alcohol use and anxiety symptoms. In line with this information, we suggested one month of abstinence, in order to be able to reassess his anxiety symptoms and if still present combining alcohol-abuse treatment with treatment interventions directed at his anxiety symptoms and his avoidance behavior. During several sessions we discussed this treatment strategy. Jan was very ambivalent about giving up drinking without first being "cured" of his anxiety. He kept on suggesting starting with the anxiety treatment first and treating the alcohol later. We repeatedly stated, however, that we still didn't know if it was the alcohol that was causing the panic attacks or whether the panic attacks were

EXTERNAL CUES

SITUATION			
	• Coming home after work • Being offered a drink • Sitting home alone • Interacting with strangers		

SPECIFIC DAYS OR TIMES OF THE DAY	SPECIFIC PLACES	SPECIFIC PEOPLE	OTHER SPECIFICS
• Weekdays 18.00 • Weekends around 13.00	• Bars • Supermarket	• Seeing William and Steve (two friends) drinking alcohol	• None (so far)

⇓

INTERNAL CUES

THOUGHTS	FEELINGS	BODILY SENSATIONS
• I'm having an attack • I'm going to lose control • People will find me strange • Life is hopeless	• Anxious • Sad	• Palpitations • Chest pains • Shortness of breath

⇓

CRAVING

PHYSICAL MANIFESTATIONS	COGNITIVE MANIFESTATIONS	BEHAVIORAL MANIFESTATIONS
• Sweating • Dry mouth	• I just need one drink	• Biting nails

⇓

BEHAVIOR

WHAT SUBSTANCE	HOW MUCH	HOW IS IT USED
• Alcohol	• Between 10-16 units a day	•

⇓

CONSEQUENCES

	POSITIVE	NEGATIVE
SHORT-TERM	• Feel less anxious • Feel less depressed	• None (so far)
LONG-TERM	• None (so far)	• Increase in anxiety symptoms • Increase in depressive symptoms • Isolation • Increase in low self-esteem • Poor health

FIGURE 4.7   Functional analysis of Jan's alcohol use

part of a disorder independent of his alcohol use. And it was our experience that treating patients with panic attacks while they are still drinking alcohol in order to cope with their anxiety is generally ineffective. Eventually, Jan had to admit that earlier treatment for his panic disorder had been unsuccessful, presumably due to his continued drinking.

After the third session Jan agreed to focus treatment on the alcohol abuse and to strive for abstinence. We discussed different options, including a two-week inpatient detoxification program. However, for Jan—being phobic—this was out the question. Eventually Jan was detoxified on an outpatient basis by his general practitioner, prescribing Librium during the first few days of detoxification and additionally prescribing Refusal to help Jan remain abstinent.

A Functional Analysis of Jan's Drinking Behavior

Using the information gathered at intake in combination with Jan's diary recordings, we constructed a functional analysis (see Figure 4.7). Jan's alcohol use was triggered by several external cues (coming home after work at a specific time) as well as internal cues (bodily sensations as well as anxiety-evoking thoughts). Jan's drinking was reinforced by the (short-term) decrease in anxiety that it brought to him.

Dealing with Craving and Exposure *In Vivo*

During the first few weeks of treatment Jan learned to deal with craving using the technique of recalling all of the negative consequences of his alcohol use in combination with doing distracting activities. After four weeks of abstinence it became clear that the panic disorder, agoraphobia, and social phobia were independent disorders given that the anxiety symptoms had not been reduced. As had been agreed upon in advance, we directed our attention to Jan's panic attacks and avoidance behavior. Standard exposure *in vivo* in combination with response prevention was used to break through Jan's avoidance behaviors. Jan made an anxiety hierarchy, a list of anxiety-evoking situations that is used as a guideline in practicing exposure (Emmelkamp, Bouman, & Scholing, 1993). Jan was recommended to continue using Refusal during the exposure treatment of his panic attacks. Otherwise chances were that Jan would use alcohol if he became anxious during exposure to phobic situations. Jan started off by practicing going to the nearby supermarket in the morning, when it was least crowded, and gradually exposed himself to more difficult situations such as going to the same supermarket in the late afternoon, when it was crowded. Although Jan found practicing exposure very hard, he experienced a lot of benefits from it early on in treatment. After he conquered his fear of going to the market on his own, it became a Saturday morning ritual for him to go out to the market and buy fresh fruit and vegetables. As a result of the exposure program, Jan's panic attacks decreased in frequency and intensity.

The Relapse Prevention Plan

After seven weeks of abstinence, Jan questioned whether he should continue using Refusal. We advised Jan to continue its use during the exposure program, but Jan was very determined that he was to test his strength and abilities in withstanding craving. All motivational interviewing techniques in vain, Jan stopped taking Refusal and during the first few weeks he lapsed into alcohol use several times. These lapses were cued by social situations in which he was offered alcohol and was unable to refuse. The most important thing Jan learned from these lapses was that lapsing increased the frequency and intensity of his panic attacks immediately and, subsequently, his avoidance behavior. Jan learned to prevent lapses from becoming full relapses mostly by contacting significant others who were supportive of his nondrinking and by not staying in bed after a night of heavy drinking, but instead getting up and doing household chores. These were activities that Jan disliked but once he had done them, his self-esteem increased.

Practicing Drinking-Refusal Skills

Analyzing under which conditions Jan had lapsed into alcohol use revealed that these were mostly social situations. We decided to use role-play to assess these situations and to have Jan practice saying no when alcohol was offered. Jan learned to stick with his original no, speak in a clear voice, and to leave the situation if others keep on offering alcoholic beverages.

Evaluation

Jan successfully changed his drinking behavior. He lapsed several times during treatment but was able to prevent full relapse (see Figure 4.8). During the last two months of treatment Jan was able to go to most stores, travel with public transportation, use elevators, and visit outdoor crowded places. Jan's score on the BDI had dropped from a score of 19 at intake to a stable score of between 4 and 7, which is considered within normal range. Jan decided he did not want to continue treatment in order to treat his social phobia. At the 6-month follow-up, Jan had lapsed into alcohol use three times but had prevented relapsing using elements from the relapse prevention plan in combination with occasional use of disulfiram. Jan's panic attacks and avoidance behaviors remained

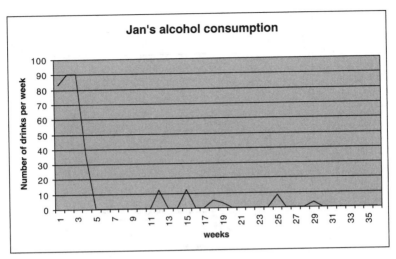

FIGURE 4.8   Jan's lapses into alcohol during treatment

in remission and his mood was stable and within normal range. He remained, however, socially anxious, but this did not hinder him much.

THE CASE OF DIANNE

Complaints

Dianne, a 52-year-old married woman with no children, increasingly called her husband Mick at work, sometimes several times a day, complaining of being lonely and craving a drink. Sometimes Mick would stop work and go to his wife to support her. When together with her husband, Dianne had been able to control her drinking, but she now had also started drinking during the times Mick was at home.

Dianne had been drinking excessively for the past four years, between 12 and 24 units a day (mostly beer and wine), for several days in a row (see Figure 4.9). After a number of days she then would collapse for two days, too sick to drink, after which she would resume drinking. Besides drinking, Dianne complained about feeling depressed, not being able to structure her day, having difficulty sleeping and eating, having sore muscles, being lonely, feeling guilty and worthless, being on edge all the time, not being able to control her worrying, and having occasional panic attacks. Until six years previous Dianne had worked as a community nurse and did not drink much. Due to some reorganization the workload increased, and this led to severe burnout. Dianne stopped

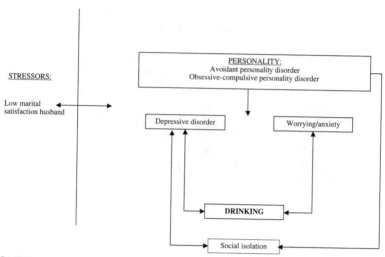

FIGURE 4.9   Macroanalysis of Dianne's complaints

working and the frequency and the quantity of her drinking increased. She started drinking at home on a daily basis and took tranquilizers (oxazepam). Two years earlier Dianne was admitted for detoxification (one-week hospitalization) and subsequently treated in a day-care program at an addiction treatment facility. She kept on drinking, however, and her depressive and anxiety symptoms only increased and her relationship with Mick deteriorated.

When we first saw Dianne and Mick, Dianne had just started using acamprosate (an anticraving drug) as prescribed by her general practitioner. Dianne was also suffering from depressive symptoms, uncontrollable worrying, and situational panic attacks. Dianne had a score of 31 on the BDI, which is considered rather severe. In view of a possible substance-related artifact, we postponed diagnosing major depression and generalized anxiety disorder. She did not meet the criteria for panic disorder. Dianne had partly started drinking because of feeling anxious and depressed, but her drinking had also made her more anxious and depressed. Using the International Personality Disorder Examination, or IPDE (Loranger, 1999), a semistructured diagnostic interview, Dianne was diagnosed as having an avoidant and obsessive-compulsive personality disorder.

Mick and Dianne had separate apartments because Mick worked in another part of the country; during the weekends and holidays Mick stayed at Dianne's place. Preparing his upcoming retirement, Mick was now going to move in with Dianne.

Marital Adjustment

According to the Maudsley Marital Questionnaire, or MMQ (Arrindell, Emmelkamp, & Bast, 1983), Mick was clearly more negative about their relationship then Dianne. On marital dissatisfaction, Mick had a score of 42 while Dianne had a score of 20. The Level of Expressed Emotion, or LEE (Cole & Kazarian, 1988), showed Mick to experience little emotional support from his wife. Dianne was more positive, finding Mick supportive in some areas. To establish if there was any form of violence or fear of violence, verbal abuse, or physical abuse, we used the Conflict Tactics Scale, or CTS (Straus, Hamby, Boney-McCoy, & Sugarman, 1996)) and interviewed both partners. In the past year Dianne had hit her husband twice while being drunk; in one of these instances Mick had hit her back. Both partners agreed these had been isolated incidences and were convinced there would be no future violence.

Macroanalysis

Concerning Dianne, there were four major related issues intertwined: her drinking, her depressive mood, her anxious symptoms, and her marital problems. In addition, Dianne met criteria for both the avoidant personality disorder and the obsessive-compulsive personality disorder.

Many of Dianne's symptoms (e.g., sleeping difficulties, muscle tension, poor concentration, and low self-esteem) could be accounted for by each of the four problem areas discussed above. We decided to focus our attention on Dianne's drinking as a first step. In general—even with severe comorbid conditions—targeting the drinking problem is the first treatment of choice. There is no evidence that, if the patient is not able to control her alcohol consumption, targeting other pathology in co-occurrence with alcohol dependence will be effective.

Prioritization of Treatment Strategies

Behavioral couple therapy is as effective as individual therapy not only with alcohol abuse but also with depression and anxiety disorders (Emmelkamp & Vedel, 2002). Because of Mick's early retirement and the consequences this was going to have on their relationship and taking into account their overall low marital satisfaction, we decided to offer Dianne and her husband behavioral couple therapy, focusing on the drinking problem as well as their relationship. If still needed, the spouse-aided therapy for alcohol abuse could be supplemented by spouse-aided therapy for depression or anxiety. Because Dianne had already started using acamprostate, we agreed that she would continue using it during the course of our treatment.

Course of Treatment and Assessment of Progress

Initially, Dianne and Mick's treatment followed a Dutch behavioral couple therapy manual, derived from the protocol described in O'Farrell (1993) and Noel and McCrady (1993).

Psychoeducation and the Sobriety Trust Contract

The first two sessions were used for psychoeducation, explaining the treatment rationale and introducing the sobriety trust contract. We agreed upon abstinence rather than moderation as a treatment goal. As to the sobriety trust contract, each day at a specific time—in order to prevent the couple from arguing about her drinking behavior through-out the day—Dianne was to initiate a brief discussion with Mick and reiterate her intention not to drink. Dianne was then to ask Mick if he had any questions or fears about possible drinking that day and answer the questions in an attempt to reassure him. Mick was not to mention past or possible future drinking beyond that day.

Behavioral Analysis (Microanalysis)

In order to obtain more information about Dianne's drinking patterns, we asked her to keep a diary. Every time she felt the urge to drink she had to write down where she was (situation), what her feelings were (emotions), what she was thinking or seeing (cognitions or images), and any physical sensations she might be experiencing (see Figure 4.10). She was also asked to rate (on a scale of 1–10) the amount of craving she had experienced, which appeared to be highly related to fluctuations in her depressed mood. The diary was used to identify high-risk situations and to detect seemingly irrelevant decisions that sometimes cumulated into high-risk situations (e.g., not getting out of bed in the morning or skipping a planned trip to the supermarket).

Using the above-mentioned daily recordings, we introduced the behavioral analysis as a framework of hypotheses with respect to ante-cedents and consequences of (drinking) behavior. Important during this first phase was to show Dianne and Mick the loop in which Dianne had caught herself: the consequences of her drinking (e.g., feeling bad

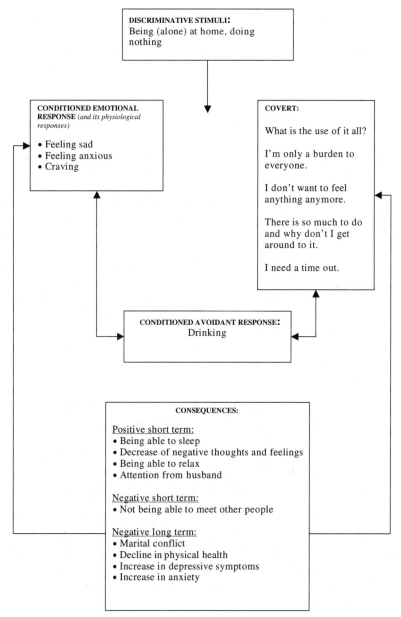

DISCRIMINATIVE STIMULI:
Being (alone) at home, doing
nothing

CONDITIONED EMOTIONAL
RESPONSE (and its physiological
responses)

• Feeling sad
• Feeling anxious
• Craving

COVERT:

What is the use of it all?

I'm only a burden to
everyone.

I don't want to feel
anything anymore.

There is so much to do
and why don't I get
around to it.

I need a time out.

CONDITIONED AVOIDANT RESPONSE:
Drinking

CONSEQUENCES:

Positive short term:
• Being able to sleep
• Decrease of negative thoughts and feelings
• Being able to relax
• Attention from husband

Negative short term:
• Not being able to meet other people

Negative long term:
• Marital conflict
• Decline in physical health
• Increase in depressive symptoms
• Increase in anxiety

FIGURE 4.10   Microanalysis of Dianne's drinking

about oneself) being also a reason for her to start drinking. During this
phase, we also addressed Mick's part in his wife's drinking behavior. We
wanted to decrease behaviors of Mick that triggered or rewarded drink-

ing and to increase behaviors that triggered or rewarded nondrinking. For example, it was explained to the couple, that, although acting out of concern, Mick's tendency to come home when Dianne complained about feeling lonely increased the frequency of phone calls and her dependency upon him.

Increasing Positive Interactions

From the second session onward we also tried to increase positive interaction between the couple. We wanted to shift Dianne and Mick's attention from recording only one another's negative behaviors (attentional bias), to also being able to recognize positive behaviors. As a homework assignment we asked both of them to write down pleasant or positive behaviors they had observed in each other (e.g., asking how your day was, getting up to make some coffee). We also attempted to increase the actual *amount* of positive behavior. Trying to identify possible pleasant activities, we asked the couple to go back in time and to talk about pleasant things they did together during the time they were dating each other. They liked going out for dinner and going to the movies. We asked them to take turns in planning comparable pleasant activities.

Identifying High-Risk Situations

Using Dianne's diary we identified the most important high-risk situations as being home alone and feeling sad or worrying about household chores. We introduced different ways of coping with craving, the two most important being getting involved in some distracting activity, and talking about it with someone who could offer support.

During these first weeks Dianne was relatively successful in remaining abstinent. Sometimes she would lapse into a one-day drinking episode but the next day she would be able to restrain herself from further drinking. Much time was spent relabeling these "failures." Rather then focusing on the notion of failure, we tried to shift attention to which antecedents had made Dianne drink in the first place (adding them to the behavioral analysis) and which thoughts/actions had helped her the next day to restrain herself.

Management of Depressed Mood

Although Dianne's sleeping and eating improved to some extent, her worrying lessened and her panic attack disappeared, Dianne kept on feeling sad and low on energy. Thus, the probable diagnosis of general anxiety disorder was not confirmed, but the diagnosis of depressive disorder was reaffirmed. Therefore, after seven sessions of alcohol treatment, the manual *Spouse-Aided Therapy with Depressive Disorders* (Emanuels-Zuurveen & Emmelkamp, 1997) was incorporated into Dianne and Mick's treatment program. Inactivity being one of Dianne's most salient high-risk situations, we introduced activity training as an intervention to tackle negative mood as well as her drinking problem. Activation training is a fairly common behavioral technique in treating depression, derived from Lewinson's (1975) theory on depression. We encouraged Mick to help his wife in organizing her week: combining basic daily activities (e.g., getting dressed in the morning), taking care of neglected activities (e.g., cleaning up the bedroom), and increasing the number of pleasant activities (e.g., listening to music, going out for a cup of coffee with a friend). Given Dianne's social anxiety, a gradual approach was used in having her engage in social situations.

Communication Training

From the ninth session onwards communication training was introduced. During this training both partners' personalities became more salient; this may be due to the fact that the drinking and the depressive symptoms had lessened. In addition, we addressed assertiveness, not only because of Dianne's social anxiety but also because both partners found it difficult to express disapproval and make a request. During these sessions it became clear that Mick had great difficulty handling Dianne's preoccupation with details and her reluctance to delegate tasks unless he submitted to exactly her way of doing things. We had the couple express their expectations about the future and about their (renewed) relationship toward one another. We found it important to address realistic goal setting, especially because Dianne had very high expectations about Mick moving in with her. In order to enhance her social support network, we encouraged Dianne to start to visit her old friends again, since she had been neglecting these contacts in the past few years. We also encouraged Dianne to start thinking about working again. She enrolled in a volunteer program, starting as a hostess in a hospital.

Relapse Prevention

Toward the end of the treatment, much time was spent planning for emergencies and coping with future (re)lapses. Dianne and Mick designed their own personal (re)lapse prevention manual using problem-solving techniques. Different alternatives were discussed, such as Dianne talking about her craving with Mick, Mick being allowed to confront Dianne with high-risk behaviors (e.g., not getting out of bed in the morning) and expressing his concern about the matter, and reintroducing the sobriety trust contract.

Evaluation

At the end of treatment (19 sessions during a seven-month period) Dianne had been abstinent for two and a half months and no longer met the criteria for major depressive disorder: her BDI score dropped to 10, which is considered to be within normal range. Via the SCQ, it was determined that Dianne's confidence in controlling her drinking increased. Results showed Dianne to be confident about remaining abstinent even when depressed or sad. She was still convinced she would not be able to limit her drinking to one or two drinks. During the course of the treatment Mick's marital dissatisfaction decreased from 41 to 22 on the MMQ. Dianne's score did not change significantly. At posttreatment both partners were near the cutoff point that differentiates maritally-distressed from non-maritally-distressed couples. The LEE showed Mick was experiencing more emotional support from his wife than he was pretreatment. Dianne seemed to find Mick somewhat less supportive, compared to pretreatment (Vedel & Emmelkamp, 2004).

THE CASE OF GUDRUN

The following case is discussed because it is often difficult in cases of co-occurrent personality disorder to decide whether treatment should first target substance abuse or should focus on the underlying personality pathology. We hope to illustrate how psychological assessment can be helpful in making a treatment plan in such cases.

Background and Complaints

Gudrun referred herself for treatment because of alcohol and drug use in combination with sudden emotional outbursts and a deep sense of emptiness. In order to prepare for intake we asked Gudrun to write an autobiography about her life and the onset and development of her present complaints:

I was born on the 12th of February 1972 in Munich. As a young child I was very close to my father. My mom was always jealous of our "bond." She was a very troubled, alcoholic, depressed mother, who frightened me because of her unpredictable outbursts. In the mornings you never went near her. I never understood why, just that you didn't. Much later I recognized the chemical symptoms of diet pills, alcohol, and antidepressants.

Around the age of 10, things started deteriorating rapidly. My mother's drinking increased and this meant that if you wanted to talk to her, it would have to be in the middle of the day, as mornings she was hateful, always screaming at anyone who came near, and in the evenings, she would just pass out. As I grew older my mother and I got into terrible fights. We would both be screaming and shouting how we hate each other, and then she'd grab a bucket full of cold water and pour it over me to "calm down my hysterics." My obsessive-compulsive behaviors developed in early childhood, became a big part of my life then. I had about five "favorite" crazy rituals and some would be an embarrassment in public, but I couldn't control it. My father completely withdrew, as my mom got worse. Our relationship was reduced to me rebelling against sudden rules and curfews. I started drinking, smoking, and developed an eating disorder. The obsessive-compulsive behaviors made place for substance abuse. I now felt I had control over the rituals and over food. I would starve myself with the help of diet pills, but became bulimic. My mother was doing the same.

At age 14, I was the first of my peers to start drinking, and smoking grass, and had a string of older boyfriends. After graduating from high school, I traveled though Europe. Due to the diet pills, wine, and hash I became an emotional wreck. After returning home, I met Jürgen, my new, older, boyfriend. After dating him over a period of four months he suddenly disappeared: that was his way of breaking up with me. Afterward I learned he had been cheating on me all the time. It feels like the trust that was broken then, poured over into all my following relationships. I always need outside affirmation.

From age 15 till now I haven't been single for more than a month. This, together with the alcohol and drugs, makes me feel I lost out on a huge part of a normal development. At age 19, I went to the University of Tübingen to study English. A new lover introduced me to LSD and XTC. I looked up to him because of his wit and intelligence. And although he was verbally abusive and told me about some terrible things he had done in the past, he could do nothing wrong in my eyes. Eventually after a lot of fights and arguments, making a fool of myself in public, I left him. At the same time, I switched from studying English to studying Journalism.

Two years later my mother died and in combination with all the diet pills, the alcohol and hash, I suffered a nervous breakdown and finally dropped out of university. During the following years I became very numb. The only good thing that happened to me in that period was meeting my current partner; in fact he helped me get off the diet pills.

A year ago I was introduced to cocaine and even crack. I had always promised myself never to do crack but I didn't think twice when it was offered to me and in a period of three weeks used it three times. When a friend offered my partner a job here in the Netherlands I was so happy we could leave Germany, I literally fled the country. For the past six months we have been living in Amsterdam; I haven't found a job yet and spend most days alone while my partner is out working. I use antidepressants but still feel moody. I drink on a daily basis; three days a week I lose control and instead of drinking three glasses, I drink a whole bottle of wine, which puts me in danger of using other substances.

Overall, I think my main problem is my self-destructive behaviors, using alcohol and drugs and finding solace in going to the pub next door, getting very drunk and high with strangers. In addition, I'm scared by the fact that I act just as hateful as my mother when my partner and I have arguments. I'm scared of losing him through this.

Assessment of Substance Abuse and Comorbid Axis-I Disorders

Reading Gudrun's autobiography, it was clear that substance abuse should be assessed. In addition, in her autobiography Gudrun describes behaviors that resemble features of a borderline personality. She had never been in any kind of treatment before and there was no previous assessment material. During initial screening Gudrun had filled out the Michigan Alcohol Screening Test (MAST), scoring on 9 of the 22 items which is indicative of problem drinking. We used the Time-Line Follow-Back method to assess the past 90 days' alcohol and drug use. For the past three months Gudrun had used alcohol on a daily basis: On an average day she would drink 4 units. Up to three times a week she would lose control and drink a bottle of wine. In addition she smoked cannabis on a nearly daily basis and she had snorted cocaine twice. To assess co-occurrent pathology we used the SCID-I. Gudrun didn't have any obsessive or compulsive symptomatology anymore. Her eating disorder was in remission. Her weight was normal, she ate three normal meals a day, she didn't binge anymore, and didn't compensate by using laxatives or excessive exercising. Currently, Gudrun didn't meet criteria for depression or dystymia. She was, however, using Efexor (an antidepressant), which stabilized her mood to some extent.

Assessment of Borderline Personality Disorder

Initially, we used the McLean Screening Instrument for Borderline Personality Disorder (MSI-BPD), a 10-item screening questionnaire. Gudrun scored positive on 7 items, which is just above the cutoff point suggesting further assessment for borderline personality. To further assess borderline features we used the SCID-II, a structured interview for the assessment of personality disorders. The diagnosis was confirmed. However, patients with a DSM-IV diagnosis of borderline personality disorder are a rather heterogeneous group. Clinicians are keenly aware of this diversity, and it relates to why we do not find the diagnosis of borderline personality disorder particularly useful for clinical decisions. We felt somewhat ambivalent about labeling Gudrun as a borderline personality because her behaviors were outside the normal range but not severely within the pathological range. For example, she didn't exhibit suicidal or parasuicidal behaviors. In order to get the personality picture more clear we used the Minnesota Multiphasic Personality-2 test (Butcher et al., 2001), the main result of which was that it confirmed the previous information gathered at intake and Gudrun's self-description. She suffered from low self-esteem and was fundamentally distrustful toward other people. She counted this distrustfulness by being extremely social, almost naive. She felt empty inside, and was restless and easily bored.

Macroanalysis and Treatment Plan

Although Gudrun appeared to be impulsive and reported having anger control issues, she did not exhibit excessive mood swings or suicidal or parasuicidal behavior. On the basis of the information available, we thought she could certainly be classified at the high-functioning end of the borderline spectrum (see Figure 4.11). Therefore, we felt no need for an integrated treatment of borderline personality and substance abuse, but decided to start with treatment for the substance abuse first. Currently, she still had some control over her substance use, but there was a risk that she would experiment with crack cocaine further when she felt lonely and met the wrong people in the wrong places. In the treatment of substance abuse the emphasis was on the acquisition of coping skills to deal with high-risk situations, including not going to pubs without trusted company and refusal skills training. Afterward we referred her to a cognitive therapist to deal with her underlying schemata with respect to self-esteem and distrust.

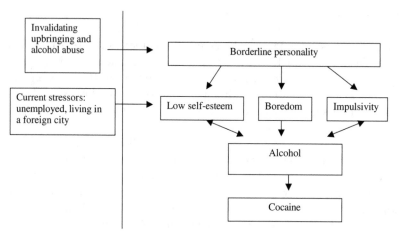

FIGURE 4.11   Macroanalysis of Gudrun

CHAPTER 5

Complicating Factors

In the previous chapters, little attention has been devoted to the fact that in a substantial number of incidences, treatment does not proceed as smoothly as portrayed in treatment manuals. Unfortunately, in the real world, there are a number of complications that might interfere with our treatment plans. In this chapter we will discuss a number of these complicating factors that, when not appropriately dealt with, will impede treatment progress. One such factor is violence. Violence can be directed to others, as is the case in domestic violence, but can also be addressed to oneself, such as in self-injury or suicide.

INTERPERSONAL VIOLENCE

Together with bipolar disorder and psychosis, substance-use disorders are associated with relatively high prevalence rates of interpersonal violence (Corrigan & Watson, 2005). The cause of this association depends somewhat on the substance that is abused. For example, in the case of the alcohol-dependent patient, violence can best be explained by the ingestion of alcohol before the violent offense. However, in the case of young marijuana-dependent patients, violent offenses can best be explained by a juvenile history of conduct disorder (Arseneault, Moffitt, Caspi, Taylor, & Silva, 2000). These findings underscore the notion that violence in patients who enter substance-abuse treatment services is caused by the use of the substance but may also be influenced by a co-occurrent disorder, such as bipolar disorder, conduct disorder, or antisocial personality disorder.

Case Example

> Carl, a 34-year-old electrician, was referred by the legal justice system because of a recent bar fight in which he, under the influence of alcohol and cocaine, had threatened one of the customers

with a knife. Assessing past violent behavior, Carl informed us about several previous arrests for vandalism and bar fights in his teens and mid-20s, but claimed that this last bar fight had just been a case of misfortune in combination with some terrible provocation by some other individuals. For the past few years, Carl told us, he had kept out of trouble and had found himself a proper job and a nice girlfriend.

During intake, Carl was openly ambivalent about his referral and although he agreed with the interviewer that his alcohol and drug use had gotten him into trouble in the past, overall he didn't find his use that problematic. The only negative side effect he could come up with was the fact that his girlfriend had become overly controlling, continuously nagging him about the amount of money he spent on alcohol, cocaine, and cannabis. Attempts of the interviewer to explore this issue any further failed, and Carl refused to invite his girlfriend to the next session.

Intimate Partner Violence

The prevalence of intimate partner violence is substantially higher among couples in which one or both partners abuse alcohol or drugs than in the normal population. Among men entering treatment for alcohol dependence, the yearly prevalence of intimate partner violence was found to be as high as 50–70%, the prevalence of severe and potentially injuring violence being 20–30%. These rates were four to eight times higher when compared to demographically matched nonalcoholic men (O'Farrell, Fals-Stewart, Murphy, & Murphy, 2003; O'Farrel & Murphy, 1995). Fals-Stewart (2003) found the odds of husband-to-wife physical violence to be 10 times higher on days when the man had been drinking compared to abstinent days, the odds of severe violence being 18 times higher on days of heavy drinking compared to sober days.

How should one deal with intimate partner violence in the treatment of substance abuse? Few studies have addressed this issue. A study by Fals-Stewart, Kashdan, O'Farrell, & Birchler (2002) is of particular interest. In a study among cohabiting or married men entering treatment for substance abuse, they found that behavioral couple therapy resulted in a significant reduction in male-to-female physical aggression during the year after treatment. However, individual-based behavioral therapy did not lead to a significant reduction of physical aggression. The results of this study (which were mediated by drinking outcome and dyadic adjustment) suggest that involving the assaulted partner in the treatment may actually reduce the risk of violence. The following example illustrates how a functional analysis of intimate violence is made partner.

Case Example

Charles, a 43-year-old computer specialist, referred himself to the addiction treatment facility because of problem drinking. At intake, Charles was accompanied by his wife Linda. The precipitating event for seeking help was a marital dispute two weeks earlier, which had escalated into a fight during which Charles had slapped Linda in the face several times. This had been the third time Charles had become physically violent toward Linda, and both were deeply upset about the incident. Charles had been under the influence of alcohol during the fight and both partners were sure that alcohol was the most important reason why Charles had become violent. We decided to explore this hypothesis by interviewing both partners about previous disputes (see Figure 5.1). Indeed, Charles and Linda seemed only to get into fights when Charles had been drinking, often in combination with Linda feeling frustrated about his drinking.

When interviewing patients about their substance use, violence is a topic not to be omitted. In general, patients are reluctant to talk about it, sometimes out of feelings of shame or fear of the negative consequences once it gets out. It is the task of the therapist to ask specific, nonjudgmental questions about the violence and to gather as much information as needed to make a balanced decision on whether to treat the patient

---

Linda makes some nasty remark about Charles drinking.

↓

Charles starts to cross-complain and starts saying nasty things back at her.

↓

Linda becomes furious ("How dare he after all he has done to me and my family") and starts summarizing all the terrible things Charles has done to her.

↓

Charles, overwhelmed by all these bad things being poured out over him, acts out by becoming verbally aggressive, telling her to shut up, and calling her names.

↓

Linda quiets down, burst into tears, and leaves the room.

FIGURE 5.1   Chain of events

for substance abuse, to combine the treatment for substance abuse with a referral to a organization specialized in anger management, or to refer him to an anger-management program before treating the substance abuse.

In dealing with (intimate partner) violence the following guidelines may be of help:

Always conceptualize violence as problem behavior needing change. Avoid labeling the aggressor ("you are bad person") but also prevent downplay of the severity of the problem ("It didn't really hurt, it was only a small bruise").

While discussing the matter, it is important to stress that the perpetrator remains responsible for his own violent behavior despite the fact that his partner or the other person in the situation may trigger feelings of anger.

If the violence only occurs under the influence of alcohol/drug use, is low in frequency, and low to mild in severity, make specific plans about how to prevent violence during a lapse/relapse and start substance-abuse treatment. Address violence every session and add assertiveness training and anger-management to your treatment package.

If the violence only occurs under the influence of alcohol/drug use, is high in frequency and mild to high in severity, substance-abuse treatment as well as specialized aggression control treatment is needed.

If the violence occurs with or without being under the influence of alcohol/drug use, specialized aggression-control treatment is needed. In addition, before starting substance-abuse treatment the therapist must have a clear agreement with the patient about which behaviors are tolerated and which are not, including a "time out" signal the patient (or therapist) may use in case emotions become too intense during the session.

Patients with severe anger-control impairments, in general, have difficulty handling (long-term) inpatient treatment programs and have difficulty dealing with emotion-focused group therapy. Skill-oriented outpatient training modules seem more appropriate for these patients.

Violence Directed Toward Oneself: Suicide

Suicidal behavior and substance abuse are linked, and working in the field of addiction treatment will expose a therapist to patients who have suicidal ideations; some of these patients will try to kill themselves, and some of them will actually succeed in committing suicide. In a review of studies on suicide in alcohol dependence, Inskip, Harris, and Barra-clough (1998) found that substance abusers were seven times more likely than non-substance-abusers to commit suicide. In opiate users and mixed intravenous drug users, the risk of committing suicide was found to be even higher (Wilcox, Conner, & Caine, 2003). This high preva-lence of suicidal behavior in patients with substance-use disorders can partly be explained by the high prevalence of other psychiatric disorders that are associated with suicide, such as depression and antisocial and/ or borderline personality disorder. However, it is not only the presence of the comorbid disorder on its own that explains the elevated risk for suicide. For example, depressed patients who abuse alcohol are more likely to commit suicide compared to nonabusing depressed patients (Dumais et al., 2005). Other risk factors for suicide among substance abusers include sexual abuse, social isolation, imprisonment, and pro-longed unemployment (Darke & Ross, 2002; Darke, Williamson, Ross, & Teesson, 2005).

In clinical practice, assessment of current suicidal thinking should be an essential part of initial assessment. Further, it is important to investigate the history of violence and self-harm (other than substance abuse). Self-harm is often associated with substance-use disorders (Evren & Evren, 2005) and significantly increases the risk of suicide. Not only with depressed patients, but also with impulsive patients (often with borderline or antisocial traits), clinicians should be particularly alert to the risk of suicide. It is a wrong assumption that impulsive aggression in substance abusers is limited to violence toward others (e.g., mari-tal violence). Many suicides are committed as an impulsive act when intoxicated.

There are certain groups of substance-abusing patients in which careful monitoring of suicidal ideation and intentionality during the course of treatment would appear warranted. Patients with multiple comorbid disorders (depression, anxiety, antisocial and borderline per-sonality disorder) are particularly at risk (Driessen et al., 1998). Heroin users also have a high risk of committing suicide: between 3% and 10% of heroin user deaths are due to suicide (Darke and Ross, 2002). Those with a recent history of suicide attempts, having no close friends, and extensive polydrug use, however, are at an even greater risk. Further, clinicians should be alert that withdrawal of stimulant drugs may be associated with mood disorders and increased risk of self-harm and suicide.

Dealing with Personality Disorders

In recent years a great deal of research attention has been given to the relationships among personality disorder, substance abuse, and harm toward self or others. Much of this attention has focused on borderline personality disorder and antisocial personality disorder, given that both are associated strongly with substance abuse. Results of epidemiological studies point to high percentages of overlap between these personality disorders; approximately 30% of patients with borderline personality disorder also meet the criteria for antisocial personality disorder, and approximately 70% of patients with antisocial personality disorder meet criteria for borderline personality disorder (Widiger & Corbitt, 1997). There is a preponderance of borderline personality disorder among women, whereas antisocial personality disorder is much more prevalent among men. Some hold that both personality disorders are expressions of one underlying disorder, which expresses itself in borderline personality disorder in women and in antisocial personality disorder in men (see, e.g., Widiger & Corbitt, 1997). In addiction treatment centers a substantial number of substance-abusing patients meet criteria of either antisocial or borderline personality disorder or both, which may interfere with successful treatment of the substance abuse.

Borderline Personality Disorder

Borderline personality disorder is a common psychiatric disorder that is often overlooked in addiction treatment settings. Levels of borderline personality disorders among substance-abusing populations have ranged from 11% to 65%, with the highest levels reported among opioid users. Borderline personality disorder is characterized by marked impulsivity, chronic feelings of emptiness, identity disturbance, lack of anger control, intense and frequent mood changes, life-threatening behaviors (e.g., self–injury and suicidal gestures), disturbed interpersonal functioning (e.g., chaotic relationship), and frantic efforts to avoid abandonment when separation is anticipated. These patients are often characterized by aggressive responses to provocation, with loss of behavioral control, which is either directed toward others in the form of uncontrolled expressions of anger and violent acts or in the form of suicide, suicidal threats and gestures, or other self-damaging acts such as self-mutilation. The risk of suicide is particularly high, and it is estimated that 8–10% of those with borderline personality disorder successfully commit suicide.

Substance-abusing patients with a borderline personality disorder are generally more disturbed than substance-abusing patients without a personality disorder. Substance-abusing patients with comorbid borderline personality disorder are more severely psychiatricly impaired (more psychopathology), have more self-destructive behavior and suicidal thoughts, and are often more extensively involved in substance abuse than substance-abusing individuals without borderline personality disorder (see, e.g., Linehan et al., 1999). The diagnosis of borderline personality disorder has been associated with higher levels of drug use and overdose. The presence of comorbid borderline personality disorder presents a host of complications for treatments focused on substance-use disorders (Dimeff, Rizvi, Brown, & Linehan, 2000; Ross, Dermatis, Levounis, & Galanter, 2003; Van den Bosch, Verheul, Schippers, & Van den Brink, 2002).

In substance-abusing individuals, routine screening for borderline personality disorder would be clinically useful to identify a group that maintains higher rates of risky, and potentially fatal, behaviors such as binge drinking, overdose, suicide threats, and needle sharing. The use of a 10-item self-report screening measure for borderline personality disorder—the McLean Screening Instrument for Borderline Personality Disorder (MSI-BPD)—may be quite useful in this respect. A MSI-BPD cutoff of 7 or more of the measure's 10 items was judged to be the best cutoff. If the diagnosis borderline personality disorder is confirmed by a structured diagnostic interview, in most cases treatment has to be adapted to the individual needs of the patient. The more severe the borderline pathology, the less likely the patient will benefit from stand-alone manualized group therapy (i.e., coping-skills training or 12-step approaches). Apart from this, having a severe borderline patient participate in a group with "normal" substance-abusing patients, the latter will probably benefit less from treatment or may drop out early in treatment.

Case Example

Cathleen, a young inpatient and mother of two children who were both placed under custodial care, was admitted to the hospital because of polydrug use. In addition, she met the criteria for borderline personality disorder. Cathleen was sexually provocative toward other patients and certain members of the staff, and she found it difficult to control her impulsive, angry behavior during group sessions. Her angry remarks ("I hate you all") and emotional outbursts ("If you are unable to help me, I will kill myself this weekend") frightened other group members, and her remarks and suicidal gestures led a number of patients to become openly hostile toward her. In return, this made Cathleen even more disruptive. Eventually, it was decided to provide

Cathleen with individual psychotherapy sessions rather than to continue group therapy attendance.

It is clinically wise to treat severe borderline patients with substance-abuse disorders individually, preferably with an add-on referral to dialectical behavior therapy (Linehan, 1993). Dialectical behavior therapy comprises strategies from cognitive and behavioral therapies and acceptance strategies adapted from Zen teaching and practice (mindfulness training). In addition to systematic behavioral analyses of dysfunctional chains of behavior, dialectic behavior therapy involves training in behavioral skills, cognitive restructuring, and exposure-based strategies aimed at reducing maladaptive emotions by blocking avoidance behaviors. Dialectal behavior therapy might help patients to cope with some of their personality problems, but is less effective in addressing substance-abuse problems. Van den Bosch et al. (2002) reported that standard dialectic behavior therapy could be effectively applied with borderline patients with comorbid substance abuse in terms of lower levels of parasuicidal and impulsive behaviors. However, dialectic behavior therapy was not more effective when compared to "treatment as usual" in reducing substance-use problems. At 6-month follow-up, the benefits of dialectic behavior therapy over care "as usual" sustained. There remained no differences between the treatment conditions for drug abuse, although patients receiving dialectic behavior therapy drank less alcohol compared to patients in the treatment-as-usual condition (Verheul et al., 2005).

Recent years have seen the development of interventions designed specifically to treat patients with both borderline personality disorder and substance abuse, the most important being adaptations in the dialectical behavior therapy program. Linehan et al. (1999) adapted the dialectical behavior therapy program for borderline patients with drug dependence. Several modifications were added to standard dialectic behavior therapy, including a dialectical stance on drug use in which total abstinence is insisted upon. However, in the case of a lapse into substance use, coping strategies from cognitive-behavior therapy are used to prevent lapses from becoming full relapse, followed by a quick return to the original treatment goal of total abstinence. Treatment also involved transitional maintenance medication in the perspective of "replacing pills with skills" later on in the program. In a randomized controlled trial, patients with borderline personality disorder and drug dependence receiving this adjusted dialectical behavior therapy program had significantly greater reduction in drug use at 16 months follow-up than control patients who had received treatment as usual. Further, dialectical behavior therapy resulted in less attrition from treatment and more improved social adjustment as compared to the controls (Linehan et al., 1999).

Antisocial Personality Disorder

Among substance abusers, antisocial personality disorder, conduct disorder, and adult antisocial behavior are very common (Compton et al., 2005). According to the fourth revised edition of the *Diagnostic and Statistical Manual of Mental Disorders*, or *DSM-IV-TR* (American Psychiatric Association, 2000), antisocial personality disorder is characterized by failure to conform to social norms, disregarding safety of self and/or others, consistent irresponsibility, lack of remorse after having hurt, mistreated, or stolen from another, impulsiveness, failure to plan ahead, irritability, aggressiveness, recklessness, deceitfulness, and manipulative behaviors. It should be noted that in a number of illicit drug users the diagnosis of antisocial personality disorders is not warranted, although they formally fulfill the necessary criteria. In a number of cases antisocial behavior is the result of the addiction to illicit drugs, rather than the result of underlying antisocial personality traits.

Unfortunately, there are no good screening measures to assess antisocial personality. Himmerich et al. (2004) found that a subscale of the Michigan Alcoholism Screening Test predicted antisocial personality disorder. Unfortunately, this subscale lacks specificity since it also predicts paranoid and borderline personality disorder.

Many clinicians hold that substance-dependent patients with antisocial personality disorder have poorer treatment outcomes when compared to patients without antisocial personality disorder. Earlier studies supported this notion, but poor prognosis and response to treatment may have been confounded by pretreatment severity. Substance-abusing patients with antisocial personality disorder often use more alcohol and drugs, and have more associated legal and psychiatric problems at baseline compared to substance-dependent patients without antisocial personality disorder (Verheul, Van den Brink, & Hartgers, 1998). Results of studies with substance-dependent patients who have co-occurring antisocial personality disorder (Cacciola, Alterman, Rutherford, & Snider, 1995; McKay, Alterman, Cacciola, Mulvaney, & O'Brien, 2000) indicated that the patients with co-occurring antisocial personality disorder were more disabled at baseline and follow-up, but improved as much as the patients without antisocial personality disorder. In a recent review of treatment outcome studies of opiate-dependent drug users meeting the criteria for comorbid antisocial personality (Havens & Strathdee, 2005), few differences were observed for those with and without antisocial personality disorder receiving treatment for opioid dependence with respect to retention, reductions in HIV risk behaviors, and drug use. However, in those continuing to use cocaine and benzodiazepines while enrolled in a methadone program, response to psychotherapy and pharmacological therapy was lower among opiate users with comorbid antisocial personality disorder.

A number of patients with antisocial personality traits are characterized by a fearful attachment style (Timmerman & Emmelkamp, 2006). This attachment style is characterized by avoidance of close relationships because of fear of rejection, a sense of personal insecurity, and a distrust of others. Most of these patients have a history of early traumatic experiences (see, e.g., Zanarini & Gunderson, 1997) in which parental figures often play a causal role in violating their trust in them. Further, in an addictive and often criminal milieu, distrusting others might be of major importance in order to "survive"; as well, many patients with a criminal history feel unfairly treated by the criminal justice system. Difficulties in the treatment of individuals with antisocial personality traits often have to do with fear of trusting therapists and fear of showing vulnerabilities. Individuals with antisocial personality traits in general are reluctant to be open about their emotions and the problems they encounter. Acting in a brutal, manipulative, or avoidant manner is often done in order to keep others at an emotionally safe distance. For clinical practice this implies that effort will be needed to build a good therapeutic relationship and a safe environment in which the patient with antisocial personality traits dares to be open about the difficulties he is facing. Even the smallest suspicion of unreliability on the part of the therapist can immediately undo the trust that was built (Timmerman & Emmelkamp, 2006). For some patients, even a trusting relationship with a therapist may be too threatening, and in these cases a more pragmatic working relationship might be more appropriate.

In sum, the research discussed in this section shows that therapeutic nihilism when working with patients with antisocial personality disorder is not justified. However, not all treatment modules may be equally suited for patients with antisocial personality disorder: favoring skill-orientated training modules over emotion-focused or insight orientated therapy modules. Finally, it should be remembered that in the Matching Alcoholism Treatments to Client Heterogeneity (MATCH) study, alcohol-dependent patients who were angry (high in hostility) at the start of treatment profited more from motivational-enhancement therapy than from 12-step approaches. Given that many patients with antisocial personality disorder are characterized by hostility, these findings suggest that a motivational rather than a confrontational approach is suited for patients with antisocial personality traits.

Case Example
   Ronald was referred to treatment by the criminal justice system.
   Meeting with his therapist for the first time, he made it very
   clear from the start he was not interested in sharing feelings or
   discussing "all the shit" from the past. The therapist decided
   not to argue with him, but asked instead in which way he might
   be of help.

Therapist: Okay, that won't work for you, but let's have a look
if there is anything that may be of use to you in order to prevent
all that shit from continuing.

Ronald: Well, I keep getting into trouble with the law because I
easily lose my temper and get into fights.

Therapist: So, if you would be able to gain control over your
temper, this would prevent you from getting into trouble with
the police, which would make your life a whole lot easier.

Ronald: Well, it wouldn't solve all my problems but it would
definitely make a difference.

Therapist: Okay, so in order to gain more control over your
impulses we need to know what actually happens when you
become angry and how this results in becoming physically
aggressive. Can you give me a recent example of losing your
temper and getting into trouble because of it?

In doing so, a working relationship was built that eventually was
quite profitable for Ronald. He accepted the expertise of the therapist with respect to problem-solving skills and was eager to use
these to his own advantage.

Dealing with Co-Occurring Axis I Disorders

The frequent co-occurrence of mental health disorders other than substance abuse has been discussed in chapter 1. In the literature the term
dual diagnosis is used to identify patients with both substance-use disorder and other psychiatric disorder(s). The term, however, is an over-
simplification. Just knowing that a patient has not only a substance-use
disorder but also fulfills the *DSM-IV-TR* criteria of another disorder
does not help much in terms of treatment planning. Actually, the so-
called dual diagnosis patients represent a rather heterogeneous group
with a variety of psychiatric disorders varying in terms of severity.
The most important indicator of the utility of making a diagnosis of

comorbidity lies in the extent to which the diagnosis guides the selection of treatment. However, the fact that a patient has a dual diagnosis does not inform us about the suitability for a specific treatment intervention. Very few studies have investigated the effectiveness of specific treatments for patients with dual diagnoses as discussed below.

When patients exhibit a comorbid disorder the clinician should gather information not only on onset and pattern of substance misuse over the individual's lifetime, but also on the onset and course of mental disorder in relation to onset and course of substance-use disorder. In treating patients with co-occurrent disorders, generally three strategies can be followed. In sequential treatment, one problem is treated first, followed by treatment of the other disorder, assuming that both disorders can be treated independently from each other. Alternatively, patients may receive parallel treatment; both disorders are then treated simultaneously. In the third method, both disorders are treated with integrated treatment approaches, which have become especially popular in severe mental illness (psychotic disorders). Although psychotherapy and pharmacotherapy can be used as stand-alone treatments targeting substance-use disorder and the co-occurrent mental disorder, respectively, in a number of instances a combined treatment approach is to be preferred.

Psychotic Disorders

The co-occurrence of substance abuse and psychotic disorder (especially schizophrenia) is one of the major problems of mental health care in recent decades. Traditional mental health and addiction treatments have not adequately addressed these co-occurring disorders, primarily due to the segregation of mental health centers and addiction centers; this approach does not sufficiently recognize the dual diagnosis patient's specific individuals needs. Most mental-health clinicians are not skilled in the core evidence-based psychotherapy approaches to treating substance-use disorders, including motivational interviewing, cognitive behavioral approaches directed at substance abuse, and 12-step facilitation. On the other hand clinicians and counselors in addiction centers are usually not versed in how to deal with schizophrenic patients.

Few treatment studies have focused on this population, and hence evidence-based findings on the management of specific co-occurring disorders, such as schizophrenia and addiction, are hardly available. In a recent conference of experts from academic institutions and state mental health systems, recommendations for improving current practice were formulated (Ziedonis et al., 2005). *Integrated treatment* is recommended for schizophrenic patients with substance-use disorders, and requires both an understanding of mental illness and addiction as well as integrating medications for both addiction and mental illness with cognitive-behavior therapy and motivational interviewing. Specific recommendations are provided concerning screening for substance-use disorders in patients with schizophrenia, selecting the most appropriate medications for such patients to maximize safety and minimize drug interactions, assessing motivation for change, and managing medical conditions that commonly occur in such patients.

Nigam, Schottenfeld, and Kosten (1992) were among the first to describe the successful use of an adjunctive group psychotherapy for substance-abusing patients with major psychiatric disorders (e.g., schizophrenia; schizoaffective, psychotic depression; and atypical psychosis). The group utilizes a psychoeducational approach that focuses on substance abuse causes and consequences, principles of recovery, and relapse prevention strategies. Most patients achieved periods of stable abstinence and improved social functioning. The positive results of such group interventions have been recently replicated (James et al., 2004). Barrowclough et al. (2001) evaluated another integrated care program. This program involved motivational interviewing, cognitive-behavior therapy, and family intervention. This integrated care program resulted in lower relapse rates, more days abstinent, and better social functioning compared to standard outpatient care.

Unfortunately, patients with schizophrenia and substance-abuse disorders often show little interest in participating in specific integrated treatment programs. Severe mental patients often become noncompliant with medication for their psychotic disorder during exacerbation of their substance abuse, and here motivational interviewing might be helpful. Bechdolf et al. (2005) reviewed the empirical evidence for the efficacy of motivational interviewing in such dual diagnosis patients and found that results are inconclusive. Although some studies found motivational interviewing either to enhance subsequent participation at integrated treatment programs or to lead to reduced substance use (e.g., Graeber, Moyers, Griffith, Guajardo, & Tonigan, 2003), other studies did not.

Finally, integrated treatment programs of substance-abusing patients with psychotic disorders need to address a number of problem areas other than substance abuse, including school or vocational training, family intervention, and social-skills straining. Given the many problems that need to be addressed, generally, intensive long-term treatments are needed (Drake, Mercer-MacFadden, Mueser, McHugo, & Bond, 1998).

Anxiety Disorders

In case of co-occurrent anxiety, the task of the clinician is first to establish whether the anxiety symptoms meet diagnostic criteria for a specific anxiety disorder, and second to determine the temporal relationship between the syndromes identified. In some anxiety disorders (e.g., specific phobias) there is usually no need to ascertain the relationship between the two disorders since in most patients the disorders run an independent course. In other disorders, however (e.g., panic disorder, social phobia, and post-traumatic stress disorder), it is important to establish whether the anxiety disorder is related to the substance-use disorder. For example, panic attacks are often associated with withdrawal syndromes. Or, in the case of social phobia, large amounts of alcohol can be consumed before patients may trust themselves to undergo social interactions. In the only controlled study that addressed this issue, Thomas, Randall, and Carrigan (2003) found support for the hypothesis that social-phobic patients use alcohol to cope with their anxiety and they concluded that individuals high in social anxiety deliberately drink alcohol to cope with their social fears. The data of their study support the assumption of the self-medication hypothesis—that alcohol is used to reduce social discomfort in socially anxious patients.

In patients with agoraphobia and social phobia the anxiety disorder usually precedes the development of alcohol-use disorders (Brady & Lydiard, 1993; Kushner, Abrams, & Brochardt, 2000). The course of the disorders can usually be established retrospectively, for example, by using the Time-Line Follow-Back interview. The association between the anxiety disorder and the substance-use disorder is not necessarily unidirectional, but in some cases a vicious cycle exists. Research in this area is scarce and provides little in the way of clinical guidelines. Research has primarily focused on alcohol abuse and dependence. Based on the frequent co-occurrence of anxiety disorders with alcohol-use disorders and the negative influence of other comorbid psychiatric disorders on the outcome of treatment of alcohol dependence, studies have investigated whether co-occurrent anxiety disorders predict worse outcome. Although it has been claimed that comorbid anxiety disorders predict poor outcome of alcoholism treatment (e.g., Kushner et al., 2000; Driessen et al., 2001), results are inconclusive given the many methodological problems in most studies (Schadé et al., 2003).

Case Example

Melanie, a 32-year-old nurse, has been socially anxious as long as she can remember. Over the years, she learned to cope with her phobic anxiety by drinking increasing quantities of alcohol, first only when she had to go to social events, but later on also when alone at home. Her increased symptoms of anxiety led to increased alcohol intake. When she attempted to stop her alcohol use, this led to a further increase in anxiety symptoms due to withdrawal from alcohol. This, in turn, led to a further increase in alcohol misuse.

In cases where anxiety disorders precede development of substance abuse, it has been suggested that many patients may ingest alcohol or drugs as self-medication to cope with the psychiatric symptoms. Would the addition of cognitive behavior strategies to directly address the anxiety disorder prevent relapse into substance abuse? Unfortunately, the results of the few studies that investigated whether dual treatments focusing both on the alcohol dependence as well as on the anxiety disorder are more effective than treatment focusing on the substance-use disorder alone are negative. Bowen, D'Arcy, Keegan, and Van Senthilsel (2000) evaluated whether a cognitive behavioral treatment for panic disorder and agoraphobia would enhance the effects of the regular alcoholism program in alcohol-dependent inpatients with comorbid panic disorder. Unfortunately, the addition of 12 hours of cognitive-behavioral therapy directed at panic and agoraphobia led neither to enhanced outcome on drinking measures nor mood and anxiety symptoms. Schadé et al. (2005) investigated whether the relapse rate in these anxiety-disordered patients could be reduced if they were given additional treatment for the comorbid anxiety disorder. Patients with a primary diagnosis of alcohol dependence and a comorbid anxiety disorder involving agoraphobia or social phobia were randomly assigned to an intensive psychosocial relapse-prevention program on its own, or in combination with an anxiety treatment program comprising cognitive behavioral therapy and optional pharmacotherapy (selective serotonin reuptake inhibitors). The addition of the treatment directed at the anxiety neither enhanced treatment outcome in terms of abstinence or a reduction in days of heavy drinking, nor reduced relapse. The additional therapy reduced the anxiety symptoms, but it had no significant effect on the outcome of alcohol treatment programs. Finally, one study yielded rather negative effects of integrated treatment with social-phobic alcohol abusers (Randall, Thomas, & Thevos, 2001). An integrated treatment addressing both the alcohol problem and social phobia resulted in worse outcome (e.g., drinking more frequently; more frequent heavy-drinking days) than the behavioral treatment focusing on alcohol use only.

Taking the results of these studies together, there does not seem to be a need to provide dual treatment in substance-dependent patients with co-occurrent anxiety disorders. Perhaps in less-substance-dependent patients evidence-based cognitive or pharmacological treatment of the "underlying" anxiety disorder may improve not only the anxiety disorder but also affect the substance abuse, but this has not yet been investigated.

Since there is considerable evidence that substance abuse may perpetuate or exacerbate anxiety symptoms, it is therapeutically wise to wait and see what happens with the anxiety symptoms when the substance use is stopped or substantially reduced. Generally, cognitive-behavior therapy targeting the substance abuse is not only likely to result in a reduction of substance use but in a reduction of anxiety symptoms as well, so within the perspective of a stepped-care approach, in most cases treatment should be directed at the substance abuse first. If the anxiety symptoms remain prevalent after a period of at least four weeks of abstinence, there is reason to consider more detailed assessment and treatment directed toward the comorbid anxiety disorder. If anxiety does not improve after reduction of substance abuse, adding treatment components directly addressing the anxiety disorder might be indicated. Besides being effective in the treatment of substance-use disorders, cognitive-behavior therapy also has strong empirical support for its efficacy in treating a range of anxiety disorders including panic disorder and agoraphobia, social phobia, generalized anxiety disorder, and obsessive-compulsive disorder (Emmelkamp, 2004). Description of these interventions falls outside the scope of this book. For detailed clinical applications of these various cognitive and behavioral approaches the reader is referred to Emmelkamp, Bouman, & Scholing (1993).

Post-Traumatic Stress Disorder

Many victims of traumatic events not only suffer from post-traumatic stress complaints, but also from substance abuse. The dual diagnosis of post-traumatic stress disorder (PTSD) and substance-use disorder (SUD) is reported to be highly prevalent. Compared to patients with either disorder alone, patients with both disorders exhibit more severe behavior, and have worse symptoms and worse treatment outcomes. The majority of studies examining the order of onset among individuals with PTSD and SUDs have found that PTSD is most often the primary disorder (i.e., it temporally precedes the onset of substance-use disorder; see chapter 1).

In clinical practice it is sometimes hard to differentiate symptoms caused by substance use, PTSD, or a combination. Some trauma victims may at first experience PTSD symptoms as a result of the trauma, but then their use of alcohol or drugs may increase the anxiety and possibly lead to the worsening of PTSD symptoms over time. For example, among a sample of combat veterans with PTSD and comorbid SUD, individuals reported that cocaine made their PTSD symptoms (particularly hyperarousal symptoms) worse (Bremner, Southwick, Darnell, & Charney, 1996).

There is some debate in the field regarding which disorder to treat first: the SUD or PTSD. Many patients in mental health settings are referred to addiction treatment centers to deal with the substance abuse first. On the other hand, in addiction treatment centers PTSD patients are often referred back to mental health settings since they are hardly motivated to give up their drinking or drug taking, which they use to control the pain released by the memories and the reexperiencing of the trauma. In addition, a commonly held belief is that addressing the PTSD in early treatment would "open Pandora's box" (Hien, Cohen, Miele, Litt, & Capstick 2004) and would interfere with achieving abstinence or staying sober.

In a study by Najavits (2002a), 147 clinicians were surveyed on their degree of difficulty and gratification in working with each disorder (PTSD, SUD) and their combination. A dual diagnosis was perceived as more difficult to treat than either disorder alone; but, notably, gratification in the work was higher than its difficulty. Areas of greatest difficulty were clients' self-destructiveness, case management, and dependency; areas of greatest gratification were teaching new coping skills, developing expertise, and helping clients achieve abstinence. Notably, clinicians with a personal history of either trauma or SUD had a more positive view of the work with dual diagnosis patients than those without such a history. Those clinicians finding the work with dual diagnosis most difficult were more likely to treat patients in a mental health setting and to have no personal history of trauma. It should be noted, however, that there is no evidence that these therapist characteristics are related to better treatment outcomes.

Little is known about how best to treat individuals with comorbid SUD and PTSD. Identifying differences by order of onset may help increase treatment utility by allowing for identification of differential treatment responders. In a study by Nisbith, Mueser, Srcic, and Beck (1997), patients with SUD secondary to PTSD evidenced significant decrease in substance use after cognitive-behavior therapy (CBT) focusing on SUD. No significant improvement in substance use was observed for patients with a primary SUD. In cocaine-dependent patients, pharmacotherapy for drug abuse resulted in a significant decrease of PTSD: approximately 60% of the dual-diagnosis participants no longer met criteria for PTSD posttreatment, although their PTSD symptoms were not directly targeted in therapy (Dansky, Brady, & Saladin, 1998). Similarly, in a study by Back, Jackson, Sonne, and Brady (2005), during treatment with CBT for alcohol abuse, which did not include specific treatment for PTSD, levels of PTSD symptoms decreased in concert with levels of alcohol consumption. Nearly two-thirds of the patients no longer fulfilled the criteria for PTSD at the posttest stage. Participants who did not show a significant reduction in PTSD symptoms had greater alcohol use during treatment. In general, alcohol-abusing patients with primary PTSD derived greater overall benefit (e.g., in physical health, alcohol use, and social functioning) when compared with patients in whom alcohol abuse preceded PTSD. Thus, the results of the studies discussed above show that patients with SUD and PTSD may profit from treatment directed at substance abuse, especially when the trauma precedes the substance abuse.

Among psychosocial treatments for PTSD, exposure-based therapies have been extensively studied and are the treatment of choice in most anxiety disorders (Emmelkamp, 2004). Patients with PTSD have shown significant reductions in PTSD and associated symptoms (e.g., depression, social adjustment) when treated with exposure therapy (Hembree & Foa, 2000). Despite these positive results of exposure-based therapies, clinicians are somewhat reluctant to use exposure for PTSD with comorbid substance abuse. Generally, clinicians hold that exposure is too emotionally distressing for SUD patients, which may lead to increased substance abuse to deal with the stress.

Brady, Dansky, Back, Foa, and Carroll (2001) investigated the feasibility of adding exposure for post-traumatic stress to treatment for substance abuse in cocaine-dependent patients. Therapy consisted of a combination of imaginal and in-vivo exposure therapy techniques to treat PTSD symptoms and cognitive-behavior techniques to treat cocaine dependence. Exposure was initiated at the seventh session, midway through the protocol. Results revealed significant improvement in PTSD at up to six months follow-up, which was comparable to results of exposure treatment in regular PTSD cases (Van Etten & Taylor, 1998). These findings suggest that some individuals with PTSD and comorbid cocaine dependence can be successfully treated with exposure therapy and that exposure therapy does not necessarily increase the risk of relapse. Significant decrease in substance use severity during the treatment and follow-up periods was also found. Importantly, and in contrast with what most clinicians would expect, patients' cocaine use did not increase during the exposure therapy. In sum, when exposure therapy is provided to treat PTSD symptoms in addition to dealing directly with the cocaine use disorder, it appears that both disorders may improve substantially in some individuals.

Few treatment programs were specifically designed to deal with substance abuse and PTSD concurrently. Triffleman, Carroll, & Kellogg (1999) have described substance-dependence PTSD therapy, a five-month, twice-weekly, two-phase individual cognitive-behavior treatment utilizing (1) relapse prevention and coping-skills training for substance abuse and (2) psychoeducation, stress inoculation training, and in-vivo exposure for PTSD. Results of their study revealed efficacy in reducing PTSD severity and reduction of substance abuse, but this study was uncontrolled.

"Seeking safety" therapy was developed by Najavits (2002b) and consists of an integrative cognitive-behavior treatment of SUD and PTSD. It is a manual-based treatment that integrates contributions from cognitive-behavior therapy of substance abuse, PTSD treatment, and educational research. The primary goals of treatment are abstinence from substances and personal safety. Seeking safety simultaneously addresses trauma and substance abuse and focuses on stabilization, coping skills, and the reduction of self-destructive behavior. Therefore, 25 topics (e.g., asking for help, coping with triggers) that address the cognitive, behavioral, interpersonal, and case management needs of persons with SUD and PTSD are dealt with. Seeking safety was found to be effective in women with comorbid PTSD and SUD. For example, in an uncontrolled study of seeking-safety therapy in a sample of community women with SUD and PTSD at the end of treatment, there were significant decreases in trauma-related symptoms, substance use, and a range of other clinical variables that included social adjustment, suicidal risk, and depression (Najavits, Weiss, & Liese, 1996). In a controlled study (Hien et al., 2004), however, seeking-safety therapy was not superior to a CBT relapse prevention program that addressed only substance abuse and focused on the identification of triggers and coping strategies for managing substance cravings and relapse. Both active treatments were more effective than routine community care.

What implications have the findings of the studies discussed above for clinical practice?

> In contrast to the prevailing view in the field, there is no reason to exclude substance-abuse patients with PTSD from treatment for their substance abuse.
> There are a number of viable treatments for co-occurring PTSD and substance abuse, including relapse prevention, seeking safety therapy, substance dependence PTSD therapy, and a combination of relapse prevention and exposure therapy. There is a clear need that these empirically supported behavioral therapies are incorporated into clinical practice.

There is no evidence that dealing with the trauma leads to worsening of symptoms and increased substance abuse.

Although the data are not yet conclusive, treatment along these lines seems most effective for patients where the substance abuse is secondary to the PTSD. In these cases substance abuse can perhaps best be conceptualized as a form of avoidance behavior.

Competent staff trained to provide these interventions are comparatively rare. There is a clear need of additional training and supervision for therapists dealing with these dual diagnosis patients, given the challenges that have to be faced and that the training and experience of most clinicians is limited to either addiction or mental health.

Major Depression and Dysthymia

Depression is highly prevalent in individuals with alcohol dependence. Comorbid depression in individuals with alcohol or drug dependence has been associated with a more severe clinical picture (e.g., Pettinati, Pierce, Wolf, Rukstalis, & O'Brien, 1997), and a poorer prognosis (Alterman, Allen, Litten, Fertig, & Barbor, 2000; Charney, Paraherakis, Negrete, & Gill, 1998; Greenfield et al., 1998; Hasin, Nunes, & Meyden, 2004), compared to patients with substance dependence without psychiatric impairment. There is, however, some controversy, since others have found that individuals with comorbid depression were actually at lower risk of substance use than those without depression (see, e.g., Charney et al., 1998; Rounsaville et al., 1998). Rounsaville (2004) has suggested that a negative prognosis of treatment outcome is likely to derive from such features of depression as low energy, pessimism, and worse withdrawal effects. In contrast, in other depressed individuals the experience of painful depressive symptoms may initiate treatment engagement and promote commitment. Alternatively, McKay (2005b) has suggested that depressed patients might do better in the short term, because their dysphoria motivates them to attend more treatment sessions. However, when depression continues and does not remit, this might eventually demotivate the patient, leading to poorer long-term outcomes. Indeed, studying patients with cocaine and alcohol-use disorders, McKay et al. (2002) found depressed patients had better treatment attendance than nondepressed patients, resulting in significantly more reduction of cocaine use than their nondepressed counterparts. However, their use of alcohol and cocaine increased more rapidly in the months after treatment when compared to the substance use of patients who were not depressed.

In a recent review of studies into the efficacy of motivational interviewing, cognitive-behavioral therapy, and contingency management in the treatment of patients with co-occurring substance use and mood disorders (Carroll, 2004), it was concluded that there is good evidence that these interventions decrease substance use. There is, however, less evidence that these interventions also lead to improvements in mood. Given that substance-dependent patients with co-occurring depression appear to manifest at least some improvement in substance use through treatment targeting their use, the question is whether treatment taking into account the co-occurring depressive disorder might enhance treatment outcome, including depression symptom severity and substance use.

Clinicians working with substance-dependent patients, however, are often reluctant to provide specific antidepressant treatment with pharmacotherapy. Although some time ago this pessimism was justified given that earlier studies showed little benefit of treatment of depression in alcohol-dependent (Liskow & Goodwin, 1987) and opiate-dependent patients (Nunes, Quitkin, Brady, & Post-Koenig, 1994), more recent studies suggest that treatment of depression and dysthymia through pharmacotherapy may hold promise in the context of treatment of substance-abuse disorder. Results of these studies were reviewed in two recent meta-analyses (Nunes & Levin, 2004; Torrens, Fonseca, Mateu, & Farre, 2005) and both reviews concluded that antidepressant medication was effective for treatment of depressive syndromes among patients with alcohol or drug dependence. Antidepressant medications proved to be effective among dual-diagnosed patients when used at adequate doses for at least six weeks, and when not used in the case of transient depressive mood due to substance abuse. However, the effects are restricted to reduction of depressed mood and, generally, do not lead to abstinence of significant reduction of substance abuse, if not targeted directly (Nunes & Levin, 2004). So, in a number of patients, the commonly held belief—that if the underlying pathology (e.g., depression) is treated this will also affect the substance-use disorder—does not hold. For example, in depressed cocaine-dependent patients, treatment directed at the depression (desipramine) resulted in improved depressive symptomatology but did not affect cocaine use (Carroll, Nich, & Rounsaville, 1995). Of interests is a recent study by McDowell et al. (2005) into the effects of combined pharmacotherapy and cognitive-behavior therapy in depressed cocaine-dependent patients. The main research question was what pharmacotherapy for depression (desipramine) would add to a standard psychosocial treatment. Therefore, all patients received weekly manual-guided cognitive-behavior therapy (relapse-prevention therapy) in combination with an antidepressant or placebo. Results revealed that desipramine alongside cognitive-behavior therapy targeting substance abuse was more effective when compared to placebo alongside cognitive-behavior therapy in patients meeting *DSM-III-R* criteria for both cocaine dependence and major depression or dysthymia. Treatment results were limited to depressed mood. Treatment groups did not differ in rate of cocaine response, but depression improvement was associated with a lessening in cocaine use, irrespective of condition.

Cognitive-behavior therapies have consistently performed as well or better than other psychotherapeutic interventions in studies of treatments for depression (Emmelkamp, 2004). It is therefore tempting to assume that cognitive-behavior treatments for substance abuse might be well suited for depressed substance abusers given the common theoretical underpinnings of the approach and overlap in therapeutic techniques, even if the intervention is directed at the substance abuse rather than targeting depression. There have not yet been any direct empirical investigations comparing pharmacotherapy versus cognitive-behavior therapy to treat comorbid depression in patients with substance-use disorders. Therefore, at this point there are no clear guidelines concerning what type of treatments (pharmacotherapy or cognitive behavior) should be added to the treatment of depressed substance abusers.

In dealing with a substance-abusing patient who is depressed one should keep in mind that depression could simply be an independent disorder with no functional relationship to substance abuse, in which case successful treatment of depression would not be expected to change substance-use outcome. According to the *DSM-IV-TR*, major depression is considered to be "independent" if the first depressive episode preceded the onset of the substance-use disorder or occurred during a persistent drug-free period. In a number of cases depressed mood is the result of toxic or withdrawal effects associated with chronic substance abuse. In these cases, we would expect that the depression would improve after a (substantial) reduction of substance use, without requiring treatment targeting the depression. Finally, in a number of patients, the depressive syndrome has preceded the onset of substance abuse or occurred during abstinent periods and promoted substance abuse. In these instances we would expect a causal link between depression and substance abuse. For example, patients may be more vulnerable to stress during depressive episodes and being less able to control the substance use, or alternatively may use alcohol or drugs to self-medicate dysphoric symptoms.

Given the complex relationship between the causes and course of mood disorders and substance-use disorders, each patient with co-occurrent mood disorders requires careful assessment to determine the sequence of depressed mood and substance abuse and to establish a causal link, if present. Assessment of the mood disorder is preferably done with a structured interview to verify the diagnosis, given that clinicians are inclined to overestimate the prevalence of a mood disorder. For example, up to 80% of individuals with an alcohol use disorder complain of one or more symptoms of depressive disorder, but only 30% meet criteria for major depressive disorder (Kessler et al., 1996).

Especially in cocaine abusers, diagnosing depression can be challenging because it is difficult to distinguish transient symptoms caused by cocaine from enduring depression syndromes. As noted by Rounsaville (2004), many symptoms of major depression can be accounted for by cocaine's intoxication or withdrawal effects including persistent dysphoric mood, sleep disturbances, appetite disturbances, anergia, anhedonia, and impaired cognition.

Clinicians are advised to undertake prospective monitoring as well as retrospective assessment to establish the nature of, and the fluctuations in, the symptoms of the mood disorder and the substance-use disorder(s). The Time-Line Follow-Back interview might be particularly helpful in investigating possible causal relationships between substance-use disorder and mood disorder. Alternatively, the Psychiatric Research Interview for Substance and Mental Disorders (Hasin et al., 1996) may be used for this purpose. If the depression is independent from the substance abuse, it will have occurred before patients started with substance abuse, or in periods of abstinence or reduced use. Such analyses may also reveal that both problems are caused by the same stressful event (e.g., loss of job, marital breakup).

Case Example

> When Catherine, a 40-year-old single woman, was referred for treatment in a mental health center, she had been unable to work for six weeks due to a severely depressed mood. Questioning revealed that she had had several episodes of major depression over the past four years and that she regularly drank up to eight glasses of wine in a row, often combined with cannabis use. The Time-Line Follow-Back technique revealed that there was a clear association between substance abuse and her depressed mood. In periods that she was not depressed she was quite able to control her drinking and hardly smoked cannabis. Each episode was related to a relationship breakup. She was longing for a stable relationship, with children of her own, and realized that—with the passage of time—the chance of having children was minimizing.

As a general clinical guideline, in cases with comorbid substance abuse and mood disorders (major depression and dysthymia) the same policy is recommended as discussed for dealing with comorbid anxiety disorders. If the level of depression allows and the patient is not suicidal, wait and see what occurs to the depressed mood when the patient manages to stop the substance use for at least four weeks. In most cocaine- and opioid-using patients, inpatient treatment or treatment in a day clinic is required, since most patients will be unable to stay abstinent for four weeks in an outpatient setting. In many cases mood will improve concurrently with a reduction in substance abuse. For example, of patients hospitalized for alcohol dependence who suffered from co-occurrent major depression, only 15% still had clinical levels of depression after four weeks of abstinence and only 6% met criteria for depressive disorder (Brown & Schuckit, 1988).

But how does one target the substance abuse in depressed patients? In contrast to anxiety disorders, depressed patients are often characterized by lack of motivation and low self-efficacy, and may profit from a few sessions of motivational interviewing. There are a few studies in which motivational interviewing was adapted for depressed inpatients with comorbid substance abuse. Although the programs differ in important aspects, they usually focus on fostering greater awareness of the negative consequences of substance use, medication adherence, and program participation during the hospital stay and after discharge. Results of these studies (Daley, Salloum, Zuckoff, Kirisci, & Thase, 1998; Martino, Carroll, Kostas, Perkins, & Rounsaville, 2002; Swanson, Pantalon, & Cohen, 1999) reveal that motivational interviewing had improved treatment engagement and led to somewhat lower substance abuse, but results on depressed mood are less clear.

A number of cognitive-behavioral approaches have been found effective in dealing with depressed mood, and these approaches can also be applied in substance-abusing patients with comorbid mood disorder. The major cognitive and behavioral approaches differ with respect to the role that they ascribe to the various factors in the etiology and functioning of depression, which leads to different emphases in the various therapeutic procedures based upon these models. Cognitive therapies focus on changing patients' depressogenic cognitions, and hence their depressed affect and behavior. Cognitive therapy aims to help patients identify the assumptions and schemas that support patterns of stereotypical negative thinking and to change specific errors in thinking (Hollon & Beck, 2004). This approach was used with the patient Catherine, described above. A disadvantage of conducting cognitive therapy is that it requires intensive training and supervision, which is usually not available in addiction centers.

Behavioral approaches attempt to change maladaptive behavior in order to increase positive reinforcement, which can be done by increasing activity level, enhancing social or relationship skills, and training in problem solving. Increasing pleasant activities by means of homework assignments is often quite useful as a first step in treatment of depressed substance-abuse patients. Typically, activities that are rated as enjoyable but not engaged in during the last few weeks are given as homework assignments. Activities that appear to be relatively easy are chosen first, while more difficult tasks are assigned in later sessions. Adding an eight-session behavioral component focusing on coping with depression to a partial-day hospitalization program for alcohol-dependent patients with elevated depressive symptoms resulted in reduction in drinking and improved mood (Brown & Lewinsohn, 1984).

Only a few studies have evaluated integrated CBT approaches directed at substance abuse and depressed mood concurrently. In these integrated approaches patients are trained to recognize the associations between worsening of depressed mood and substance-abuse lapses or relapse. Brown, Evans, Miller, Burgess, and Mueller (1997) investigated whether CBT focusing on depression could enhance the effects of routine alcohol treatment and prevent relapse. At six months follow-up, 47% of the patients who had been treated for their depression as well as for alcohol problems were completely abstinent as compared to 13% of the control patients, who had received the standard alcohol treatment plus relaxation.

Jerrell & Ridgely (1995) have examined the relative effectiveness of three intervention models for treating people with severe mental illness and substance-abuse disorders: 12-step recovery, behavioral-skills training, and intensive case management. Patients in the behavioral-skills group demonstrated the most positive and significant differences in psychosocial functioning and symptomatology, compared with the 12-step approach. The case management intervention was less effective compared to the behavioral-skills group but more effective compare to the 12-step approach. Results were maintained in an 18-month follow-up. Similar results were reported by Maude-Griffin et al. (1998) in cocaine-dependent individuals. In this study, CBT emphasizing mood-control strategies was significantly more effective than a 12-step approach in patients who had a history of major depression.

The effectiveness of contingency management in dual-diagnosis patients has hardly been investigated. However, studies evaluating contingency management procedures in substance abusers found that depressed substance abusers respond as well to contingency management procedures compared with those without comorbid mood disorders (see, e.g., Gonzalez, Feingold, Oliveto, Gonsai, & Kosten, 2003; McNamara, Schumacher, Milby, Wallace, & Usdan, 2001).

The following clinical guidelines may be helpful when dealing with co-occurrent depression:

In moderately depressed substance-abusing patients, direct treatment at substance abuse and monitor depressed mood.

Cognitive-behavioral programs directed at substance-use disorder are moderately effective with respect to reduction in substance abuse, but somewhat less effective with respect to depressed mood.

Twelve-step-oriented approaches are less effective with substance-abusing patients with concurrent depression or dysthymia than is cognitive-behavioral treatment.

In cocaine- and opioid-dependent patients the effectiveness of contingency management procedures is not impeded by depressed mood.

If mood does not improve after reduction of substance abuse, adding treatment components that directly address depressed mood might be indicated (e.g., coping with depression).

Motivational interviewing may facilitate initial engagement and retention in treatment and after-care programs.

Patients with comorbid dysthymia and major depression can be treated with either cognitive-behavioral procedures or pharmacotherapy (selective serotonin reuptake inhibitors).

Pharmacotherapy leads to moderate reduction in depressed mood, but generally does not affect substance abuse.

Bipolar Disorder

There is some evidence that patients who have bipolar disorder with associated alcoholism have an increased likelihood of rapid cycling, increased rate of suicide attempts, and a slower time to recovery from affective episodes. Generally, alcoholism is related to poor outcome for the bipolar disorder, presumably related to medication noncompliance (Strakowski et al., 2005; Tohen, Waternaux, & Tsuang, 1990). When patients are in remission from a bipolar episode, the absence of symptoms can be a major reason for medication noncompliance.

Few studies have investigated the effects of intervention specifically directed toward changing substance abuse in patients with bipolar disorder. Bipolar patients may also profit from motivational interviewing. Carey, Purnine, Maisto, & Carey (2001, 2002) have evaluated the effectiveness of a four-session, individual, motivational interview in a small group of bipolar patients. As a result of treatment, patients better acknowledged the negative consequences of substance use and increased their motivation to change.

Usually substance-abusing patients are treated either sequentially or concurrently in an addiction treatment center and a mental health center for the substance abuse and the bipolar disorder, respectively. Weiss, Najavits, and Greenfield (1999) developed a group intervention designed specifically for patients with bipolar disorder and substance-use disorder. The goals of treatment include education regarding the relationship between the substance use and bipolar disorder, provision of mutual support through group interactions, abstinence from substance use, and adherence to prescribed medication regimens. The treatment uses an integrated approach by discussing topics that are relevant to both disorders and by highlighting common aspects of recovery from, and relapse into, each disorder. The manual is based partly on the relapse prevention approach (coping-skills training). It was argued that relapse prevention treatment addresses some of the major issues that patients with both substance-use disorder and bipolar disorder frequently face, including ambivalence about complying with treatment; self-monitoring of craving, moods, and thought patterns; coping with high-risk situations; and developing better interpersonal relationships (Weiss et al., 1999). The group therapy consists of 20 one-hour-long weekly sessions, each devoted to a specific topic. Whenever feasible, group sessions are designed to discuss topics that are relevant to both disorders. Throughout the sessions, patients receive psychoeducation on the capacity of certain drugs to trigger manic or depressive episodes; the potential adverse effect of substance use on medication adherence; and advice on sleep hygiene in order to prevent relapse. Many elements of the treatment are borrowed from coping-skills training, including discussion of the "abstinence violation effect" and the difference between a lapse and a relapse, recognizing high-risk situations and triggers not only for substance use but also for depressive and manic episodes. In addition, patients learned how to cope with mood changes. Patients are taught to monitor their moods and their desire for substance use as a way of identifying these early warning signs. Another aim of this therapy is to promote greater awareness in patients that substance use can trigger affective symptoms and reduce medication adherence. Special emphasis is given to the pros and cons of taking medication for both bipolar disorder (e.g., mood stabilizers) and for substance-use disorder (e.g., naltrexone, disulfiram).

In a randomized controlled trial this group therapy was investigated in 45 individuals with both bipolar disorder and substance dependence (Weiss et al., 2000). Weiss et al. reported significantly improved substance abuse outcomes among those assigned to this group intervention as compared to care as usual. Although the treatment described above has been designed as a group intervention, there are no a priori reasons why the same combination of strategies directed at the bipolar disorder and the substance abuse would also not be effective in individual cases.

Attention Deficit Hyperactivity Disorder

Attention Deficit Hyperactivity Disorder (ADHD) is a neurobiological disorder that results in core deficits such as disinhibition, impulsivity, and attentional deficits. There is growing evidence that ADHD plays an important role in the etiology and pathogenesis of substance abuse. Addiction treatment centers are increasingly becoming aware of the fact that a relatively large proportion of their patients have comorbid ADHD and that they are much more vulnerable to substance abuse than individuals without ADHD. The prevalence of ADHD appears elevated not only among stimulant users, but is common among alcohol, opiate, and other substance users as well (Clure et al., 1999, King, Brooner, Kidorf, Stoller, & Mirsky, 1999; Molina, Bukstein, & Lynch, 2002). Biederman, Wilens, and Mick (1995) found a much higher lifetime risk for substance abuse in adults with ADHD (52%) than in controls (27%). In adolescents with ADHD, increased substance abuse may be explained by comorbid conduct disorder and/or bipolar disorder, but in the case of adult ADHD, substance abuse is also more prevalent when comorbid disorders are absent (Schubiner, 2005). Generally, substance use is more severe and relapses more likely for those substance abusers with comorbid ADHD (Ercan, Coŵjunol, Varan, & Toksözet, 2003; Wilens, Biederman, & Mick, 1998).

Why is there an increased risk of substance abuse in adults with ADHD? There are no robust data yet, but a number of ADHD patients report using alcohol and drugs for self-medication purposes.

Case Example

> Frank, a 34-year-old man, was admitted because of cocaine and alcohol dependence. During the first weeks of treatment, staff became increasingly irritated by Frank's lack of treatment motivation. Frank didn't keep his appointments, was often late for group sessions, and left these sessions with no apparent reason. At breakfast he was restless, unable to sit down, and inappropriately talkative, causing quite a stir between himself and some of the other patients. Moreover, Frank seemed to benefit little from treatment, lapsing into cocaine and alcohol use regularly.

Although he seemed to grasp the concept of avoiding high-risk situations, he kept on entering these situations impulsively and unprepared. When he had been clean for three weeks, it was decided to screen Frank for ADHD. Eventually, Frank was diagnosed with ADHD and put on medication (methylphenidate), which was effective in reducing his restlessness and impulsive behavior. This in return improved his treatment compliance, reduced the need for self-medication by using cocaine and alcohol, reduced the number of lapses, and improved his relationship with the other patients and members of staff.

Generally, the prognosis of outcome of substance-abuse treatment in adult ADHD cases is worse when no due attention is given to ADHD. A careful assessment of ADHD is needed in order to plan treatment. It is often difficult to distinguish symptoms of ADHD from effects of substance abuse (Sullivan & Rudnik-Levin, 2001). In patients whose ADHD emerged in childhood, the presenting clinical picture may be due partly to chronic ADHD and partly to the effects of substance use. In patients whose ADHD symptoms did not emerge until after a period of regular alcohol or drug use, symptoms may be due entirely to drug use. Therefore, information is needed with respect to the developmental history of ADHD and substance abuse, respectively. Although it is important to require information about ADHD symptoms in periods of abstinence of alcohol and drugs, this is often not feasible, or the information gathered is unreliable.

To enable a formal diagnosis of ADHD, a prolonged period of abstinence (length depending on the substances used) is a condition sine qua non. In addition to a structured interview through the *DSM-IV-TR*, the use of an observer rating scale is recommended. Conners, Erhardt, & Sparrow (1998) developed a set of self-report and observer rating instruments—the Conners Adult ADHD Rating Scales (CAARS)—to measure current adult ADHD symptoms. For adults both in the general population and adults with ADHD, this scale results in four subscales: (1) inattention/memory problems; (2) hyperactivity; (3) impulsivity; and (4) problems with self-concept. The CAARS had good internal consistency, test-retest reliability, and concurrent validity in samples of adults in the general population, adults referred to an outpatient ADHD clinic, and adults meeting *DSM-IV* criteria for ADHD (Cleland, Magura, Foote, Rosenblum, & Kosanke, 2006). Although the CAARS cannot provide a diagnosis of ADHD, it may be a useful measure of ADHD symptoms, which is not only relevant for treatment planning but also for the evaluation of its effects.

If a formal diagnosis of ADHD is obtained, what does this mean for the treatment to be provided? Sequential treatment is of no use in ADHD with substance-abuse disorder, and both disorders should be treated concurrently. The positive effects of stimulant medication (e.g., methylphenidate) for ADHD have now been well established. Despite many controlled studies demonstrating their effectiveness, these kinds of medication have been controversial because of concerns that they might kindle substance abuse when used for many years. Meta-analyses of longitudinal studies reveal, however, that the use of stimulant medication in ADHD reduces the risk for substance-use disorder by 50% (Faraone & Wilens, 2003; Wilens, Faraone, Biederman, & Gunawardene, 2003).

Although behavioral treatment can be effective in ADHD as well, a recent meta-analysis of the available studies comparing pharmacotherapy and behavior therapy revealed that stimulant drugs are more effective than behavior therapy, and that there is no evidence that behavior therapy enhances the effects of stimulant drugs (Van der Oord, Prins, Oosterlaan, & Emmelkamp, 2006). These analyses suggest that for individuals with ADHD, medication should be the first-line treatment for the disorder, provided that drug treatment is successfully titrated. These conclusions, however, are based on studies with children and adolescents. Recently, Safren et al. (2005) reported a study in which CBT directed at ADHD symptoms was effective in adults with ADHD who did not fully respond to medication alone. The results suggest that CBT might have additional value in some adults with ADHD.

Although stimulants are now also widely prescribed for adults with ADHD, relatively few studies have reported on the use (efficacy) of stimulants for ADHD in adults. Several controlled studies found that methylphenidate had a positive effect on ADHD in adults, although the effect was less robust than in children (Kooij et al., 2004; Spencer et al., 1995). Since most patients in these studies did not have a comorbid substance-abuse disorder, it is unclear whether in adults with substance abuse, pharmacotherapy for ADHD influences the course of their substance abuse. At present, only two placebo-controlled studies have been conducted on the efficacy of stimulant medication in adult substance abusers with ADHD. Schubiner et al. (2002) found stimulant medication more effective than placebo in cocaine-dependent ADHD patients with respect to ADHD symptoms, but this did not affect the use of cocaine. Another double-blind, placebo-controlled study (Carpentier, De Jong, Dijkstra, Verbrugge, & Krabbe, 2005) failed to show any definite effect of methylphenidate in ADHD patients with various substance-abuse disorders. The positive response to methylphenidate treatment (nine patients; 36%) was not significantly higher than that to placebo (five patients; 20%). The effectiveness of stimulant medication in this study was limited, probably due to suboptimal dosage of methylphenidate.

Apparently, treatment directed at the substance abuse is still needed, even when patients are successfully treated for ADHD symptoms. In ADHD patients with substance-use disorder, a combination of medication directed at the ADHD and CBT directed at the substance abuse (as described in chapter 4) is recommended. The best evidence-based medication for ADHD is pharmacotherapy by stimulants, but there is a risk of abuse by the patient. Actually, few patients abuse the drug, given that rapid euphoric feelings are absent, because orally administered methylphenidate is cleared much more slowly in the brain than, for example, cocaine. Nevertheless, clinicians should be alert for abuse. It has been argued that newer forms of prescribed long-acting methylphenidate have less abuse potential (Schubiner, 2005) and are therefore to be preferred in substance-abusing ADHD patients.

Concluding Remarks

Given the high psychiatric comorbidities associated with substance-use disorders, a better management of comorbid psychiatric disorders is highly desirable. Historically, addiction treatment centers have been developed outside mental health centers, not only in the United States but in most countries in the world, which is rather unfortunate. Comorbid patients with more severe psychopathology (e.g., schizophrenia and bipolar disorder) and more moderate substance abuse are most commonly treated in specialized mental health settings, whereas patients with moderate to severe substance abuse and moderate psychopathology (e.g., anxiety, depression, dysthymia, and ADHD) are treated in substance-abuse centers. There is a clear need of a better integration of mental health services into treatment programs for substance-use disorders. Similarly, a better integration of addiction treatment programs into mental health services is needed. Such problems need to be addressed through formal mechanisms of liaison. Often the boundaries of responsibility may be unclear, and clearly identified lines of responsibility are essential to good quality care (Scott, Gilvarry, & Farrell, 1998). Further, staff in both mental health and addiction settings may need training to improve their skills to screen, assess, and treat patients with substance-use disorder and comorbid mental disorders (Hall & Farrell, 1997; McLellan, Carise, & Kleber, 2003).

As discussed above, several integrated treatment protocols have been developed that target co-occurring disorders, including *dialectical behavior therapy* for borderline patients with substance-use disorders, *seeking safety* for substance-dependent patients with post-traumatic stress disorder, and *integrated group therapy* for substance-dependent patients with bipolar disorder. In any case, there is clearly a need for more research on approaches for treating co-occurring substance use and other psychiatric disorders.

Given the considerable heterogeneity in symptoms and course among individuals with co-occurring substance use and psychiatric disorders, it seems therapeutically wise to base the treatment planning on a macro-analysis of the problems, as discussed in chapter 4. In most cases treatment should first target the substance-use disorder, but in some patients treatment of the psychiatric disorder (e.g., psychosis) should have priority provided that their substance abuse is well-managed over time. In other patients concurrent treatment of substance-use disorder and psychiatric disorder may be needed. Such flexible approaches to treatment are likely to yield better outcomes than providing dual-diagnosis patients with standardized treatments, irrespective of the course of the disorders and the causal relationship between the psychiatric disorder and the substance-use disorder.

Obstacles in the Therapeutic Relationship

An important distinction in psychotherapy efficacy research has been between common and unique factors of treatment. *Common factors* refer to dimensions of treatment that are shared across most psychotherapies, including psychoeducation, a convincing rationale, support, expectations of improvement, an experienced therapist, and the quality of the therapeutic relationship. Of the common factors investigated in various psychotherapies, the therapeutic alliance has emerged as a robust mediator of positive outcome across psychotherapies of different types and with diverse clinical samples (Lambert, 2004).

A number of studies have specifically addressed the role of the therapeutic relationship in the treatment of substance-use disorder. Given the ambivalence most patients have with respect to changing alcohol and drug use, the therapist's style with this population is rather important. In substance-abuse treatment the relationship between the quality of the therapeutic relationship, on the one hand, and the treatment process and outcomes, on the other, has yielded convincing evidence that better therapeutic alliance early in treatment may prevent dropout and facilitate patient engagement (see, e.g., Carroll, Nich, & Rounsaville, 1997; Öjehagen, Berglund, & Hansson, 1997; Meier, Barrowclough, & Donmall, 2005; Raytek, McCrady, Epstein, & Hirsch, 1999). As well, in behavioral couple therapy for substance use the therapeutic relationship is important. Raytek et al. (1999) have found that experienced therapists developed better therapeutic alliances than less-experienced therapists. The quality of the therapeutic alliance and therapists' competence was found to be related to number of sessions attended and dropout from treatment. However, the evidence is less convincing that a good therapeutic relationship is a robust predictor of substance abuse after treatment (Meier, Donmall, Barrowclough, McElduff, & Heller, 2005). Notably, Carroll et al. (1997) found that therapeutic alliance scores were rated as significantly more positive in cognitive-behavioral treatment than in routine clinical management. However, a good therapeutic alliance was more closely associated with outcome in the clinical management than in the cognitive-behavioral treatment. This suggests that the relationship between common factors such as the therapeutic alliance may be quite different for cognitive-behavior therapies than in supportive therapies.

Meier, Barrowclough, & Donmall (2005) have found that patients with higher readiness to change, more successful relationship histories, secure attachment style, and better social support find it easier to establish a successful alliance with their therapist. That attachment is related to the quality of the therapeutic relationship does not come as a surprise, because patients who feel safe with others and are able to successfully interact with others will be more likely to establish a good relationship with their therapist. Unfortunately, many substance-abusing patients who are referred to treatment do not have good social support, lack adequate coping skills, are ambivalent about changing their behavior, and are often characterized by insecure and avoidant attachment styles rather than by secure attachment. This means that with many patients, the therapists need to invest extra efforts in establishing a therapeutic relationship.

If there are obstacles in the therapeutic alliance that become evident in the treatment, repairing the therapeutic alliance should receive the highest priority. When these problems are not recognized and properly dealt with, the chances are high that the patient will drop out of treatment. Many patients are lost in the initial engagement phase of treatment due to therapists' failures to respect and empathize with the client's concerns and definition of the problem. This is particularly important in dual-diagnosis patients. Meier, Barrowclough, & Donmall (2005), in reviewing the literature in this area, found evidence that a good therapeutic relationship may be especially important in retaining drug-using individuals with psychiatric comorbidity.

There are some common misconceptions regarding the nature of the therapeutic relationship in cognitive-behavior therapy. It is often thought of as distant, one-sided, and somewhat authoritarian. Arguably, cognitive-behavior therapists themselves are partly responsible for this prejudice as they—in contrast to, for example, psychodynamic therapists and experientially oriented therapists—pay scarce attention to the therapeutic relationship in their published work, apart from those therapists associated with motivational interviewing. However, most cognitive-behavior therapists recognize the importance of a strong treatment alliance and invest time and effort in establishing a cooperative relationship.

There currently is ample literature demonstrating that "Rogerian" concepts such as warmth and empathy are also characteristic of the therapeutic relationship in cognitive-behavior therapy. However, in contrast to other therapy schools, these variables are not thought of as merely facilitative for the therapeutic process. In cognitive-behavior therapy these concepts are thought of as significant situational variables in the promotion of a learning process and changing problem behavior. This conceptualization implies that not every patient needs equal amounts of warmth, empathy, structuring, support, and the like. Relevant aspects can also differ from one phase of therapy to the next. In the early stage with patients who are not yet ready for change, the therapist will prefer a more emphatic supportive style, while later on in the treatment, when a patient is ready for action-oriented interventions, a more directive style may be indicated.

What are other good characteristics of a therapeutic alliance in the treatment of substance abuse? Unfortunately, apart from motivational interviewing (see chapter 2), there are few specific clinical guidelines available that are based on empirical investigations. As a general rule, the clinician should meet the patient without preconceived ideas about the patient's needs and appropriate goals. By accepting the client's definition of the problem the therapist will meet the patient's needs, which will facilitate the development of a productive treatment alliance. A collaborative stance that aims to have client and clinician working toward shared goals is likely to strengthen the alliance.

Further, the therapeutic style should not be rigid, but adapted to the needs of the patient. Karno & Longabaugh (2003) have found an interaction between specific therapist behaviors and depressive symptoms in patients treated in the MATCH project. Depressed alcohol-dependent patients had better drinking outcomes when the therapist focused less on painful emotional material in the sessions when compared to patients treated by therapists who focused highly on emotional material. The results of this study nicely illustrate that not all patients are similar, which means that the therapeutic style should be flexible and adapted to the needs of an individual patient in a specific phase of the treatment process. To give another example, the therapeutic style should be markedly different with a substance-abusing patient with a dependent personality disorder versus a patient with clear narcissistic or paranoid features (Van Velzen & Emmelkamp, 1996). When working with a substance-abusing patient with dependent personality disorder at the start of treatment, it may be advisable to enquire by telephone how the homework assignments are coming along. With a narcissistic patient, however, the therapist had better refrain from this as it may reinforce the narcissistic tendency to demand excessive attention. The same applies for the paranoid patient, as this patient may interpret the therapist's good intentions as doubts as to whether she is completing the homework assignments. Of note, later in therapy one should fade out the telephone inquiries with the dependent personality patient as well, as these calls may end up reinforcing the undesired dependent behaviors.

As in other therapies, the therapist may be faced with phenomena such as resistance or transference. Its perceived significance and the way these behaviors are dealt with by the cognitive-behavior therapist, however, are different from how psychodynamic therapists perceive and act. Generally, in dealing with resistance behavior, the therapist will not use confrontation but may see this as problematic behavior that needs to be studied and understood. When a patient displays resistance—for instance, by being consistently late, or by avoiding specific subjects, being taciturn or overly talkative, not complying with homework assignments, and so on—the therapist might want to examine what factors might be eliciting such behaviors The therapeutic stance regarding resistance is thus in fact quite similar to how other problem behaviors are regarded and approached. Making use of his observations and, if needed, additional probing, the therapist will attempt to formulate a functional analysis of the resistance behavior. As a result, the therapist may learn that the behaviors are better understood by other factors than by the initial impression of treatment resistance.

OTHER COMPLICATING FACTORS

Cognitive Deficits

Presumably, cognitive deficits associated with substance abuse may contribute to poor treatment outcome. Over the past decade, research has emerged that shows that a substantial number of substance abusers suffer from damage in cortical and subcortical brain regions and impairments across cognitive domains (see chapter 1). In individuals with substance abuse and dependence, cognitive impairments were found to impede learning and acquisition of new coping behaviors (Alterman & Hall, 1989; McCrady & Smith, 1986), and to enhance the risk of treatment dropout (Aharonovich, Nunes, & Hasin, 2003; Fals-Stewart & Schafer, 1992; Teichner, Horner, Roitzsch, Herron, & Thevos, 2002). In cocaine-dependent patients, dropouts from cognitive-behavior therapy had significantly poorer cognitive functioning than completers on attention, memory, spatial ability, speed, accuracy, global functioning, and cognitive proficiency.

Clinicians should be alert to cognitive deficits in their patients. If cognitive impairment is likely to impede treatment progress, the clinician should consider alternatives. Generally, treatment in group format is less suited for cognitively impaired patients, because the pace of therapy cannot be adapted to the needs of the individual patient. Therefore, in mildly to moderately impaired patients individual therapy is recommended, in which the treatment is adapted to the patients' abilities. Memory aids are quite useful, as may be the engaging in treatment of a concerned other (e.g., a partner or family member), provided that this person is not addicted herself. Specific homework assignments are usually of little avail: these tend to be forgotten or will be too difficult to understand or to perform. In more severely cognitively impaired patients the evidence-based treatments discussed in this book are probably too complex and the principles on which these treatments are based are likely not to be understood. In some of these cases residential placement under close supervision may be considered.

The Homeless

In order to be effective, the evidence-based treatments discussed throughout this book are more suited for substance-abusing patients who live in a safe environment with at least some supportive social contacts than for the homeless. Understandably, many homeless patients without resources give higher priority to where they will spend the night than in overcoming their addiction. In these cases the primary needs are food and shelter, and as long as these needs are not met, treatment only directed at the substance abuse is usually of little avail. It is a bit optimistic to expect homeless patients who are seen by a clinician once or twice a week to stay abstinent while spending the rest of their time on the streets with other homeless people and other substance abusers. Although hospitalization may seem to circumvent this problem, immediate relapse after discharge from the treatment program is the rule rather than the exception if post-treatment safe housing is not organized. At present, community reinforcement in combination with contingency management is the only treatment program addressing this issue (see chapter 2).

CHAPTER 6

Maintenance and Follow-Up Strategies

Patients with substance-use disorders frequently go through periods of abstinence or nonproblematic use after receiving treatment. However, a number of these patients will eventually engage in problematic drinking or drug use again. A subgroup of substance users will cycle through periods of relapse, treatment reentry, and recovery.

RELAPSE

Despite the fact that substance-abuse treatment is associated with major reductions in substance use (see chapter 3), studies in adults have demonstrated that after discharge, relapse is a common phenomenon, particularly in dual-diagnosis patients. Most patients initiate three to four episodes of treatment over an average of eight years before reaching a stable state of abstinence (Dennis, Scott, Funk, & Foss, 2005). Relapse following treatment for drug-use disorders among adolescents is especially high, relapses typically occurring soon following the completion of treatment (Chung & Maisto, 2006). Brown, Tapert, Tate, and Abrantes (2000) have reported that the majority of their inpatient adolescent sample returned to drug use within three months after discharge from treatment, and over three-fourths had relapsed at the one-year follow-up point.

Thus, despite the documented benefits of psychological interventions, positive treatment outcomes often gradually decline over time. Relapse rates are high, and thus, besides changing drinking or drug-taking behavior, preventing or minimizing relapse is an extremely important goal in the treatment of addictive behaviors (Marlatt & Gordon, 1985). Relapse to substance abuse after treatment of alcoholism is a multifactorial phenomenon and most likely results from a combination of a number of variables. Apart from genetic vulnerability (Meyer, 2001), a number of risk factors for resuming substance abuse have been established, including stress (Koob, 2000; Miller, Westerberg, Harris, & Tonigan, 1996); poor self-efficacy and lack of coping skills (Connors, Maisto, & Zywiak, 1996; Hall, Havassy, & Wasserman, 1991; McKay, Maisto, & O'Farrell, 1993; Miller et al., 1996; Rohsenow, Martin, & Monti, 2005); social isolation (Longabaugh, Wirtz, Beattie, Noel, & Stout, 1995); neuroticism/negative affectivity (e.g., feeling sad, anxious; Hall et al., 1991; Miller et al., 1996); co-occurring psychiatric disorders and life context of substance abuse (e.g., other family members drinking); and living in neighborhoods with high levels of crime and drug abuse (McKay, 2005a, 2005b). In addition, a substantial number of patients who relapsed reported frustrating situations in which they were unable to adequately express their anger prior to their relapse (Marlatt, 1996). The vulnerability to relapse exhibited by many substance abusers appears to be a function of poor compliance with treatment, homework assignments, and continuing care as well. On the other hand, a social network that supports abstinence or controlled substance use may buffer against relapse.

Anxiety and Depression

Concurrent depression and anxiety symptoms are among the most common problems reported by persons seeking treatment for alcohol and/or drug abuse (see chapter 1). When anxiety and depression persist beyond detoxification and the remission of addictive behavior, patients may be at higher risk for relapse. A number of studies have indicated that patients with concurrent anxiety and depressive disorders have an increased vulnerability to relapse into substance abuse than do those with no psychopathology (see, e.g., Charney, Palacios-Boix, Negrete, Dobkin, & Gill, 2005; Driessen et al., 2001; Greenfield et al., 1998; Willinger et al., 2002). For example, Driessen et al. (2001) found higher relapse rates among alcohol-dependent patients with concurrent anxiety and depression disorders: 40% for patients with no psychopathology, 69% for those with anxiety, and 77% for those with both anxiety and depression. Similarly, Charney et al. (2005) found higher relapse rates among patients with combined depression and anxiety symptoms. Depression on its own (without a comorbid anxiety disorder), however, may have less impact on relapse (see, e.g., Charney et al., 2005; Rounsaville, Dolinsky, Babor, & Meyer, 1987).

If comorbid anxiety disorders and depression persist after treatment directed at substance use, these comorbid disorders merit appropriate psychological or medical treatment, as discussed in chapter 5. After some improvement in both disorders is achieved, low-intensity monitoring may be an effective method for the long-term management of patients with co-occurring disorders (McKay et al., 2005a). This enables the clinician to increase the level of care, including hospitalization, if needed.

Should Patients Be Allowed to Continue Cannabis Use?

Many patients who have been treated for alcohol dependence or illicit drug use such as cocaine and heroin (continue to) use cannabis after treatment. Clinicians often do not feel the need to change cannabis use in substance-dependent patients as long as it is used in a controlled way. The widely held belief among clinicians that cannabis use is relatively harmless is based on lack of knowledge of the much higher potency of marijuana as compared to its potency 15 years ago (see chapter 1). If patients who have been treated for alcohol or drug dependence use cannabis, cannabinoids may continue to trigger pleasant cues previously associated with other substances such as cocaine, alcohol, or heroin. In cannabis use, the cannabinoid-reward effect is produced by increasing the activity of the dopaminergic neurons in the mesolimbic-dopamine system, similar to the effect of other addictive substances.

Clinically, it is important to know whether use of cannabis enhances relapse in patients treated for alcohol and drug dependence. Studies by De Vries and colleagues (De Vries et al., 2001; De Vries, Homberg, Binnekade, Raaso, & Schoffelmeer, 2003) demonstrated that synthetic cannabinoid agonists induced relapse to cocaine and heroin in rats after periods of abstinence. However, would cannabinoids also enhance the risk of relapse in treated substance-abuse patients? Aharonovich et al. (2005) have found that cannabis use after discharge from treatment programs increased the hazard of relapse to alcohol and cocaine, and strongly reduced the likelihood of stable remission from use of any substance. As the authors conclude, potential negative clinical implications of cannabis use should be taken more seriously by clinicians when treating dependence on alcohol and other substances.

MAINTENANCE TREATMENT

There is an assumption in psychotherapy that the processes underlying the changes that occurred during therapy should persist after the termination of treatment, preferably as long as the patient lives. If such permanence does not occur, the individual relapses and thus becomes a treatment failure (Emmelkamp & Foa, 1983). This assumption is not always justified. There may be a psychological condition, such as substance-use disorders that require continued intervention or booster sessions as is often the case in many medical problems, such as diabetes, obesity, and hypertension, but also in psychiatric disorders such as schizophrenia and mood disorders. For example, at our present state of knowledge, nobody expects that severe hypertension will not recur when medication is discontinued; although blood pressure will increase with termination of drug treatment, the patient will not be considered a treatment failure. Yet, despite often weak interventions in the area of substance-use disorders, many individuals (clinicians and patients alike), but also managed-care agencies, insurance companies, and the general public expect treatment of substance-use disorders to produce durable changes. However, if a certain set of unwanted behaviors are triggered by unchanged environmental stimuli and maintained by environmental reinforcements that persist after treatment, why should we expect that these behaviors will not be resumed when the patient returns to her natural environment?

In the medical and psychiatric disorders discussed above it is now widely accepted that continued treatment programs are needed in order to maintain the initial improvements achieved. In contrast, many treatment approaches for patients with substance-use disorders are rather brief. In the United States, there is a trend in recent years toward making these programs even shorter due to pressures from managed-care and insurance companies. Recent figures of treatment of substance-use disorders in the United States reveal that most care is provided in outpatient settings where the planned duration of care is usually 90 days or less, and actual length of stay is often less than 30 days (Substance Abuse and Mental Health Services Administration, 2002). As noted by McKay (2005a), after the end of more or less successful treatment, there are generally no provisions to manage patients' disorders through ongoing monitoring or "check-ups" that are common with other chronic disorders: "Eventually, many individuals with substance-use disorders end up with 'treatment careers' that consist of a number of relatively short treatment episodes over time but these episodes are typically not integrated in any way" (p. 1595).

Booster Sessions

The treatment effectiveness of evidence-based cognitive-behavioral interventions might be enhanced with posttreatment follow-up contacts designed to facilitate the maintenance of treatment gains. So-called booster sessions have been proposed as a vehicle for maximizing the longer-term benefits of treatment for substance-use disorders. Booster sessions may serve several purposes. In the case of behavioral couple therapy, O'Farrell, Kleinke, and Cutter (1998) have found that in patients with severe marital and drinking problems, those who received booster sessions had better nondrinking outcomes throughout the 30-month follow-up. Similarly, McCrady, Epstein, and Kahler (2004) have found that attendance at booster sessions was related to better outcome at the 18-month follow-up.

Being still in treatment may remind patients of the decided-upon goal, be it abstinence or moderation. Further, booster sessions may provide assistance to patients in dealing with stressors and lapses that may occur after treatment. Finally, these sessions can be used to repeat key elements of treatment.

Follow-Up Visits

The high rate of relapse among clients discharged from substance-abuse treatment facilities suggests a need to strengthen posttreatment care. Treatment research studies find consistently that longer retention is associated with better outcomes, but controlled studies that have directly compared shorter versus longer versions of the same treatment did not find better substance-use outcomes for those with longer durations. McKay (2005a) recently reviewed the research into the effects of extended treatment, including interventions described as "aftercare," "stepped care," "continuing care," and "disease management." "Extended interventions" are defined as therapeutic protocols that have a planned duration of longer than six months; many extended interventions that were reviewed, however, have a planned duration of at least a year. The findings of the review indicate that maintaining therapeutic contact for extended periods of time with individuals with alcohol and other drug disorders appears to promote better long-term outcomes than does "treatment as usual." Not only extended cognitive-behavioral interventions, but also extended pharmacotherapies are found to be more effective than "treatment as usual."

Given these positive results of extended care, it seems therapeutically wise to keep some degree of regular contact with patients after completion of treatment so that worsening of symptoms can be monitored and patients can be reengaged in treatment when necessary. From this perspective, a continuing-care program developed by Scott, Dennis, & Foss (2005) is particularly interesting. This recovery management checkup model was designed to provide early detection of individuals who relapsed, and to link them to treatment, thus shortening the pathway between relapse and treatment. This intervention was designed as a model that could be integrated into the continuum of care offered by substance-abuse treatment agencies. In the recovery management checkup protocol, substance abusers who have entered treatment are followed and interviewed every three months. The goal of the protocol is to identify people who are living in the community and have restarted using substances and to quickly link them to treatment, thus expediting the recovery process. Briefly, recovery management checkup involves the following steps:

determining eligibility for the intervention (i.e., verifying that the person is not already in treatment or jail and is living in the community)
determining the need for treatment based on the criteria listed below
completing the assessment
transfering the participants in need of treatment to the linkage manager

The criteria for needing further treatment consist of meeting any of the following over the past three months:

use of any substances on 13 or more days
being drunk or high for most of one or more days
not meeting work/school/home responsibilities on one or more days
having substance-use-related problems in the prior month
having withdrawal symptoms in the prior week
desire to return to treatment

The intervention utilizes motivational interviewing techniques to provide feedback to participants about their substance use and related problems, and to help the participants recognize their substance-use problems and consider returning to treatment. Linkage managers actively initiate linkage activities with individuals to substance-abuse treatment during the 14 days following their checkup, and address any existing barriers to reentering treatment. It is explained to the patients that it is the participants' task to resolve their ambivalence, and the linkage manager helps participants explore the factors contributing to their ambivalence about treatment. Further, the linkage manager arranges scheduling and transportation to treatment if the patients have decided that they would like to return to treatment.

The effects of this program have recently been evaluated (Scott et al., 2005). Patients assigned to recovery management checkup are significantly more likely to return to treatment sooner and receive more treatment than patients in the control condition who receive assessment sessions only. Further, patients in the recovery management checkup have better substance-use outcomes over the course of the follow-up period (two years) than do those in the control condition. Many of the patients eventually agree to reenter treatment in spite of their low level of motivation if the linkage manager successfully helps them improve their understanding of how their problems are related to substance use, facilitates access to treatment, and helps participants think through ways to address their barriers to accessing treatment.

Telephone-Based Continuing Care

Another continuing-care intervention was developed by McKay, Lynch, Shepard, and Pettinati (2005) that consists of weekly phone calls. After a four-week intensive outpatient program (of 10 group therapy sessions per week) patients made one 15-minute telephone call per week to their therapist. During the phone conversation specific goals for the next week were discussed; if needed, it could include some face-to-face contact. This intervention was evaluated in patients with alcohol and cocaine dependence and proved to be quite effective in preventing relapse. In this study, phone intervention was at least as effective as continuing treatment consisting of either individual cognitive-behavioral relapse prevention or 12-step facilitation. All three interventions lasted 12 weeks. At the two-year follow-up, patients from the telephone-based continuing care intervention produced higher rates of abstinence than those using the 12-step approach.

Given the positive effects of such continuing care interventions as these booster sessions, recovery management checkups, and weekly phone calls, such interventions are highly recommended in order to prevent relapse.

Self-Help Groups

Many substance-abuse programs provide referrals to self-help groups. Self-help groups often differ in their approaches, although most organizations focus on helping individuals maintain and achieve sobriety. Alcoholics Anonymous (AA) and Narcotics Anonymous (NA) are the best known self-help organizations. As described in chapter 2, AA and

NA membership implies that the individual endorses a particular 12-step philosophy of recovery that emphasizes the importance of accepting addiction as a disease that can be arrested but never eliminated, enhancing individual spiritual growth, and minimizing self-centeredness. Individuals who improve with 12-step facilitation therapy are inclined to attend AA meetings to consolidate their gains (Etheridge, Craddock, Hubbard, & Rounds-Bryant, 1999; Fiorentine & Hillhouse, 2000). Given the fact that approximately one-fourth of patients who are referred by clinicians to AA will not attend the first meeting (Fiorentine, 1999) and that half of the patients who do attend will drop out within three months (McIntire, 2000), AA is clearly not suited for all substance-dependent patients. However, AA and NA are not the only options available as after-care self-help groups. Also based on the 12-step philosophy is Double Trouble in Recovery, a self-help organization for addicted individuals who also have a serious mental illness. Currently, in many countries there exist several alternatives, including the Secular Organization for Sobriety, which does not include any spiritual content, and Women for Sobriety, which organizes all-female feminist groups that emphasize self-esteem and trying to achieve enhanced emotional and spiritual growth in order to be able to stay abstinent.

Other alternative self-help groups are organized by Moderation Management and SMART (Self-Management and Recovery Training) Recovery, both based on social-learning principles. Moderation Management and SMART Recovery view excessive use of alcohol and other drugs as a maladaptive behavior rather than a disease. SMART Recovery is based on the principles of rational emotive therapy (Ellis, 1988) and introduces its members to using cognitive self-analyses to secure abstinence and cognitive-behavioral techniques to cope with cravings.

Although there are currently other options for self-help, AA and associated groups such as NA are still the "market leader." AA has an estimated U.S. membership of over a million. Unfortunately, current referral practices to self-help groups are less determined by the needs of the patient and more by staff beliefs on addiction and their views of 12-step groups. Staff members of older age, or of less education; staff members who themselves are substance abusers in remission; positive attitudes toward 12-step programs; and an agency's endorsement of 12-step or abstinence-only treatment approaches all have been associated with higher rates of referral to 12-step groups (Fenster, 2006; Laudet, 2003). In New York City, many substance-abuse workers held highly positive views of 12-step groups as a method of after care, but a large percentage had some potential resistance to 12-step groups—in particular, the emphasis such groups place on spirituality and powerlessness (Laudet & White, 2005).

The 12-step approach is the most widely available option for continuing care, as noted in a recent U.S. cross-sectional sample obtained from the Substance Abuse and Mental Health Services Administration (Fenster, 2006). Substance-abuse workers still most frequently recommend AA or NA as after care. However, three-fourths of clinicians are likely to refer clients to other options (including treatment with cognitive-behavior therapy, or moderation-oriented groups) as well as to 12-step programs. Further, there is a tendency for a subgroup of clinicians to continue to refer only to 12-step programs, apparently being based on a lack of knowledge about the effectiveness of alternatives to such programs (Fenster, 2006).

While 12-step based self-help groups have certainly played a role in the after care of substance-abusing patients, the best practice seems to be to assess for each patient individually what type of after care would be most beneficial. We recommend taking the following issues into consideration:

Not all patients need to be referred to some form of after care, including self-help groups. Self-help groups may be particularly useful for patients with a lack of a social support system, or whose support system does not adhere to either abstinence or moderation.

Be aware as a therapist of your own possible biases toward or against particular self-help groups.

Be informed about all available options for self-help groups in your region. As recommended by Humphreys et al. (2004), "given the variety of pathways to recovery, clinicians should have a menu of treatment and self-help group options available for use when selecting care alternatives in consultation with the client and other stakeholders" (p. 155).

Fit referrals to self-help groups to patients' individual needs and preferences.

Patients' goals should be congruent with the aims and philosophies of the self-help group. Therefore, knowledge of clients' own abstinence or moderation goals (rather than therapists' own beliefs) is important. It seems of little avail to refer patients with a goal of 'abstinence' to a moderation-oriented self-help group or patients with a goal of 'moderation' to self-help groups as Moderation Management, or a cognitive-behavioral-therapy-based self-help group.

Ascertain a client's religious beliefs before making a referral to AA or NA, as recommended by the American Psychiatric Association (1995). Although research with respect to the influence of religious involvement on 12-step programs is inconclusive (Kelly, 2003), it seems of little avail to refer a patient to a 12-step program if the patient does not have any positive attitudes toward religion or spirituality. Patients who are uncomfortable with AA's focus on spirituality are better referred to another abstinence-oriented self-help group with less emphasis on this aspect.

Given that women do profit less from AA than men (Tonigan & Hiller-Strumhofel, 1994), consider other self-help options in the case of female patients, such as the Secular Organization for Sobriety, Women for Sobriety, Moderation Management, and SMART Recovery.

Although some youth appear to benefit from AA, many do not attend or may not continue attendance given the predominantly adult composition of such groups. As noted by Kelly (2003), the sharing of specific experiences at AA meetings by older members may not be perceived by adolescents as helpful in dealing with their own life-stage problems.

In dual-diagnosis patients, referral to AA groups is not recommended given the rejection of any drugs including pharmacotherapy. Since medication compliance is often an important prerequisite for successful treatment, such patients are better referred to Double Trouble in Recovery (Magura, Laudet, Mohmood, Rosenblum, & Knight, 2002).

Use empirically validated methods (e.g., 12-step facilitation counseling, motivational enhancement techniques) when seeking to foster self-help group engagement (Humphreys et al., 2004).

Begin orientation to self-help groups and attendance before outpatient treatment completion or discharge from the hospital.

HARM REDUCTION

Harm reduction is an important new development in the substance-use treatment field, and has been proposed as an alternative to the disease models of drug use and addiction (Marlatt, 1996a; Marlatt & Roberts, 1998). For many drug users living in an area full of poverty and violence, using drugs may be seen as the only way to get some pleasure. For many, the substances have come to serve life-sustaining functions as long as no better alternative solutions are available. Apart from being a primary source of pleasure, for a number of (poly) drug users substance use is their only way of coping with negative emotions and pain related to constant frustration and deprivation, and may provide to them a sort of identity that they are not willing to give up. Over time, the drugs them-selves become a problem as the cycle of physical dependence becomes a motivator as well.

Although a life without drugs is laudable, many substance-abusing individuals will not be able to achieve this. Given that for a number of substance abusers lifelong abstinence is unthinkable, it seems realis-tic and pragmatic to accept other goals than abstinence and to aim at reducing the harm associated with continued substance abuse. Many cognitive-behavioral programs that were developed for the moderation of drinking have already been discussed (see chapters 2 and 3), and this will not be reiterated here, as the emphasis here is on drug dependence.

The essence of harm reduction is that mental health workers accept the personal goals of substance abusers, but try to reduce the damages associated with substance abuse as much as possible. Harm-reduction practice involves the provision of self-management strategies that are effective in reducing the personal harm and harm to the society asso-ciated with continued drug use. In the context of motivational inter-viewing (see chapter 2), the clinician discusses what is harmful about substance use, and tries to get a commitment from the patient toward setting harm-reduction goals that are realistic. Making the harm-reduc-tion position explicit is a way to counter the client's expectations of being treated coercively. The process of setting harm-reduction target goals in the context of a nonevaluative supportive relationship supports the patient in becoming more aware of the dangers associated with con-tinued substance abuse. A cost-benefit analysis of the current pattern of substance use may facilitate the patient in recognizing the current bal-ance between positive consequences of use and negative aspects. In this approach, harmful aspects of substance use are identified, and harm-reduction goals are agreed upon that minimize costs or risks.

Where substance use has become excessive and self-defeating, a harm-reduction approach would initially aim to support the patient to moderate use of substances to reduce the harmful impact. In drug-dependent patients, other harm-reducing goals include

better management of drug use
switching to less dangerous substances; for example, methadone
    maintenance as replacement for illegal opiates such as heroin,
    or methylphenidate as a replacement for illicit stimulants
learning safer drug-using practices, including the utilization
    of clean syringes
being informed about dose limits and overdose risk

It is important to realize that patients' enrollment in harm-reduction programs may not be a lifelong goal. Some patients will eventually switch to Prochaska and DiClemente's (1982) contemplation or action stages (discussed in chapter 2) and be willing to undergo treatment directed at changing substance abuse.

REFERENCES

WORKS CONSULTED

Aas, H., Leigh, B. C., Anderssen, N., & Jakobsen, R. (1998). Two-year longitudinal study of alcohol expectancies and drinking among Norwegian adolescents. *Addiction, 93*, 373–384.

Aharonovich, E., Hasin, D. S., Brooks, A. C., Liu, X., Bisaga, A., & Nunes, E. V. (in press). Cognitive deficits predict low treatment retention in cocaine dependent patients. *Drug and Alcohol Dependence.*

Aharonovich, E., Liu, X. H., Samet, S., Nunes, E., Waxman, R., & Hasin, D. (2005). Postdischarge cannabis use and its relationship to cocaine, alcohol, and heroin use: A prospective study. *American Journal of Psychiatry, 162*, 1507–1514.

Aharonovich, E., Nguyen, H. T., & Nunes, E. V. (2001). Anger and depressive states among treatment-seeking drug abusers: Testing the psychopharmacological specificity hypothesis. *American Journal of Addiction, 10*, 327–334.

Aharonovich, E., Nunes, E., & Hasin, D. (2003). Cognitive impairment, retention and abstinence among cocaine abusers in cognitive-behavioral treatment. *Drug and Alcohol Dependence, 71*, 207–211.

Alcoholics Anonymous UK (2005). *Membership.* Online at www.alcoholics-anonymous.org.uk.

Alcoholics Anonymous World Services. (1986). *Alcoholics Anonymous* (3rd ed.). New York: Author.

Allen, J. P., Litten, R. Z., Fertig, J. B., & Babor, T. F. (1997). A review of research on the alcohol use disorders identification test (AUDIT). *Alcoholism: Clinical and Experimental Research, 21*, 613–619.

Alterman, A. I., Allen, J. P., Litten, R. Z., Fertig, J. B., & Barbor, T. (1997). A review of research on the alcohol use disorders identification test (AUDIT). *Alcoholism, Clinical and Experimental Research, 21*, 613–619.

Alterman, A. I., & Hall, J.G. (1989). Effects of social drinking and familial alcoholism risk of cognitive functioning: Null findings. *Alcoholism: Clinical and Experimental Research, 13*, 799–803.

Alterman, A. I., McKay, J. R., Mulvaney, F. D., Cnaan, A., Cacciola, J. S., & Tourian, K. A. (2000). Baseline prediction of 7-month cocaine abstinence for cocaine-dependence patients. *Drug and Alcohol Dependence, 59*, 215–221.

Alterman, A. I., McKay, J. R., Mulvaney, F. D., & McLellan, A. T. (1996). Prediction of attrition from day hospital treatment in lower socioeconomic cocaine-dependent men. *Drug and Alcohol Dependence, 40,* 227–233.

American Psychiatric Association. (1994). *DSM-IV: Diagnostic statistical manual of mental disorder* (4th ed.). Washington, DC: Author.

American Psychiatric Association. (1995). *Practice guidelines for the treatment of patients with substance abuse disorders: Alcohol, cocaine, opioids.* Washington, DC: Author.

American Psychiatric Association. (2000) *DSM-IV-TR: Diagnostic statistical manual of mental disorder* (4th ed., text rev.). Washington, DC: Author.

Ames, S. C., & Roitzsch, J. C. (2000). The impact of minor stressful life events and social support on cravings: A study of inpatients receiving treatment for substance dependence. *Addictive Behaviors, 25,* 539–547.

Amrhein, P. C., Miller, W. R., Yahne, C. E., Palmer, M., & Fulcher, L. (2003). Client commitment language during motivational interviewing predicts drug use outcomes. *Journal of Consulting and Clinical Psychology, 71,* 862–878.

Andréasson, S., & Öjehagen, A. (2003). Psychosocial treatment for alcohol dependence. In M. Berglund, E. Johnsson, & S. Thelander (Eds.), *Treatment of alcohol and drug abuse: An evidence-based review* (pp. 43–188). Weinheim, Germany: Wiley-VCH.

Anglin. M. D., Hser, Y.-I., & Grella, C. E. (1997). Drug addiction and treatment careers among clients in the Drug Abuse Treatment Outcome Study (DATOS). *Psychology of Addiction, 11,* 308–323.

Annis, H. M. (1982). Inventory of drinking situations (IDS). Toronto: Addiction Research Foundation.

Annis, H.M., and Graham, J.M. (1988). Situational Confidence Questionnaire (SCQ-39) users guide. Toronto: Alcoholism and Drug Addiction Research Foundation.

Annis, H. M., & Martin, G. (1985). Inventory of drug-taking situations (IDTS). Toronto: Addiction Research Foundation.

Anthony, J. C., Tien, A. Y., & Petronis, K. R. (1989). Epidemiologic evidence on cocaine use and panic attacks. *American Journal of Epidemiology, 129,* 543–549.

Anton, R. F., Moak, D. H., Waid, R., Latham, P. K., Malcolm, R. J., & Dias, J. K. (1999). Naltrexone and cognitive behavioral therapy for the treatment of outpatient alcoholics: Results of a placebo-controlled trial. *American Journal of Psychiatry, 156,* 1758–1764.

Arrindell, W. A., Emmelkamp, P. M. G., & Bast, S. (1983). The Maudsley Marital Questionnaire (MMQ): A further step towards its validation. *Journal of Personality and Individual Differences, 4,* 457–464.

Arseneault, L., Cannon, M., Witton, J., & Murray, R. (2004). Cannabis as a potential causal factor in schizophrenia. In D. Castle & R. Murray (Eds.), *Marijuana and madness: Psychiatry and neurobiology* (pp. 101–118). Cambridge: Cambridge University Press.

Arseneault, L., Moffitt, T. E., Caspi, A., Taylor, P. J., and Silva, P. A. (2000). Mental disorders and violence in a total birth cohort: Results from the Dunedin Study. *Archives of General Psychiatry, 57,* 979–986.

Azrin, N. H. (1976). Improvements in the community reinforcement approach to alcoholism. *Behaviour Research and Therapy, 14,* 339–348.

Azrin, N. H., & Besalel, V.A. (1980). *Job club counselor's manual: A behavioral approach to vocational counseling.* Baltimore: Pro-Ed.

Azrin, N. H., McMahon, P. T., Donahue, B., Besalel, V. A., Lapinski, K. J., Kogan, E. S., et al. (1994). Behavior therapy for drug abuse: A controlled treatment outcome study. *Behaviour Research and Therapy, 32,* 857–866.

Azrin, N. H., Sisson, R. W., Meyers, R., & Godley, M. (1982). Alcoholism treatment by disulfiram and community reinforcement therapy. *Journal of Behavior Therapy and Experimental Psychiatry, 13,* 105–112.

Babor, F., Higgins-Biddle, J. C., Saunders, J. B., & Monteiro, M.G. (2001). *The alcohol use disorders identification test: Guidelines for use in primary care* (2nd ed.). World Health Organization Department of Mental Health and Substance Dependence. Online at whqlibdoc.who.int/hq/2001/WHO_MSD_MSB_01.6a.pdf.

Babor, T. F., Hofmann, M., Del Boca, F. K., Hesselbrock, V., Meyer, R. E., & Dolinsky, Z. S., et al. (1992). Types of alcoholics: I. Evidence for an empirically derived typology based on indicators of vulnerability and severity, *Archives of General Psychiatry, 49,* 599–608.

Back, S. E., Jackson, J. C., Sonne, S., & Brady, K. T. (2005). Alcohol dependence and posttraumatic stress disorder: Differences in clinical presentation and response to cognitive-behavioral therapy by order of onset. *Journal of Substance Abuse Treatment, 29,* 29–37.

Baker, A., Lee, N. K., Claire, M., Lewin, T. J., Grant, T., Pohlman, S., et al. (2005). Brief cognitive behavioural interventions for regular amphetamine users: a step in the right direction. *Addiction, 100,* 367–373.

Baker, A., Lewin, T., Reichler, H., Clancy, R., Carr, V., Garrett, R., et al. (2002). Motivational interviewing among psychiatric in-patients with substance use disorders. *Acta Psychiatria Scandinavia, 106,* 233–240.

Balldin, J., Berglund, M., Borg, S., Mansson, M., Bendtsen, P., Franck, J., et al. (2003). A 6-months controlled naltrexone study: Combined effect cognitive behavioural therapy in outpatient treatment of alcohol dependence. *Alcoholism: Clinical and Experimental Research, 27,* 1142–1149.

Bandura, A. (1977). Self-efficacy: Toward a unifying theory of behavioral change. *Psychology Review, 84,* 191–215.

Bandura, A. (1997). *Self-efficacy: The exercise of control.* New York: Freeman.

Barber, J. G., Cooper, B. K., & Heather, N. (1991). The situational confidence questionnaire. *International Journal of Addiction, 26,* 565–575.

Barnett, P. G., Rodgers, J. H., & Bloch, D. A. (2001). A meta-analysis comparing buprenorphine to methadone for treatment of opiate dependence. *Addiction, 96,* 683–690.

Barrowclough, C., Haddock, G., Tarrier, N., Lewis, S. W., Moring, J., O'Brien, R., et al. (2001). Randomized controlled trial of motivational interviewing, cognitive behavior therapy, and family intervention for patients with comorbid schizophrenia and substance use disorders. *American Journal of Psychiatry, 158,* 1706–1713.

Bates, M. E., & Convit, A. (1999). Neuropsychology and neuroimaging of alcohol and illicit drug abuse. In A. Calev (Ed.), *The assessment of neuropsychological functions in psychiatric disorders* (pp. 373–445). Washington, DC: American Psychiatric Association.

Bates, M. E., Voelbel, G. T., Buckman, J. F., Labouvie, E. W., & Barry, D. (2005). Short-term neuropsychological recovery in clients with substance use disorders. *Alcoholism: Clinical and Experimental Research, 29,* 367–377.

Bean-Bayog, M. (1993). AA processes and change: How does it work? In B. S. McCrady and W. R. Miller (Eds.), *Research on Alcoholics Anonymous: Opportunities and alternatives* (pp. 113–135). New Brunswick, NJ: Rutgers Center of Alcohol Studies.

Bechdolf, A., Pohlmann, B., Geyer, C., Ferber, C., Klosterkötter, J., Gouzoulis-Mayfrank, E. (2005). Motivationsbehandlung bei Patienten mit der Doppeldiagnose Psychose und Sucht. *Fortschritte der Neurologie und Psychiatrie, 73,* 728–735.

Beck, A. T., Steer, A., & Brown, G. K. (1996). *Manual for Beck Depression Inventory-II,* San Antonio, TX: Psychological Corporation.

Beidel, D. C., Turner, S. M., & Stanley, M. A. (1989). The Social Phobia and Anxiety Inventory: Concurrent and external validity. *Behavior Therapy, 20*, 417–427.

Berglund, M. (2005). A better widget? Three lessons for improving addiction treatment from a meta-analytical study. *Addiction, 100*, 742–750.

Berglund, M., Thelander, S., & Jonsson, E. (Eds.). (2003). *Treating alcohol and drug abuse: An evidence based review.* Weinheim, Germany: Wiley-VCH.

Bickel, W. K., Amass, L., Crean, J. P., & Badger, G. J. (1999). Buprenorphine dosing every 1–3 days in opioid-dependent patients. *Psychopharmacology, 146*, 111–118.

Bickel, W. K., Amass, L., Higgins, S. T., Badger, G. J., & Esch, R. A. (1997). Effects of adding behavioral treatment to opioid detoxification with buprenorphine. *Journal of Consulting and Clinical Psychology, 65*, 803–810.

Biederman, J., Wilens, T. E., & Mick, E. (1995). Psychoactive substance use disorders in adults with attention-deficit hyperactivity disorder (ADHD): Effects of ADHD and psychiatric comorbidity. *American Journal of Psychiatry, 152*, 1652–1658.

Bisaga, A., Aharonovich, E., Garawi, F., Levin, F. R., Rubin, E., Raby, W. N., et al. (in press). A randomized placebo-controlled trial of gabapentin for cocaine dependence, *Drug and Alcohol Dependence.*

Blume, A. W. (2004). Understanding and diagnosing substance use disorders. In R. Holman Coombs (Ed.), *Handbook of addictive disorders* (pp. 63–93). New York: Wiley.

Bohn, M. J., Babor, T. F., & Kranzler, H. R. (1995). The Alcohol Use Disorders Identification Test (AUDIT): Validation of a screening instrument for use in medical settings. *Journal of Studies on Alcohol, 56*, 423–432.

Bolla, K. I., Eldreth, D. A., London, E. D., Kiehl, K. A., Mouratidis, M., Contoreggi, C., et al. (2003). Orbitofrontal cortex dysfunction in abstinent cocaine abusers performing a decision-making task. *Neuroimage, 19*, 1085–1094.

Booth, R. E., Kwiatkowski, C., Iguchi, M. Y., Pinto, F., & John, D. (1998). Facilitating treatment entry among out-of-treatment injection drug users. *Public Health Reports, 113*(Suppl. 1), 116–128.

Bowen, R. C., D'Arcy, C., Keegan, D., & Van Senthilsel, A. (2000). A controlled trial of cognitive behavioral treatment of panic in alcoholic inpatients with comorbid panic disorder. *Addictive Behavior, 4*, 593–597.

Brady, K. T., Dansky, B. S., Back, S. E., Foa, E. B., & Carroll, K. B. (2001). Exposure therapy in the treatment of PTSD among cocaine-dependent individuals: Preliminary findings. *Journal of Substance Abuse Treatment, 21,* 47–54.

Brady, K. T., & Lydiard, R. B. (1993). The association of alcoholism and anxiety. *Psychiatric Quarterly, 64,* 135–149.

Brady, S., Rierdan, J., Peck, W., Losardo, M., & Meschede, T. (2003). Post-traumatic stress disorder in adults with serious mental illness and substance abuse. *Journal of Trauma and Dissociation, 4,* 77–90.

Brady, T. M., Krebs, C. P., & Laird, G. (2004). Psychiatric comorbidity and not completing jail-based substance abuse treatment. *American Journal of Addiction, 13,* 83–101.

Bremner, J. D., Southwick, S. M., Darnell, A., & Charney, D. S. (1996). Chronic PTSD in Vietnam combat veterans: Course of illness and substance abuse. *American Journal of Psychiatry, 153,* 369–375.

Breslin, F. C., Sobell, L. C., Sobell, M. B., & Agrawal, S. (2000). A comparison of a brief and long version of the situational confidence questionnaire. *Behaviour Research and Therapy, 38,* 1211–1220.

Broers, B., Giner, F., Dumont, P., & Mino, A. (2000). Inpatient opiate detoxification in Geneva: Follow-up at 1 and 6 months. *Drug and Alcohol Dependence, 58,* 85–92.

Brookhof, D., O'Brien, K. K., Cook, C. S., Thompson, T. D., & Williams, C. (1997). Characteristics of participants in domestic violence. *Journal of the American Medical Association, 277,* 1369–1373.

Brown, H. P., Peterson, J. H., & Cunningham, O. (1988). Rationale and theoretical basis of a behavioral/cognitive approach to spirituality. *Alcoholism Treatment Quarterly, 5,* 47–59.

Brown, R. A., Evans, D. M., Miller, I. W., Burgess, E. S., & Mueller, T. I. (1997). Cognitive-behavioral treatment for depression in alcoholism. *Journal of Consulting and Clinical Psychology, 65,* 715–726.

Brown, R. A., & Lewinsohn, P. M. (1984). A psychoeducational approach to the treatment of depression: Comparison of group, individual, and minimal-contact procedures. *Journal of Consulting and Clinical Psychology, 52,* 774–783.

Brown, S. (1985). *Treating the alcoholic: A development model of recovery.* New York: Wiley.

Brown, S. (1993). Therapeutic processes in Alcoholics Anonymous. In B. S. McCrady & W. R. Miller (Eds.) *Research on Alcoholics Anonymous: Opportunities and alternatives* (pp. 137–152). New Brunswick, NJ: Rutgers Center of Alcohol Studies.

Brown, S. A., Christiansen, B. A., & Goldman, M. S. (1987). The Alcohol Expectancy Questionnaire: An instrument for the assessment of adolescent and adult expectancies. *Journal of Studies on Alcohol, 48,* 483–491.

Brown, S. A., & Schuckit, M. A. (1988). Changes in depression among abstinent alcoholics. *Journal of Studies on Alcohol, 49,* 412–417.

Brown, S. A., Tapert, S. F., Tate, S. R., Abrantes, A. M. (2000). The role of alcohol in adolescent relapse and outcome. *Journal of Psychoactive Drugs, 32,* 107–115.

Budney, A. J., & Higgins, S. T. (1998). *National Institute on Drug Abuse Therapy Manuals for Drug Addiction: Manual 2. A Community Reinforcement Approach: Treating Cocaine Addiction* (NIH Publication No. 98-4309). Rockville, MD: U.S. Department of Health and Human Services.

Budney, A. J., Hughes, J. R., Moore, B. A., & Vandrey, R. (2004). Review of the validity and significance of cannabis withdrawal syndrome. *American Journal of Psychiatry, 161,* 1967–1977.

Budney, A. J., Sigmon, S. C., & Higgins, S. T. (2004). Contingency management in the substance abuse treatment clinic. In F. Rotgers, J. Morgenstern, & S. T. Walters (Eds.), *Treating substance abuse: Theory and technique* (pp. 248–277). New York: Guilford.

Burke, B. L., Arkowitz, H., & Menchola, M. (2002). The efficacy of motivational interviewing: A meta-analysis of controlled clinical trials. *Journal of Consulting and Clinical Psychology, 71,* 843–861.

Butcher, J. N., Graham, J. R., Ben-Porath, Y. S., Tellegen, A., Dahlstrom, W. G., & Kaemmer, B. (2001). Minnesota Multiphasic Personality Inventory-2: Manual for administration and scoring (2nd ed.). Minneapolis: University of Minnesota Press.

Cacciola, J. S., Alterman, A. I., Rutherford, M. J., & Snider, E. C. (1995). Treatment response of antisocial substance abusers. *Journal of Nervous and Mental Disease, 183,* 166–171.

Campbell, T. C., Catlin, L., Bentzler, J., Fuller, S., Barrett, D. E., Brondino, M.J. (2004). Test-retest reliability of the Alcohol Use Disorders Identification Test: Revised to include other drugs (AUDIT-ID). *Alcoholism: Clinical and Experimental Research 28,* 110.

Carey, K. B. (2002). Clinically useful assessments: Substance use and comorbid psychiatric disorders. *Behaviour Research and Therapy, 40,* 1345–1361.

Carey, K. B., Maisto, S. A., Kalichman, S. C., Forsythe, A. D., Wright, E. M., & Johnson, B. T. (1997). Enhancing motivation to reduce the risk of HIV infection for economically disadvantaged urban women. *Journal of Consulting and Clinical Psychology, 65,* 531–541.

Carey, K. B., Purnine, D.M., Maisto, S.A., & Carey, M. P. (2001). Enhancing readiness to change substance abuse in persons with schizophrenia: A four session motivation based intervention. *Behavior Modification, 25*, 331–384.

Carey, K. B., Purnine, D. M., Maisto, S. A., & Carey, M. P. (2002). Correlates of stages of change for substance abuse among psychiatric outpatients. *Psychology of Addictive Behaviors, 16*, 283–289.

Carey, M. P., Braaten, L. S., Maisto, S. A., Gleason, J. R., Forsyth, A. D., Durant, L. E., et al. (2000). Using information, motivational enhancement, and skills training to reduce the risk of HIV infection for low-income urban women: A second randomized clinical trial. *Health Psychology, 19*, 3–11.

Carpentier, P. J., De Jong, C. A. J., Dijkstra, B. A. G., Verbrugge, C. A. G., & Krabbe, P. F. M. (2005). A controlled trial of methylphenidate in adults with attention deficit/hyperactivity disorder and substance use disorders. *Addiction, 100*, 1868–1876.

Carrigan, H. M., & Randall, C. L. (2003). Self-medication in social phobia: Review of the alcohol literature. *Addictive Behaviors, 28*, 269–284.

Carroll, K.M. (1998). A cognitive-behavioral approach: treating cocaine addiction. National Institute on Drug Abuse, NIH Publication Number 98–4308.

Carroll, K.M. (1999). Behavioral and cognitive behavioral treatments. In B. S. McCrady & E. E. Epstein (Eds.), *Addictions: A comprehensive guidebook* (pp. 250–267). New York: Oxford University Press.

Carroll, K. M. (2004). Behavioral therapies for co-occurring substance use and mood disorders. *Biological Psychiatry, 56*, 778–784.

Carroll, K. M., Ball, S. A., Nich, C., O'Connor, P. G., Eagen, D. A., Frankforter, T. L., et al. (2001). Targeting behavioral therapies to enhance naltrexone treatment of opioid dependence. *Archives of General Psychiatry, 58*, 755–761.

Carroll, K. M., Fenton, L. R., Ball, S. A., Nich, C., Frankforter, T.L., Shi, J., et al. (2004). Efficacy of disulfiram and cognitive behavior therapy in cocaine-dependent outpatients: a randomized placebo-controlled trial. *Archives of General Psychiatry, 61*, 264–272.

Carroll, K. M., Nich, C., & Ball, S. A. (2005). Practice makes progress? Homework assignments and outcome in treatment of cocaine dependence. *Journal of Consulting and Clinical Psychology, 73*, 749–755.

Carroll, K. M., Nich, C., Ball, S. A., McCance, E., & Rounsaville, B. J. (1998). Treatment of cocaine and alcohol dependence with psychotherapy and disulfiram. *Addiction, 93*, 713–727.

Carroll, K.M., Nich, C., & Rounsaville, B.J. (1995). Differential symptom reduction in depressed cocaine abusers treated with psychotherapy and pharmacotherapy. *Journal of Nervous and Mental Disease, 181*, 71–79.

Carroll, K. M., Nich, C., & Rounsaville, B. J. (1997). Contribution of the therapeutic alliance to outcome in active versus control psychotherapies. *Journal of Consulting and Clinical Psychology, 65*, 510–514.

Carroll, K. M., Power, M. D., Bryant, K., & Rounsaville, B. J. (1993). One-year follow-up of treatment seeking cocaine abusers: Psychopathology and dependence severity as predictors of outcome. *Journal of Nervous and Mental Disease, 181*, 71–79.

Carroll, K. M., & Rounsaville, B. J. (2002). On beyond urine: Clinically useful assessment instruments in the treatment of drug dependence. *Behaviour Research and Therapy, 40*, 1329–1344.

Carroll, K. M., Rounsaville, B. J., & Gawin, F. H. (1991). A comparative trial of psychotherapies for ambulatory cocaine abusers: Relapse prevention and interpersonal psychotherapy. *American Journal of Drug and Alcohol Abuse, 17*, 229–247.

Carroll, K. M., Rounsaville, B. J., Gordon, L. T., Nich, C., Jatlow, P., Bisinghini, R. M., et al. (1994). Psychotherapy and pharmacotherapy for ambulatory cocaine abusers. *Archives of General Psychiatry, 51*, 177–187.

Carroll, K. M., Rounsaville, B. J., Nich, C., Gordon, L. T., Wirtz, P. W., & Gawin, F. (1994). One-year follow-up of psychotherapy and pharmacotherapy for cocaine dependence: Delayed emergence of psychotherapy effects. *Archives of General Psychiatry, 51*, 989–997.

Carroll, K. M., Sinha, R., Nich, C., Babuscio, B., & Rounsaville, B. J. (2002). Contingency management to enhance naltrexone treatment of opioid dependence: A randomized clinical trial of reinforcement magnitude. *Experimental and Clinical Psychopharmacology. 10*, 54–63.

Carter, B. L., & Tiffany, S. T. (1999). Meta-analysis of cue-reactivity in addiction research. *Addiction, 94*, 327–340.

Chambless, D. L., Caputo, G. C., Bright, P., & Gallagher, R. (1984). Assessment of fear in agoraphobics: The Body Sensations Questionnaire and the Agoraphobic Cognitions Questionnaire. *Journal of Consulting and Clinical Psychology, 52*, 1090–1097.

Chaney, E. F., O'Leary, M. R., & Marlatt, G. A. (1978). Skill training with problem drinkers. *Journal of Consulting and Clinical Psychology, 46*, 1092–1104.

Charney, D. A., Palacios-Boix, J., Negrete, J. C., Dobkin, P. L., & Gill, K. J. (2005). Association between concurrent depression and anxiety and six-month outcome of addiction treatment. *Psychiatric Services, 56*, 927–933.

Charney, D. A., Paraherakis, A. M., Negrete, J. C., & Gill, K. J. (1998). The impact of depression on the outcome of addictions treatment. *Journal of Substance Abuse Treatment, 15*, 123–130.

Childress, A. R., Hole, A. V., Ehrman, R. N., Robbins, S. J., McLellan, A. T., & O'Brien, C. P. (1993). Cue reactivity and cue reactivity interventions in drug dependence. In L. S. Onken, J. D. Blaine, & J. J. Boren (Eds.), *Behavioral treatment for drug abuse and dependence* (pp. 73–95). Rockville, MD: National Institute on Drug Abuse.

Christo, G., & Franey, C. (1995). Drug users' spiritual beliefs, locus of control and the disease concept in relation to Narcotics Anonymous attendance and six-month outcomes. *Drug and Alcohol Dependence, 38*, 51–56.

Chung, T., & Maisto, S. A. (2006). Relapse to alcohol and other drug use in treated adolescents: Review and reconsideration of relapse as a change point in clinical course. *Clinical Psychology Review, 26*, 149–161.

Chutuape, M. A., Jasinski, D. R., Fingerhood, F. I., & Stitzer, M. L. (2001). One, three, and six month outcomes following brief inpatient opioid detoxification. *American Journal of Drug and Alcohol Abuse, 27*, 19–44.

Clark, N., Lintzeris, N., Gijsbers, A., Whelan, G., Dunlop, A., Ritter, A., et al. (2004). *LAAM maintenance vs. methadone maintenance for heroin dependence (Cochrane review)* (Cochrane Library, Issue 1). Chichester, England: Wiley.

Cleland, C., Magura, S., Foote, J., Rosenblum, A., & Kosanke, N. (2006) Factor structure of the Conners Adult ADHD Rating Scale (CAARS) for substance users. Online at http://www.pearsonassessments.com/tests/caars.htm.

Cloninger, C. R., Sigvardsson, S., & Bohman, M. (1996). Type I and Type II alcoholism: An update. *Alcohol Health and Research World, 20*, 18–23.

Clure, C., Brady, K. T., Saladin, M. E., Johnson, D., Waid, R., & Rittenbury, M. (1999). Attention-deficit/hyperactivity disorder and substance use: Symptom pattern and drug choice. *American Journal of Drug and Alcohol Abuse, 25*, 441–448.

Cocco, K. M., & Carey, K. B. (1998). Psychometric properties of the Drug Abuse Screening Test in psychiatric outpatients. *Psychological Assessment, 10*, 408–414.

Cohen, P., & Sas, A. (1994). Cocaine use in Amsterdam in non deviant subcultures. *Addiction Research, 2,* 71–94.

Cole, J. D., & Kazarian, S. S. (1988). The Level of Expressed Emotion scale: A new measure of expressed emotion. *Journal of Clinical Psychology, 44,* 392–397.

Collins, B. N., & Brandon, T. H. (2002). Effects of extinction context and retrieval cues on alcohol cue reactivity among nonalcoholic drinkers. *Journal of Consulting and Clinical Psychology, 70,* 390–397.

Conners, C., Erhardt, D., & Sparrow, E. (1998). *The Conners adult ADHD rating scale (CAARS),* Toronto: Multi-Health Systems.

Connors, G. J., Maisto, S. A., & Zywiak, W. H. (1996). Understanding relapse in the broader context of post-treatment functioning. *Addiction, 91*(Suppl.), 173–190.

Cooney, N. L., Kadden, R. M., Litt, M. D., & Getter, H. (1991). Matching alcoholics to coping skills or interactional therapies. Two-year follow-up results. *Journal of Consulting and Clinical Psychology, 59,* 598–601.

Cooper, M. L., Russell, M., Skinner, J. B., & Windle, M. (1992). Development and validation of a three-dimensional measure of drinking motives. *Psychological Assessment, 4,* 123–132.

Corby, E. A., Roll, J. M., Ledgerwood, D. M., & Schuster, C. R. (2000). Contingency management interventions for treating the substance abuse of adolescents: A feasibility study. *Experimental and Clinical Psychopharmacology, 8,* 371–376.

Cornelius, J. R., Maisto, S. A., Martin, C. S., Bukstein, O. G., Salloum, I. M., Daley, D. C., et al. (2004). Major depression associated with earlier alcohol relapse in treated teens with AUD. *Addictive Behaviors, 29,* 1035–1038.

Cornelius, J. R., Salloum, I. M., Thase, M. E., Haskett, R. F., Daley, D. C., Jones-Block, A., et al. (1998). Fluoxetine versus placebo in depressed alcoholic cocaine abusers. *Psychopharmacological Bulletin, 34,* 117–121.

Corrigan, P. W., & Watson, A. C. (2005). Findings from the national comorbidity survey on the frequency of violent behavior in individuals with psychiatric disorders. *Psychiatry Research, 136,* 153–162.

Crits-Christoph, P., Connolly Gibbons, M., Barber, J. P., Gallop, R., Beck, A. T., Mercer, D.,et al. (2003). Moderators of outcome of psychosocial treatment for cocaine dependence. *Journal of Consulting and Clinical Psychology, 71,* 918–925.

Crits-Christoph, P., Liqueland, L., Blaine, J., Frank, A., Luborsky, L. Onken, L. S., et al. (1999). Psychosocial treatments for cocaine dependence: National Institute on Drug Abuse Collaborative Cocaine Treatment Study. *Archives of General Psychiatry, 56,* 493–502.

Cubells, J. F., Feinn, R., Pearson, D., Burda, J., Tang, Y., Farrer, L. A., et al. (2005). Rating the severity and character of transient cocaine-induced delusions and hallucinations with a new instrument, the Scale for Assessment of Positive Symptoms for Cocaine-Induced Psychosis (SAPS-CIP). *Drug and Alcohol Dependence, 80,* 23–33.

Daley, D. C., Salloum, I. M., Zuckoff, M. A., Kirisci, L., & Thase, M. E. (1998). Increased treatment adherence among outpatients with depression and cocaine dependence: Results of a pilot study. *American Journal of Psychiatry, 155,* 1611–1613.

Dallery, L., Silverman, K., Chutuape, M. A. D., Bigelow, G. E., & Stitzer, M. L. (1996). Voucher-based reinforcement of opiate plus cocaine abstinence in treatment-resistant methadone patients: Effects of reinforcer magnitude. *Experimental and Clinical Psychopharmacology, 9,* 317–325.

Dallery, L., Silverman, K., Chutuape, M. A. D., Bigelow, G. E., & Stitzer, M. L. (2001). Voucher-based reinforcement of opiate plus cocaine abstinence in treatment-resistant methadone patients: Effects on reinforer magnitude. *Experimental and Clinical Psychopharmacology, 9,* 317–325.

Dalton, E.J., Cate-Carter, T.D., Mundo, E., Parikh, S.V., & Kennedy, J.L. (2003). Suicide risk in bipolar patients: The role of comorbid substance use disorders. *Bipolar Disorder, 5,* 58–61.

Dansky, B. S., Brady, K. T., & Saladin, M. E. (1998). Untreated symptoms of PTSD among cocaine-dependent individuals. *Journal of Substance Abuse Treatment, 15,* 499–504.

Darke, S., & Ross, J. (2002). Suicide among heroin users: Rates, risk factors and methods. *Addiction, 97,* 1383–1394.

Darke, S., Williamson, A., Ross, J., & Teesson, M. (2005). Attempted suicide among heroin users: 12-month outcomes from the Australian Treatment Outcome Study (ATOS). *Drug and Alcohol Dependence, 78,* 177–186.

Davies, J. B. (1992). *The myth of addiction.* Chur, Switserland: Harwood.

Dawe, S., Powell, J. H., Richards, D., Gossop, M., Marks, I., Strang, J., & Gray, J. (1993). Does post-withdrawal cue exposure improve outcome in opiate addiction? A controlled trial. *Addiction, 88,* 1233–1245.

Dawe, S., Rees, V. W., Sitharthan, T., Mattick, R. P., & Heather, N. (2002). Efficacy of moderation-oriented cue-exposure for problem drinkers: A randomised controlled trial. *Journal of Consulting and Clinical Psychology, 70,* 1045–1050.

Dawkins, M.P. (1997). Drug use and violent crime among adolescents. *Adolescence, 32,* 395–504.

Day, B. M., Lopez Gaston, C., Furlong, E., Murali, V., & Copello, A. (2005). United Kingdom substance misuse treatment workers' attitudes toward 12-step self-help groups. *Journal of Substance Abuse Treatment, 29,* 321–327.

De los Cobos, J. P., Trujols, J., Ribalta, E., & Casas, M. (1997). Cocaine use immediately prior to entry in an inpatient heroin detoxification unit as a predictor of discharges against medical advice. *American Journal of Drug and Alcohol Abuse, 23,* 43–59.

Delbello, M. P., & Strakowski, S. M. (2003). Understanding the problem of co-occurring mood and substance use disorders. In J. J. Westermeyer, R. D. Weiss, & D. M. Ziedonis (Eds.), *Integrated treatment for mood and substance use disorders* (pp. 17–41). Baltimore, MD: Johns Hopkins University Press.

Dennis, M., Godley, S. A., Diamond, G., Tims, F.M., Babor, T., Donaldson, J., et al. (2004). The Cannabis Youth Treatment (CYT) Study: Main findings from two randomized trials *Journal of Substance Abuse Treatment, 27,* 197–213.

Dennis, M. L., Scott, C. K., Funk, R., & Foss, M. A. (in press). The duration and correlates of addiction and treatment careers. *Journal of Substance Abuse Treatment.*

De Sousa, A., & De Sousa, A. (2004). A one-year pragmatic trial of naltrexone versus disulfiram in the treatment of alcohol dependence. *Alcohol and Alcoholism, 39,* 528–531.

De Sousa, A., & De Sousa, A. (2005). An open randomized study comparing disulfiram and acamprosate in the treatment of alcohol dependence. *Alcohol and Alcoholism, 40,* 545–548.

De Vries, T. J., Homberg, J. R., Binnekade, R., Raaso, H., & Schoffelmeer, A. N. (2003). Cannabinoid modulation of the reinforcing and motivational properties of heroin and heroin-associated cues in rats. *Psychopharmacology, 168,* 164–169.

De Vries, T. J., Shaham, Y., Homberg, J. R., Crombag, H., Schuurman, K., Dieben, J., et al. (2001). A cannabinoid mechanism in relapse to cocaine seeking. *Nature Medicine, 7,* 1151–1154.

De Wildt, W. A. J. M., Schippers, G. M., Van den Brink, A. S., Potgieter, A. S., Deckers, F., & Bets, D. (2002). Does psychosocial treatment enhance the efficacy acamprosate in patients with alcohol problems? *Alcohol and Alcoholism, 37,* 375–382.

DiClemente, C. C. (1993). Alcoholics Anonymous and the structure of change. In B. S. McCrady & W. R. Miller (Eds.), *Research on Alcoholics Anonymous: Opportunities and alternatives* (pp. 79–97). New Brunswick, NJ: Rutgers Center of Alcohol Studies.

DiClemente, C. C., & Hughes, S. O. (1990). Stages of change profiles in outpatient alcoholism treatment. *Journal of Substance Abuse, 2*, 217–235.

Dimeff, L., Rizvi, S. L., Brown, M., & Linehan, M. M. (2000). Dialectical behavior therapy for substance abuse: A pilot application to methamphetamine-dependent women with borderline personality disorder. *Cognitive and Behavioral Practice, 7*, 457–468.

Dishion, T., McCord, J., & Poulin, F. (1999). When interventions harm: Peer groups and problem behavior. *American Psychologist, 54*, 755–764.

Donohue, B. (2004). Coexisting child neglect and drug abuse in young mothers. *Behavior Therapy, 28*, 206–233.

Donovan, D. M., Rosengren, D. B., Downey, L., Cox, G. C., & Sloan, K. L. (2001). Attrition prevention with individuals awaiting publicly funded drug treatment. *Addiction, 96*, 1149–1160.

Drake, R. E., Mercer-MacFadden, C., Mueser, K. T., McHugo, G. J., & Bond, G. R. (1998). Review of integrated mental health and substance abuse treatment for patients with dual disorders. *Schizophrenia Bulletin, 24*, 589–608.

Driessen, M., Meier, S., Hill, A., Wetterling, T., Lange, W., & Junghanns, K. (2001). The course of anxiety, depression and drinking behaviours after completed detoxification in alcoholics with and without comorbid anxiety and depressive disorders. *Alcohol and Alcoholism, 36*, 249–255.

Driessen, M., Veltrup, C., Weber, J., John, U., Wetterling, T., & Dilling, H. (1998). Psychiatric co-morbidity, suicidal behaviour and suicidal ideation in alcoholics seeking treatment. *Addiction, 93*, 889–894.

Drummond, D. C., & Glautier, S. (1994). A controlled trial of cue exposure treatment in alcohol dependence. *Journal of Consulting and Clinical Psychology, 62*, 809–817.

Dumais, A., Lesage, A. D., Alda, M., Rouleau, G., Dumont, M., Chawky, N., et al. (2005). Risk factors for suicide completion in major depression: A case-control study of impulsive and aggressive behaviors in men. *American Journal of Psychiatry, 162*, 2116–2124.

D'Zurilla, T. J., Sanna, L. J., & Chang, E. (2004). Social problem solving: Current status and future directions. In E. Chang, T. J. D'Zurilla, & L. J. Sanna (Eds.), *Social problem solving: Theory, research, and training* (pp. 241–253). Washington, DC: American Psychological Association.

Edens, J. F., & Willoughby, F. W. (1999). Motivational profiles of poly-substance dependent patients: Do they differ from alcohol-dependent patients? *Addictive Behaviors, 24*, 195–206.

Edens, J. F., & Willoughby, F. W. (2000). Motivational patterns of alcohol dependent patients: A replication. *Psychology of Addictive Behaviors, 14*, 397–400.

Edwards, G., Marshall, E. J., & Cook, C. C. H. (2003). *The treatment of drinking problems.* Cambridge: Cambridge University Press.

Eissenberg, T., Bigelow, G. E., Strain, E. C., Walsh, S. L., Brooner, R. K., Stitzer, M. L., et al. (1997). Dose-related efficacy of levo-methadyl acetate for treatment of opiate dependence. *Journal of the American Medical Association, 227*, 1945–1951.

El-Bassel, N., Gilbert, L., Wu, E., Go, H., & Hill, J. (2005). Relationship between drug abuse and intimate violence. *American Journal of Public Health, 95*, 465–470.

Ellis, A. (1988). *Rational-Emotive Therapy with Alcoholics and Substance Abusers.* New York: Pergamon.

ElSohly, M. A., Ross, S. A., Mehmedic, Z., Arafat, R., Yi, B., & Banahan, B. F. (2000). Potency trends of delta9-THC and other cannabinoids in confiscated marijuana from 1980–1997. *Journal of Forensic Science, 45*, 24–30.

Emanuels-Zuurveen, L., & Emmelkamp, P.M.G. Spouse-aided therapy with depressed patients: A comparative evaluation. *Behavior Modification, 21*, 62–77.

Emmelkamp, P. M. G. (1986). Behavior therapy with adults. In S. Garfield & A. Bergin (Eds.), *Handbook of psychotherapy and behavior change* (3rd ed., pp. 383–442). New York: Wiley.

Emmelkamp, P. M. G. (1994). Behavior therapy with adults. In A. Bergin & S. Garfield (Eds.), *Handbook of psychotherapy and behavior change* (4th ed., pp. 379–427). New York: Wiley.

Emmelkamp, P. M. G. (2004). Behavior therapy with adults. In M. Lambert (Ed.), *Bergin and Garfield's handbook of psychotherapy and behavior change* (5th ed., pp. 393–446). New York: Wiley.

Emmelkamp, P. M. G., Bouman, T. K., & Scholing, A. (1993). *Anxiety disorders: A practitioners guide.* Chichester, England: Wiley.

Emmelkamp, P. M. G., & Foa, E. B. (1983). The study of failures. In E. B. Foa & P. M. G. Emmelkamp (Eds.), *Failures in behavior therapy* (pp. 1–9). New York: Wiley.

Emmelkamp, P. M. G., & Gerlsma, C. (1994). Marital functioning and the anxiety disorders. *Behavior Therapy, 25*, 407–429.

Emmelkamp, P. M. G., & Heeres, H. (1988). Drug addiction and parental rearing style: A controlled study. *International Journal of Addiction, 23*, 207–216.

Emmelkamp, P. M. G., & Kamphuis, J. H. (2002). Aversion relief therapy. In M. Hersen & W. Sledge (Eds.), *The encyclopedia of psychotherapy* (Vol. 1, pp. 139–143). New York: Academic.

Emmelkamp, P. M. G., & Kamphuis, J. H. (2005). Aversion relief. In M. Hersen (Ed.), *Encyclopedia of behavior modification and cognitive behavior therapy* (Vol. 1, pp. 39–40). Thousand Oaks, CA: Sage.

Emmelkamp, P. M. G., & Vedel, E. (2002). Spouse-aided therapy. In M. Hersen & W. Sledge (Eds.), *The encyclopedia of psychotherapy* (pp. 693–698). New York: Academic.

Emmelkamp, P. M. G., & Vedel, E. (2005). Spouse-aided-therapy. In M. Hersen (Ed.), *Encyclopedia of behavior modification and cognitive behavior therapy* (Vol. 1, pp. 558–562). Thousand Oaks, CA: Sage.

Emrick, C. D., Tonigan, J. S., Montgomery, H., & Little, L. (1993). Alcoholics Anonymous: What is currently known? In B. S. McCrady & W. R. Miller (Eds.), *Research on Alcoholic Anonymous: Opportunities and alternatives* (pp. 41–76). New Bruswick, NJ: Rutgers Center of Alcohol Studies.

Ercan, E. S., Coḡjunol, H., Varan, A., & Toksöz, K. (2003). Childhood attention deficit/hyperactivity disorder and alcohol dependence: A 1-year follow-up. *Alcohol and Alcoholism, 38,* 352–356.

Etheridge, R. M., Craddock, S. G., Hubbard, R. L., & Rounds-Bryant, J. L. (1999). The relationship of counseling and self-help participation to patient outcomes in DATOS. *Drug and Alcohol Dependence, 57,* 99–112.

Evren, C., & Evren, B. (2005). Self-mutilation in substance-dependent patients and relationship with childhood abuse and neglect, alexithymia and temperament and character dimensions of personality. *Drug and Alcohol Dependence, 80,* 15–22.

Fals-Stewart, W. (2003). The occurrence of partner physical aggression on days of alcohol consumption: a longitudinal diary study. *Journal of Consulting and Clincial Psycholgy, 71,* 41–52.

Fals-Stewart, W., & Birchler, G. R. (2002a). A national survey of the use of couples therapy in substance abuse treatment. *Journal of Substance Abuse Treatment, 20,* 277–283.

Fals-Stewart, W., & Birchler, G. R. (2002b). Behavioral couples therapy with alcoholic men and their intimate partners: The comparative effectiveness of bachelor's and master's level counselors. *Behavior Therapy, 33,* 123–147.

Fals-Stewart, W., Birchler, G. R., & O'Farrell, T. J. (1996). Behavioral couples therapy for male substance-abusing patients: Effects on relationship adjustment and drug-using behavior. *Journal of Consulting and Clinical Psychology, 64,* 959–972.

Fals-Stewart, W., Kashdan, T.B., O'Farrell, T.J., & Birchler, G.R. (2002). Behavioral couples therapy for drug-abusing patients: Effects on partner-violence. *Journal of Substance Abuse Treatment, 22*, 87–96.

Fals-Stewart, W., Klostermann, K., O'Farrell, T. J., Yates, B. T., & Birchler, G. R. (2005). Brief relationship therapy for alcoholism: A randomized clinical trail examining clinical efficacy and cost-effectiveness. *Psychology of Addictive Behaviors, 19*, 362–371.

Fals-Stewart, W., Leonard, K. E., & Birchler, G. R. (2005). The occurrence of male-to-female intimate partner violence on days of men's drinking: The moderating effects of antisocial personality disorder. *Journal of Consulting and Clinical Psychology, 73*, 239–248.

Fals-Stewart, W., Marks, A. P., & Schafer, J. (1993). A comparison of behavioral group therapy and individual behavior therapy in treating obsessive-compulsive disorder. *Journal of Nervous and Mental Disease, 181*, 189–193.

Fals-Stewart, W., O'Farrell, T. J., & Birchler, G. R. (2001). Behavioral couples therapy for male methadone maintenance patients: Effects on drug-using behavior and relationship adjustment. *Behavior Therapy, 32*, 391–411.

Fals-Stewart, W., O'Farrell, T. J., Feehan, M., Birchler, G. R., Tiller, S., & McFarlin, S. K. (2000). Behavioral couples therapy versus individual-based treatment for male substance-abusing patients: An evaluation of significant individual change and comparison of improvement rates. *Journal of Substance Abuse Treatment, 18*, 249–254.

Fals-Stewart, W., & Schafer, J. (1992). The relationship between length of stay in drug-free therapeutic communities and neurocognitive functioning. *Journal of Clincial Psychology, 48*, 539–543.

Faraone, S. V., & Wilens, T. (2003). Does stimulant treatment lead to substance use disorders? *Journal of Clinical Psychiatry, 64*(Suppl. 11), 9–13.

Farber, P. D., Khavari, K. A., & Douglass, F. M. (1980). A factor analytic study of reasons for drinking: Empirical validation of positive and negative reinforcement dimensions. *Journal of Consulting and Clinical Psychology, 48*, 780.

Fenster, J. (in press). Characteristics of clinicians likely to refer clients to 12-step programs versus a diversity of post-treatment options. *Drug and Alcohol Dependence.*

Fergusson, D. M., & Horwood, L. J. (2000). Does cannabis use encourage other forms of illicit drug use? *Addiction, 95*, 505–520.

Fergusson, D. M., Horwood, L. J., Lynskey, M. T., & Madden, P. A. F. (2003). Early reactions to cannabis predict later dependence. *Archives of General Psychiatry, 60,* 1033–1039.

Finney, J., & Moos, R. (1995). Entering treatment for alcohol abuse: A stress and coping model. *Addiction, 90,* 1223–1240.

Finney, J. W., Noyes, A., Coutts, I., & Moos, R. H. (1998). Evaluating substance abuse treatment process models, I: Changes on proximal outcome variables during 12-step and cognitive-behavioral treatment. *Journal of Studies on Alcohol, 59,* 371–380.

Fiorentine, R. (1999). After drug treatment: Are twelve-step programs effective in maintaining abstinence? *American Journal of Drug and Alcohol Abuse, 25,* 93–116.

Fiorentine, R., & Hillhouse, M. P. (2000). Drug treatment and 12-step program participation: the addictive effects of integrated recovery activities. *Journal of Substance Abuse Treatment, 18,* 65–74.

First, M. B., Spitzer, R. L., Gibbon, M., & Williams, J. B. W. (1995). Structured Clinical Interview for *DSM-IV* Axis Disorders—Patient Edition (SCID-I/P, Version 2.0). New York: New York State Psychiatric Institute.

First, M. B., Spitzer, R. L., Gibbon, M., Williams, J. B. W., & Benjamin, L. (1995). Structured Clinical Interview for *DSM-IV* Axis II Personality Disorders—Patient Edition (SCID-II, Version 2.0). New York: New York State Psychiatric Institute.

Fisher, M. S., & Bentley, K. J. (1996). Two group therapy models for clients with a dual diagnosis of substance abuse and personality disorder. *Psychiatric Services, 4,* 1244–1250.

Foreman, R. F., Bovasso, G., & Woody, G. (2001). Staff beliefs about addiction treatment. *Journal of Substance Abuse Treatment, 21,* 1–9.

Franken, I. H. A., De Haan, H. A., Van Der Meer, C. W., Haffmans, P. M. J., & Hendriks, V. M. (1999). Cue reactivity and effects of cue exposure in abstinent post-treatment drug users. *Journal of Substance Abuse Treatment, 16,* 81–85.

Fu, Q., Heath, A. C., Bucholz, K. K., Nelson, E., Goldberg, J., Lyons, M. J., et al. (2002). Shared genetic risk of major depression, alcohol dependence, and marijuana dependence: Contribution of antisocial personality disorder in men. *Archives of General Psychiatry, 59,* 1125–1132.

Fudala, P. J., Vocci, F., Montgomery, A., & Trachtenberg, A. I. (1997). Levomethadyl acetate (LAAM) for the treatment of opiate dependence: A multisite, open label study of LAAM safety and an evaluation of the product labeling and treatment regulations. *Journal of Maintenance Addiction, 1,* 9–39.

Fuller, R. K., Branchey, L., Brightwell, D. R., Derman, R. M., Emrick, C. D., et al. (1986). Disulfiram treatment of alcoholism: A Veterans Administration cooperation study. *Journal of the American Medical Association, 256*, 1449–1455.

Fuller, R. K., & Gordis, E. (2004) Does disulfiram have a role in alcoholism treatment today? *Addiction, 99*, 21–24.

Galai, N., Safaeian, M., Vishov, D., Bolotin, A., & Celentano, D. D. (2003). Longitudinal patterns of drug injection behavior in the alive study cohort, 1988–2000. *American Journal of Epidemiology, 158*, 695–704.

Garbutt, J. C., West, S. L., Carey, T. S., Lohr, K. N., & Crews, F. T. (1999). Pharmacological treatment of alcohol dependence: A review of the evidence. *Journal of the American Medical Association, 281*, 1318–1325.

Goldman, M. S. (1994) The alcohol expectancy concept: Applications to assessment, prevention, and treatment of alcohol abuse. *Applied and Preventive Psychology, 3*, 131–144.

Goldstein, R. Z., & Volkow, N. D. (2002). Drug addiction and its underlying neurobiological basis: Neuroimaging evidence for the involvement of the frontal cortex. *American Journal of Psychiatry, 159*, 1642–1652.

Gonzalez, G., Feingold, A., Oliveto, A., Gonsai, K., & Kosten, T. A. (2003). Comorbid major depressive disorder as a prognostic factor in cocaine-abusing buprenorphine maintained patients treated with desipramine and contingency management. *American Journal of Drug and Alcohol Abuse, 29*, 497–514.

Gonzalez-Pinto, A., Gonzalez, C., Enjuto, S., Fernandez de Corres, B., Lopez, P., Palomo, J., et al. (2004). Psychoeducation and cognitive-behavioral therapy in bipolar disorder: An update. *Acta Psychiatrica Scandinavia, 109*, 83–90.

Gorman, D. M., & Derzon, J. H. (2002). Behavioral traits and marijuana use and abuse: A meta-analysis of longitudinal studies. *Addictive Behaviors, 27*, 193–206.

Gossop, M., Marsden, J., Stewart, D., & Kidd, T. (2003). The National Treatment Outcome Research Study (NTORS): 4–5 years follow-up results. *Addiction, 98*, 291–303.

Gouzoulis-Mayfrank, E., Fischermann, T., Rezk, M., Thimm, B., Hensen, G., & Daumann, J. (2005). Memory performance in polyvalent MDMA (ecstasy) users who continue or discontinue MDMA use. *Drug and Alcohol Dependence, 78*, 317–323.

Graeber, A. D., Moyers. T. B., Griffith, G., Guajardo, E., & Tonigan, S. (2003). A pilot study comparing motivational interviewing and an educational intervention in patients with schizophrenia and alcohol use disorders. *Community Mental Health Journal, 39*, 189–202.

Grant, B. (1998). The impact of family history of alcoholism on the relationship between age at onset of alcohol use and *DSM-III* alcohol dependence. *Alcohol Health Research World, 22*, 144–147.

Grant, B. F., Stinson, F. S., Dawson, D. A., Chou, S. P., Dufour, M. C., Compton, W., et al. (2004). Prevalence and co-occurrence of substance use use disorders and independent mood and anxiety disorders. *Archives of General Psychiatry, 61*, 807–816.

Green, A. R., Mechan, A. O., Elliott, J. M., O'Shea, E., & Colado, M. N. I. (2003). The pharmacology and clinical pharmacology of 3,4-methylenedioxymethamphetamine (MDMA, "ecstasy"). *Pharmacological Review, 55*, 463–508.

Greenfield, S. F., Weiss, R. D., Muenz, L. R., Vage, L. M., Kelly, J. F., Bello, L. R., et al. (1998). The effect of depression on return to drinking: A prospective study. *Archives of General Psychiatry, 55*, 259–265.

Griffith, J. D., Rowan-Szal, G. A., Roark, R. R., & Simpson, D. D. (2000). Contingency management in outpatient methadone treatment: A meta-analysis. *Drug and Alcohol Dependence, 58*, 55–66.

Gruber, K., Chutuape, M. A., & Stitzer, M. L. (2000). Reinforcement-based intensive outpatient treatment for inner city opiate abusers: A short-term evaluation. *Drug and Alcohol Dependence, 57*, 211–223.

Haasen, C., Prinzleve, M., Zurhold, H., Rehm, J., Guttinger, F., & Fischer, G. (2004). Cocaine use in Europe: A multi-centre study. Methodology and prevalence estimates. *European Addiction Research, 10*, 139–146.

Haley, J. (1963). *Strategies of psychotherapy*. New York: Grunne & Straton.

Hall, S. M., Havassy, B. E., & Wasserman, D. A. (1991). Effects of commitment to abstinence, positive moods, stress, and coping on relapse to cocaine use. *Journal of Consulting and Clinical Psychology, 59*, 526–532.

Hall, W., & Farrell, M. (1997). Comorbidity of mental disorders with substance misuse. *British Journal of Psychiatry, 171*, 4–5.

Hammersley, R., & Ditton, J. (1994). Cocaine careers in a sample of Scottish users. *Addiction Research, 2*, 51–70.

Hasin, D., Trautman, K., Miele, G., Samet, S., Smith, M., & Endicott, J. (1996). Psychiatric Research Interviews for Substance and Mental Disorders (PRISM): Reliability for substance abusers. *American Journal of Psychiatry, 153*, 1195–2001.

Hasin, D. S., Nunes, E., & Meydan, J. (2004). Comorbidity of alcohol, drug, and psychiatric disorders: epidemiology. In H. R. Kranzler & J. A. Tinsley (Eds.), *Dual diagnosis and psychiatric treatment: Substance abuse and comorbid disorders* (2nd ed., pp. 1–34). New York: Marcel Dekker.

Havens, J. R., & Strathdee, S. A. (2005). Antisocial personality disorder and opioid treatment outcomes: A review. *Addictive Disorders and Their Treatment, 4*, 85–97.

Hawkins, J., Catalano, R., Gillmore, M., & Wells, E. (1989). Skills training for drug abusers: Generalization, maintenance and effects on drug use. *Journal of Consulting and Clinical Psychology, 57*, 559–563.

Heather, N., Booth, P., & Luce, A. (1998). Impaired Control Scale: Cross-validation and relationships with treatment outcome. *Addiction, 93*, 761–771.

Heather, N., Brodie, J., Wale, S., Wilkinson, G., Luce, A., Webb, E., et al. (2000) A randomized controlled trial of Moderation-Oriented Cue Exposure. *Journal of Studies on Alcohol, 61*, 561–570.

Heather, N., & Dawe, S. (2005). Level of impaired control predicts outcome of moderation-oriented treatment for alcohol problems. *Addiction, 100*, 945–952.

Heather, N., Rollnick, S., Bell, A., & Richmond, R. (1996). Effects of brief counselling among heavy drinkers identified on general hospital wards. *Drug and Alcohol Review, 15*, 29–38.

Heather, N., Tebbutt, J. S., Mattick, R. P., & Zamir, R. (1993). Development of a scale for measuring impaired control over alcohol consumption: A preliminary report. *Journal of Studies on Alcohol, 54*, 700–709.

Heinälä, P., Alho, H., Kiianmaa, K., Lönnqvist, J. K., & Sinclair, J. D. (2001). Targeted use of naltrexone without prior detoxification in the treatment of alcohol dependence: A factorial double-blind placebo controlled trial. *Journal of Clinical Psychopharmacology, 21*, 287–292.

Helzer, J. E., & Pryzbeck, T. R. (1988). The co-occurrence of alcoholism with other psychiatric disorders in the general population and its impact on treatment. *Journal of Stidies on Alcohol, 49*, 219–224.

Hembree, E. A., & Foa, E. B. (2000). Posttraumatic stress disorder: psychological factors and psychosocial interventions. *Journal of Clinical Psychiatry, 61*(Suppl. 7), 33–39.

Henman, J. O., & Henman, S. (1990). Cognitive-perceptual reconstruction in the treatment of alcoholism. In C. M. Sterman (Ed.), *Neurolinguistic programming in alcoholism treatment* (pp. 105–124). New York: Haworth Press.

Henquet, C., Krabbendam, L., Spauwen, J., Kaplan, C., Lieb, R., Wittchen, H.U., et al. (2005). Prospective cohort study of cannabis use, predisposition for psychosis, and psychotic symptoms in young people. *British Medical Journal, 330,* 11–14.

Hesselbrock, M. N., Hesselbrock, V. N., & Epstein, E. E. (1999). Theories of etiology of alcohol and other drug use disorders. In B. S. McCrady & E. E. Epstein (Eds.), *Addictions: A comprehensive guidebook* (pp. 50–74). New York: Oxford University Press.

Hesselbrock, V. M., Hesselbrock, M. N., & Workman-Daniels, K. L. (1986). Effect of major depression and antisocial personality on alcoholism: Course and motivational patterns. *Journal of Studies on Alcohol, 47,* 207–212.

Hester, R. K., & Miller, W. R. (1989). Self-control training. In: R. K. Hester & W. R. Miller (Eds.), *Handbook of alcoholism treatment approaches: Effective alternatives* (pp. 141–149). New York: Pergamon.

Hettema, J., Steele, J., & Miller, W. R. (2005). Motivational interviewing. *Annual Review of Clinical Psychology, 1,* 91–111.

Hien, D. A., Cohen, L. R., Miele, G. M.,Litt, L.C., & Capstick, C.(2004). Promising empirically supported treatments for women with comorbid PTSD and substance use disorders. *American Journal of Psychiatry, 161,* 1426–1432.

Higgins, S. T., Alessi, S., & Dantona, R. L. (2000). Voucher-based incentives: A substance abuse treatment innovation. *Addictive Behaviors, 27,* 887–910.

Higgins, S. T., Budney, A. J., Bickel, W. K., Foerg, F. E., Ogden, D., & Badger, G. J. (1995). Outpatient behavioral treatment for cocaine dependence: One year outcome. *Experimental and Clinical Psychopharmacology, 3,* 205–212.

Higgins, S. T., Budney, A. J., Bickel, W. K., & Badger, G. J. (1994). Participation of significant others in outpatient behavioral treatment predicts greater cocaine abstinence. *American Journal of Drug and Alcohol Abuse, 1,* 47–56.

Higgins, S. T., & Wong, C. J. (1998). Treating cocaine abuse: What does research tell us? In S. T. Higgins & J. L. Katz (Eds.), *Cocaine abuse: Behavior, pharmacology, and clinical applications* (pp. 343–361). New York: Academic.

Higgins, S. T., Wong, C. J., Badger, G. J., Ogden, D. E. H., & Dantona, R. L. (2000). Contingent reinforcement increases cocaine abstinence during outpatient treatment and 1 year of follow-up. *Journal of Consulting and Clinical Psychology, 68*, 64–72.

Himmerich, H., Müller, M. J., Anghelescu, I., Klawe, L., Scheurich, A., & Szegedi, A. (2004). *German Journal of Psychology, 28*, 12–19.

Hingson, R. W., Heeren, T., Jamanka, A., & Howland, J. (2000). Age of drinking onset and unitential injury involvement after drinking. *Journal of the American Medical Association, 284*, 1527–1533.

Holahan, C. J., Moos, R. H., Holahan, C. K., Cronkite, R. C., & Randall, P. K. (2003). Drinking to cope and alcohol use and abuse in unipolar depression: A 10 year model. *Journal of Abnormal Psychology, 112*, 159–165.

Hollon, S. D., & Beck, A. T. (2004). Cognitive and cognitive-behavioral therapy. In M. Lambert (Ed.), *Bergin and Garfield's handbook of psychotherapy and behavior change* (5th ed., pp. 447–492). New York: Wiley.

Humphreys, K., Huebsch, P. D., Finney, J. W., & Moos, R. H. (1999). A comparative evaluation of substance abuse treatments: V. Treatment can enhance the effectiveness of self-help groups. *Alcoholism: Clinical and Experimental Research, 23*, 558–563.

Humphreys, K., Wing, S., McCarty, D., Chappel, J., Gallant, L., Haberle, B., et al. (2004). Self-help organizations for alcohol and drug problems: Toward evidence-based practice and policy. *Journal of Substance Abuse Treatment, 26*, 151–158.

Hunt, G. M., & Azrin, N. H. (1973). A community-reinforcement approach to alcoholism. *Behaviour Research and Therapy, 11*, 91–104.

Hyler, S. E. (1994). *The Personality Disorder Questionnaire-4+ (PDQ-4+)*. New York: New York State Psychiatric Institute.

Iguchi, M.Y., Belding, M. A., Morral, A. R., & Lamb, R. (1997). Reinforcing operants other than abstinence in drug abuse treatment: An effective alternative for reducing drug use. *Journal of Consulting and Clinical Psychology, 65*, 421–428.

Iguchi, M. Y., Lamb, R. J., Belding, M. A., Platt, J. J., Husband, S.D., & Morral, A. R. (1996). Contingent reinforcement of group participation versus abstinence in a methadone maintenance program. *Experimental and Clinical Psychopharmacology, 4*, 1–7.

Inskip, H. M., Harris, E. C., & Barraclough, B. (1998). Lifetime risk of suicide for affective disorder, alcoholism and schizophrenia. *British Journal of Psychiatry, 172*, 35–37.

Irvin, J. E., Bowers, C. A., Dunn, M. E., & Wang, M. C. (1999). Efficacy of relapse prevention: A meta-analytic review. *Journal of Consulting and Clinical Psychology, 67*, 563–570.

Ito, J. R., Donovan, D. M., & Hall, J. J. (1988). Relapse prevention in alcohol aftercare: Effects on drinking outcome, change process, and aftercare attendance. *British Journal of Addiction, 83,* 171–181.

James, W., Preston, N. J., Koh, G., Spencer, C., Kisely, S. R., & Castle, D. J. (2004). A group intervention which assists patients with dual diagnosis reduce their drug use: A randomized controlled trial. *Psychological Medicine, 34,* 983–990.

Jerrell, J. M., & Ridgeley, M. S. (1995). Comparative effectiveness of three approaches to serving people with severe mental illness and substance abuse disorders. *Journal of Nervous and Mental Disease, 183,* 566–576.

Johnson, H. L., & Johnson, P. B. (1995). Children's alcohol-related cognitions: Positive versus negative alcohol effects. *Journal of Alcohol and Drug Education, 40,* 112.

Johnson, N. P., Phelps, G. L., & McCuen, S. K. (1990). Never try to carry a drunk by yourself: Effective use of self-help groups. *Journal of the South Carolina Medical Association, 86,* 7–31.

Johnson, R. E., Jaffe, J. H., & Fudala, P. J. (1992). A controlled trial of buprenorphine treatment for opioid dependence. *Journal of the American Medical Association, 267,* 2750–2755.

Johnson, S. D., Phelps, D. L., & Cottler, L. B. (2004). The association of sexual dysfunction and substance use among a community epidemiological sample. *Archives of Sexual Behavior, 33,* 55–63.

Jones, H. E., Haug, N. A., Silverman, K., Stitzer, M. L., & Svikis, D. S. (2001). The effectiveness of incentives in enhancing treatment attendance and drug abstinence in methadone maintained pregnant women. *Drug and Alcohol Dependence, 61,* 297–306.

Jones, H. E., Strain, E. C., Bigelow, G. E., Walsh, S. L., Stitzer, M. L., Eissenberg, T. E., et al. (1998). Induction with levomethadyl acetate: Safety and efficacy. *Archives of General Psychiatry, 55,* 729–736.

Jones, H. E., Wong, C. J., Tuten, M., & Stitzer, M. L. (2005). Reinforcement-based therapy: 12-month evaluation of an outpatient drug-free treatment for heroin abusers. *Drug and Alcohol Dependence, 79,* 119–128.

Kadden, R. M., Cooney, N. L., Getter, H., & Litt, M. D. (1989). Matching alcoholics to coping skills or interactional therapies: Posttreatment results. *Journal of Consulting and Clinical Psychology, 57,* 698–704.

Kamon, J., Budney, A., & Stanger, C. (2005). A contingency management intervention for adolescent marijuana abuse and conduct problems. *American Academy of Child and Adolescent Psychiatry, 44,* 513–521.

Karkowski, L. M., Prescott, C. A., & Kendler, K. S. (2000). Multivariate assessment of factors influencing illicit substance use in twins from female-female pairs. *American Journal of Medical Genetics, 96,* 665–670.

Karno, M. P., & Longabaugh, R. (2003). Patient depressive symptoms and therapist focus on emotional material: A new look at Project MATCH. *Journal of Studies on Alcohol, 64,* 607–615.

Karno, M. P., & Longabaugh, R. (2005). Less directiveness by therapists improves drinking outcomes of reactant clients in alcoholism treatment. *Journal of Consulting and Clinical Psychology, 73,* 262–267.

Katz, E. C., Gruber, K., Chutuape, M. A., & Stitzer, M. L. (2001). Reinforcement-based outpatient treatment for opiate and cocaine abusers. *Journal of Substance Abuse, 20,* 93–98.

Kavanagh, D. J., Waghorn, G., Jenner, J., Chant, D. C., Carr, V., Evans, M., et al. (2004). Demographic and clinical correlates of comorbid substance use disorders in psychosis: Multivariate analyses from an epidemiological sample. *Schizophrenia Research, 66,* 115–124.

Kellam, S. G., Brown, C., Rubin, B., & Ensminger, M. E. (1983). Paths leading to teenage psychiatric symptoms and substance use: Developmental epidemiological studies in Woodlawn. In S. Cuze, F. Earls, and J. Barrett (Eds.), *Childhood psychopathology and development* (pp. 17–51). New York: Raven.

Kelly, J. F. (2003). Self-help for substance-use disorders: History, effectiveness, knowledge gaps, and research opportunities. *Clinical Psychology Review, 23,* 639–663.

Kelly, T. M., Cornelius, J. R., & Lynch, K. G. (2002). Psychiatric and substance use disorders as risk factors for attempted suicide among adolescents: A case-control study. *Suicide and Life Threatening Behavior, 32,* 301–309.

Kendler, K. S., Jacobson, K. C., Prescott, C. A., & Neale, M. C. (2003). Specificity of genetic and environmental risk factors for use and abuse/dependence of cannabis, cocaine, hallucinogens, sedatives, stimulants, and opiates in male twins. *American Journal of Psychiatry, 160,* 687–695.

Kendler, K. S., Prescott, C. A., Myers, J., & Neale, M. C. (2003). The structure of genetic and environmental risk factors for common psychiatric and substance use disorders in men and women. *Archives of General Psychiatry, 60,* 929–937.

Kessler, R. C. (2004). Impact of substance abuse on the diagnosis, course, and treatment of mood disorders: The epidemiology of dual diagnosis. *Biological Psychiatry, 56,* 730–737.

Kessler, R. C., Crum, R. M., Warner, L. A., Nelson, C. B., Schulen-berg, J., & Anthony, J. C. (1997). The lifetime co-occurrence of *DSM-III-R* alcohol abuse and dependence with other psychiatric disorders in the National Comorbidity Survey. *Archives of General Psychiatry, 54,* 313–321.

Kessler, R. C., Nelson, C. B., McGonagle, M. A., Edlund, M. B., Frank, R. G., & Leaf, P. J. (1996). The epidemiology of co-occurring addic-tive and mental disorders: Implications for prevention and service utilization. *American Journal of Orthopsychiatry, 66,* 17–31.

Khantzian, E. J., & Mack, J. E. (1994). Alcoholics Anonymous and con-temporary psychodynamic theory. In M. Galanter (Ed.), *Recent developments in alcoholism, 7,* pp. 67–89. New York: Plenum.

Kidorf, M., Disney, E. R., King, V. L., Neufeld, K., Beilenson, P. L., & Brooner, R. K. (2004). Prevalence of psychiatric and substance use disorders in opioid abusers in a community syringe exchange pro-gram. *Drug and Alcohol Dependence, 74,* 115–122.

Kiefer, F., Jahn, H., Tarnaske, T., Helwig, H., Briken, P., Holzbach, R., et al. (2003). Comparing and combining naltrexone and acampro-sate in relapse prevention of alcohol a double-blind, placebo-con-trolled study. *Archives of General Psychiatry, 60,* 92–99.

Killeen, T. K., Brady, K. T., Gold, P. B., Simpson, K. N., Faldowski, R. A., Tyson, C., et al. (2004). Effectiveness of naltrexone in a com-munity treatment program. *Alcoholism: Clinical and Experimen-tal Research, 28,* 1710–1717.

Kilpatrick, D. G., Acierno, R., Resnick, H. S., Saunders, B. E., & Best, C. L. (1997). A 2-year longitudinal analysis of the relationships between violent assault and substance use in women. *Journal of Consulting and Clinical Psychology, 65,* 834–837.

Kim-Cohen, J., Caspi, A., Moffitt, T. E., Harrington, H., Milne, B. J., & Poulton, R. (2003). Prior juvenile diagnoses in adults with mental disorder: Developmental follow-back of a prospective-longitudinal cohort. *Archives of General Psychiatry, 60,* 709–717.

King, A. C., Volpicelli, J. R., Frazer, A., & O'Brien, C. P. (1997). Effect of naltrexone on subjective alcohol response in subjects at high and low risk for future alcohol dependence. *Psychopharmacology, 129,* 15–22.

King, V. L., Brooner, R. K., Kidorf, M. S., Stoller, K. B., & Mirsky, A. F. (1999). Attention deficit hyperactivity disorder and treatment outcome in opioid abusers entering treatment. *Journal of Nervous and Mental Disease, 187,* 487–495.

Kirby, K. C., Marlowe, D. B., Festinger, D. S., Lamb R. J., & Platt, J. J. (1998). Schedule of voucher delivery influences initiation of cocaine abstinence. *Journal of Consulting and Clinical Psychology, 66,* 761–767.

Kleber, H. D. (2005). Future advances in addiction treatment. *Clinical Neuroscience Research, 5,* 201–205.

Knopik, V. S., Heath, A. C., Madden, P. A. F., Bucholz, K. K., Slutske, W. S., Nelson, E. C., et al. (2004). Genetic effects on alcohol dependence risk: Re-evaluating the importance of psychiatric and other heritable risk factors. *Psychological Medicine, 34,* 1519–1530.

Koob, G. F. (2000). Stress, corticotropin-releasing factor and drug addiction. *Annals of the New York Academy of Science, 897,* 27–45.

Kooij, J. J. S., Burger, H., Boonstra, A. M., Van der Linden, P. D., Kalma, L. E., & Buitelaar, J. K. (2004). Efficacy and safety of methylphenidate in 45 adults with attention-deficit/hyperactivity disorder (ADHD). A randomised placebo-controlled double-blind cross-over trial. *Psychological Medicine, 34,* 973–982.

Kosten, T. R. (2005). Advances in pharmacotherapy of stimulant dependence: From alcohol antagonist to Xenova vaccines. *Clinical Neuroscience Research, 5,* 169–173.

Kosten, T. R., & O'Connor, P. G. (2003). Management of drug and alcohol withdrawal. *New England Journal of Medicine, 348,* 1786–1795.

Kownacki, R. J., & Shadish, W. R. (1999). Does Alcoholics Anonymous work? The results from a meta-analysis of controlled experiments. *Substance Use and Misuse, 34,* 1897–1916.

Kranzler, H. R., & Van Kirk, J. (2001). Efficacy of naltrexone and acamprosate for alcoholism treatment: A meta-analysis. *Alcohol Clinical and Experimental Research, 25,* 1335–1341.

Kranzler, H. R., Wesson, D. R., & Billot, L. (Drug Abuse Sciences Naltrexone Depot Study Group). (2004). Naltrexone depot for treatment of alcohol dependence: A multicenter, randomized, placebo-controlled clinical trial. *Alcohol Clinical and Experimental Research, 28,* 1051–1059.

Krystal, J. H., Cramer, J. A., Krol, W. F., Kirk, G. F., & Rosenheck, R.A. (2001). Naltrexone in the treatment of alcohol dependence. *New England Journal of Medicine, 345,* 1734–1739.

Kushner, M. G., Abrams, K., & Brochardt, C. (2000). The relationship between anxiety disorders and alcohol use disorders: A review of major perspectives and findings. *Clinical Psychology Review, 20,* 149–171.

Laberg, J. C., & Ellertsen, B. (1987). Psychophysiological indicators of craving in alcoholics: Effects of cue exposure. *British Journal of Addiction, 82,* 1341–1348.

Lambert, M. (Ed.). (2004). *Bergin and Garfield's handbook of psychotherapy and behavior change* (5th ed.). New York: Wiley.

Langeland, W., Draijer, N., & Van den Brink, W. (2004). Psychiatric comorbidity in treatment-seeking alcoholics: The role of childhood trauma and perceived parental dysfunction. *Alcoholism: Clinical and Experimental Research, 28,* 441–447.

Larimer, M. E., Palmer, R. S., & Marlatt, G. A. (1999). Relapse prevention: An overview of Marlatt's cognitive-behavioral model. *Alcohol Health Research World, 23,* 151–160.

Laudet, A. (2003). Attitudes and beliefs about 12-step groups among addiction treatment clients and clinicians: Toward identifying obstacles to participation. *Substance Use and Misuse, 14,* 2017–2047.

Laudet, A., & White, W. (2005). An exploratory investigation of the association between clinicians' attitudes toward twelve-step groups and referral rates. *Alcoholism Treatment Quarterly, 23,* 31–45.

Lejuez, B. C. W., Daughters, S. B., Rosenthal, M. Z., & Lynch, T. R. (2005). Impulsivity as a common process across borderline personality and substance use disorders. *Clinical Psychology Review, 25,* 790–812.

Leshner, A. I. (1998). Drug addiction research: Moving toward the 21st century. *Drug and Alcohol Dependence, 51,* 5–7.

Levin, F. R., & Hennessy, G. (2004). Bipolar disorder and substance abuse. *Biological Psychiatry, 56,* 738–748.

Lewinsohn, P. M. (1975). The behavioral study and treatment of depression. In M. Hersen, R. M. Eisler, & P. M. Miller (Eds.), *Progress in behavior modification* (Vol. 1, pp. 19–65). New York: Academic.

Lewinsohn, P. M., Rohde, P., Seeley, J. R., Klein, D. N., & Goblib, I. H. (2000). Natural course of adolescent major depressive disorder in a community sample: Predictors of recurrence in young adults. *American Journal of Psychiatry, 157,* 1584–1591.

Lewis, M. W., & Petry, N. M. (2005). Contingency management treatments that reinforce completion of goal-related activities: Participation in family activities and its association with outcomes. *Drug and Alcohol Dependence, 79,* 267–271.

Liberman, R.P. (1988). Social skills training. In R.P.Liberman (Ed.), *Psychiatric rehabilitation of chronic mental patients.* Washington: American Psychiatric Press.

Linehan, M. M. (1993). *Cognitive-behavioral treatment for borderline personality disorder: The dialectics of effective treatment.* New York: Guilford.

Linehan, M. M., Amstrong, H. E., Suarez, A., Allmon, D. J., & Heard, H. L. (1991). Cognitive-behavioral treatment of chronically suicidal borderline patients. *Archives of General Psychiatry, 48,* 1060–1064.

Linehan, M. M., Schmidt, H., Dimeff, L. A., Craft, J. C., Kanter, J., & Comtois, K. A. (1999). Dialectical behavior therapy for patients with borderline personality disorder and drug-dependence. *American Journal on Addictions, 8,* 279–292.

Liskow, B. I., & Goodwin, D. W. (1987). Pharmacologic treatment of alcohol intoxication, withdrawal, and dependence: A critical review. *Journal of Studies on Alcohol, 48,* 356–370.

Litman, G. K., Stapleton, J., Oppenheim, A. N., O'Brien, C. P., Childress, A. R., & McLellan, T. (1990). Integrating systematic cue exposure with standard treatment in recovering drug dependent patients. *Addictive Behaviors, 15,* 355–365.

Litt, M. D., Babor, T. F., Del Boca, F. K., Kadden, R. M., & Cooney, N. L. (1992). Types of alcoholics, II: Application of an empirically derived typology to treatment matching. *Archives of General Psychiatry, 49,* 609–614.

Litt, M. D., Kadden, R. M., Cooney, N. L., & Kabela, E. (2003). Coping skills and treatment outcomes in cognitive-behavioral and interactional group therapy for alcoholism. *Journal of Consulting and Clinical Psychology, 71,* 118–128.

Litt, M. D., Kadden, R. M., Stephens, R. S., & the Marijuana Treatment Project Research Group (2005). Coping and self-efficacy in marijuana treatment: Results from the Marijuana Treatment Project. *Journal of Consulting and Clinical Psychology, 73,* 1015–1025.

Liu, I. C., Blacker, D. L., Xu, R., Fitzmaurice, G., Lyons, M. J., & Tsuang, M. T. (2004). Genetic and environmental contributions to the development of alcohol dependence in male twins. *Archives of General Psychiatry, 61,* 897–903.

Longabaugh, R., Wirtz, P. W., Beattie, M. C., Noel, N., & Stout, R. L. (1995). Matching treatment focus to patient social investment and support: 18 month follow-up results. *Journal of Consulting and Clinical Psychology, 63,* 296–307.

Longabaugh, R., Wirtz, P. W., Zweben, A., & Stout, R. (1998). Network support for drinking, Alcoholics Anonymous and long-term matching effects. *Addiction, 93,* 1313–1333.

Longshore, D., Annon, J., Anglin, M. D., & Rawson, R. A. (2005). Levo-alpha-acetylmethadol (LAAM) versus methadone: Treatment retention and opiate use. *Addiction, 100,* 1131–1139.

Loranger, A. W. (1999). *International Personality Disorder Eximina-tion Manual:* DSM-IV *Module.* Washington, DC: American Psychiatric Press.

Lussier, J. P., Heil, S. H., Mongeon, J. A., Badger, G. J., & Higgins, S. T. (2006). A meta-analysis of voucher-based reinforcement therapy for substance use disorders. *Addiction, 101,* 192–203.

Luty, J. (2004). Treatment preferences of opiate-dependent patients. *Psychiatric Bulletin, 28,* 47–50.

Macleod, J., Oakes, R., Copello, A., Crome, I., Egger, M., & Hickman, M. (2004). Psychological and social sequelae of cannabis and other illicit drug use by young people: A systematic review of longitudinal, general population studies. *Lancet, 363,* 1579–1588.

MacPhillamy, D. J., & Lewinsohn, P. M. (1982). The Pleasant Events Schedule. *Journal of Consulting and Clinical Psychology, 50,* 363–380.

Magura, S., Laudet, A. B., Mahmood, D., Rosenblum, A., & Knight, E. (2002). Adherence to medication regimens and participation in dual focus self-help. *Psychiatric Sevices, 53,* 310–316.

Maisto, S. A., Carey, M. P., Carey, K. B., Gleason J. G., & Gordon, C. M. (2000). Use of the AUDIT and the DAST-10 to identify alcohol and drug use disorders among adults with a severe and persistent mental illness. *Psychological Assessment, 12,* 186–192.

Maisto, S. A., Conigliaro, J., McNeil, M., Kraemer, K., Conigliaro, R. L.., & Kelley, M. E. (2001). Effects of two types of brief intervention and readiness to change on alcohol use in hazardous drinkers. *Journal of Studies on Alcohol, 62,* 605–614.

Maisto, S.A., Zywiak, W. H., & Connors, G. J. (in press). Course of functioning 1 year following admission for treatment of alcohol use disorders. *Addictive Behaviors.*

Margolese, H. C., Malchy, L., Negrete, J. C., Tempier, R., & Gill, K. (2004). Drug and alcohol use among patients with schizophrenia and related psychoses: Levels and consequences. *Schizophrenia Research, 67,* 157–166.

Mann, K. (2004). Pharmacotherapy of alcohol dependence: A review of clinical data. *CNS Drugs, 18,* 485–504.

Mann, K., Lehert, P., & Morgan, M. Y. (2004). The efficacy of acamprosate in maintaining abstinence in alcohol dependent individuals: Results of a meta-analysis. *Journal of Studies Alcohol, 65,* 136–139.

Marissen, M. A. E., Franken, I. H. A., Blanken, P., Van den Brink, W., & Hendriks, V. M. (2005). Cue eposure therapy for opiate dependent clients. *Journal of Substance Use, 10,* 97–105.

Marlatt, G. A. (1996a). Harm reduction: Come as you are. *Addictive Behaviors, 21*, 779–788.

Marlatt, G. A. (1996b). Taxonomy of high-risk situations for alcohol relapse: Evolution and development of a cognitive-behavioral model. *Addiction, 91*(Suppl.), S37–S49.

Marlatt, G. A., & Gordon, J. R. (1980). Determinants of relapse: Implications for the maintenance of behavior change. In P. Davidson (Ed.), *Behavioral medicine: Changing health lifestyles.* New York: Brunner/Mazel.

Marlatt, G. A., & Gordon, J. R. (Eds). (1985). *Relapse prevention: Maintenance strategies in the treatment of addictive behaviors.* New York: Guilford.

Marlatt, G. A., Larimer, M. E., Baer, J. S., & Quigley, L. A. (1993). Harm reduction for alcohol problems: Moving beyond the controlled drinking controversy. *Behavior Therapy, 24*, 461–504.

Marlatt, G. A., & Roberts, L. J. (1998). Introduction: Special Issue. *In-session-Psychotherapy in Practice, 4*, 1–8.

Marlowe, D. B., Kirby, K. C., Festinger, D. S., Husband, S. D., & Platt, J .J. (1997). Impact of comorbid personality disorders and personality disorder symptoms on outcomes of behavioral treatment for cocaine dependence. *Journal of Nervous and Mental Disease, 185*, 483–490.

Marsch, L. A., Bickel, W. K., Badger, G. J., & Jacobs, E. A. (2005). Buprenorphine treatment for opioid dependence: The relative efficacy of daily, twice and thrice weekly dosing. *Drug and Alcohol Dependence, 77*, 195–204.

Marsh, A., Smith, L., Saunders, B., & Piek, J. (2002). The Impaired Control Scale: Confirmation of factor structure and psychometric properties for social drinkers and drinkers in alcohol treatment. *Addiction, 97*, 1339–1346.

Martin, D. J., Graske, P. J., & Davis, M. K. (2000). Relation of the therapeutic alliance with outcome and other variables: A meta-analytic review. *Journal of Consulting and Clinical Psychology, 68*, 438–450.

Martino, S., Carroll, K. M., Kostas, D., Perkins, J., & Rounsaville, B. J. (2002). Dual diagnosis motivational interviewing: A modification of motivational interviewing for substance abusing patients with psychotic disorders. *Journal of Substance Abuse and Treatment, 23*, 297–308.

Martino, S., Carroll, K. M., O'Malley, S. S., & Rounsaville, B. J. (2000). Motivational interviewing with psychiatrically ill substance abusing patients. *American Journal on Addiction, 9* , 88–91.

Mason, B. J., Salvato, F. R., Williams, L. D., Ritvo, E. C., & Cutler, R. B. (1999). A double-blind, placebo-controlled study of oral nalmefene for alcohol dependence. *Archives of General Psychiatry, 56,* 719–724.

Mattick, R. P., Kimber, J., Breen, C., & Davoli, M. (2002). Buprenorphine maintenance versus placebo or methadone maintenance for opioid dependence. *Cochrane Database Systematic Reviews, 4,* CD002207.

Maude-Griffin, P. M., Hohenstein, J. M., Humfleet, G. L., Reilly, P. M., Tusel, D. J., & Hall, S. M. (1998). Superior efficacy of cognitive-behavioral therapy for crack cocaine abusers: Main and matching effects. *Journal of Consulting and Clinical Psychology, 66,* 832–837.

Mayfield, D., McLeod, G., & Hall, P. (1974). The CAGE questionnaire: Validation of a new alcoholism screening instrument. *American Journal of Psychiatry, 13,* 1121–1123.

McClanahan, S. F., McClelland, G. M., Abram, K. M., & Teplin, A. (1999). Pathways into prostitution among female jail detainees and their implications for mental health service. *Psychiatric Services, 50,* 1606–1613.

McCrady, B. S. (1994). Alcoholics Anonymous and behavior therapy: Can habit be treated as diseases? Can diseases be treated as habits? *Journal of Consulting and Clinical Psychology, 62,* 1159–1166.

McCrady, B. S., Epstein, E. E., & Kahler, C. W. (2004). Alcoholics Anonymous and relapse prevention maintenance strategies after conjoint behavioral alcohol treatment for men: 18-month outcomes. *Journal of Consulting and Clinical Psychology, 72,* 870–878.

McCrady, B. S., Noel, N. E., & Abrams, D. B. (1986). Comparative effectiveness of three types of spouse involvement in outpatient behavioral alcoholism treatment. *Journal of Studies on Alcohol, 47,* 459–467.

McCrady, B. S., & Smith, D. E. (1986). Implications of cognitive impairment for the treatment of alcoholism. *Alcoholism: Clinical & Experimental Research, 10,* 145–149.

McCrady, B. S., Stout, R., Noel, N., Abrams, D., & Nelson, H. F. (1991). Effectiveness of 3 types of spouse-involved behavioral alcoholism-treatment. *British Journal of Addiction, 86,* 1415–1424.

McCusker, C. G., & Brown, K. (1990). Alcohol-predictive cues enhance tolerance to and precipitate "craving" for alcohol in social drinkers. *Journal of Studies on Alcohol, 51,* 494–499.

McDowell, D., Nunes, E. V., Seracini, A. M., Rothenberg, J., Vosburg, S. K., Ma, G. J., & Petkov, E. (2005). Desipramine treatment of cocaine-dependent patients with depression: A placebo-controlled trial. *Drug and Alcohol Dependence, 80,* 209–221.

McGovern, M. P., Fox, T. S., Xie, H., & Drake, R. E. (2004). A survey of clinical practices and readiness to adopt evidence-based practices: Dissemination research in an addiction treatment system. *Journal of Substance Abuse Treatment, 26,* 305–312.

McGue, M. (1999). Behavioral genetic models of alcoholism and drinking. In K. E. Leonard & H. T. Blane (Eds.), *Psychological theories of drinking and alcoholism* (pp. 372–421). New York: The Guilford Press.

McIntire, D. (2000). How well does A.A. work? An analysis of published A.A. surveys 1968–1996 and related analyses/comments. *Alcoholism Treatment Quarterly, 18,* 1–18.

McKay, J. R. (2005a). Is there a case for extended interventions for alcohol and drug use disorders? *Addictions, 100,* 1594–1610.

McKay, J. R. (2005b). Co-occurring substance dependence and depression: Practical implications and next questions. *Addiction, 100,* 1755–1762.

McKay, J. R., Alterman, A. I., Cacciola, J. S., Mulvaney, F. D., & O'Brien, C. P. (2000). Prognostic significance of antisocial personality in cocaine-dependent patients entering continuing care. *Journal of Nervous and Mental Disease, 188,* 287–296.

McKay, J. R., Alterman, A. I., Cacciola, J. S., Rutherford, M. J., O'Brien, C. P., & Koppenhaver, J. (1997). Group counseling versus individualized relapse prevention aftercare following intensive outpatient treatment for cocaine dependence: Initial results. *Journal of Consulting and Clinical Psychology, 65,* 778–788.

McKay, J. R., Lynch, K. G., Shepard, D. S., Morgenstern, J., Forman, R. F., & Pettinati, H. M. (2005). Do patient characteristics and initial progress in treatment moderate the effectiveness of telephone-based continuing care for substance use disorders? *Addiction, 100,* 216–226.

McKay, J. R., Lynch, K. G., Shepard, D. S., & Pettinati, H. M. (2005). The effectiveness of telephone-based continuing care for alcohol and cocaine dependence. *Archives of General Psychiatry, 62,* 199–207.

McKay, J.R., Maisto, S.A., & O'Farrell, T.J. (1993). End-of-treatment self-efficacy, aftercare, and drinking outcomes of alcoholic men. *Alcoholism:Clinical and Experimental Research, 17,* 1078–1083.

McKay, J. R., Pettinati, H. M., Morrison, R., Feeley, M., Mulvaney, F. D., & Gallop, R. (2002). Relation of depression diagnoses to 2-year outcomes in cocaine dependent patients in a randomized continuing care study. *Psychology of Additive Behaviors, 16,* 225–235.

McKay, J. R., & Weiss, R. V. (2001). A review of temporal effects and outcome predictors in substance abuse treatment studies with long-term follow-ups: Preliminary results and methodological issues. *Evaluation Review, 25,* 113–161.

McKellar, J., Stewart, E., & Humphreys, K. (2003). Alcoholics Anonymous involvement and positive alcohol-related outcomes: Cause, consequence, or just a correlate? *Journal of Consulting and Clinical Psychology, 71,* 302–308.

McLellan, A. T., Carise, D., & Kleber, H. D. (2003). The national addiction treatment infrastructure: Can it support the public's demand for quality care? *Journal of Substance Abuse Treatment, 25,* 117–121.

McLellan, A. T., Kushner, H., Metzger, D., Peters, R., Smith, I., Grissom, G., et al. (1992). The fifth edition of the Addiction Severity Index. *Journal of Substance Abuse Treatment, 9,* 199–213.

McNamara, C., Schumacher, J. E., Milby, J. B., Wallace, D., & Usdan, S. (2001). Prevalence of nonpsychotic mental disorders does not affect treatment outcome in a homeless cocaine-dependent sample. *American Journal of Drug and Alcohol Abuse, 27,* 91–106.

Meichenbaum, D. (1977). *Cognitive-behavior modification: An integrative approach.* New York: Plenum.

Meier, P. S., Barrowclough, C., & Donmall, M. C. (2005). The role of the therapeutic alliance in the treatment of substance misuse: A critical review of the literature. *Addiction, 100,* 304–316.

Meier, P. S., Donmall, M. C., Barrowclough, C., McElduff, P., & Heller, R. F. (2005). Predicting the early therapeutic alliance in the treatment of drug misuse. *Addiction, 100,* 500–511.

Merikangas, K. R., Metha, R. L., Molnar, B. E., Walters, E. E., Swendsen, J. D., Aguilar-Gaxiola, S., et al. (1998). Comorbidity of substance use disorders with mood and anxiety disorders: Results of the international consortium in psychiatric epidemiology. *Addictive Behaviors, 23,* 893–907.

Merikangas, K.R., Stolar, M., Stevens, D. E., Goulet, J., Preisig, M.A., Fenton, B., Zhang, H., O'Malley, S.S., & Rounsaville, B.J. (1998). Familial transmission of substance use disorders. *Archives of General Psychiatry, 55,* 973–979.

Merline, A. C., O'Malley, P. M., Schulenberg, J. E., Bachman, J. G., & Johnston, L. D. (2004). Substance use among adults 35 years of age: Prevalence, adulthood predictors, and impact of adolescent substance use. *American Journal of Public Health, 94*, 96–102.

Mertens, J. R., Lu, Y. W., Parthasarathy, S., Moore, C., & Weisner, C. M. (2003). Medical and psychiatric conditions of alcohol and drug treatment patients in an HMO: Comparison with matched controls. *Archives of Internal Medicine, 163*, 2511–2517.

Metzger, D. S., Woody, C. E., McLellan, A. R., O'Brien, C. P., Druley, P., Navaline, et al. (1993). Human immunodeficiency virus seroconversion among intravenous drug users in- and out-of-treatment: An 18 month prospective follow-up. *Journal of Acquired Immune Deficiency Syndrome, 6*, 1049–1056.

Meyer, R. E. (2001). Finding paradigms for the future of alcholism research: An interdisciplinary perspective. *Alcoholism: Clinical and Experimental Research, 25*, 1393–1406.

Meyers, J. R., Miller, W. R., Smith, J. E., & Tonigan, J. S. (2002). A randomized trail of two methods for engaging treatment refusing drug users through concerned significant others. *Journal of Consulting and Clinical Psychology, 70*, 1182–1185.

Meyers, R. J., and Smith, J. E. (1995). *Clinical guide to alcohol treatment: The community reinforcement approach.* New York: Guilford.

Milby, J. B., Schumacher, E., McNamara, C., Wallace, D., Usdan, S., McGill, T., et al. (2000). Initiating abstinence in cocaine abusing dually diagnosed homeless persons. *Drug and Alcohol Dependence, 60*, 55–67.

Miller, N. S., & Hoffman, N. G. (1995). Addictions treatment outcomes. *Alcoholism Treatment Quarterly, 12*, 41–55.

Miller, W. R. (1983). Motivational interviewing with problem drinkers. *Behavioural Psychotherapy, 11*, 441–448.

Miller, W. R. (1987). Motivation and treatment goals. *Drugs and Society, 1*, 133–151.

Miller, W. R. (1996). Motivational interviewing: Research, practice and puzzles. *Addictive Behaviors, 21*, 835–842.

Miller, W. R., Andrews, N. R., Wilbourne, P., & Bennett, M. E. (1998). A wealth of alternatives. In W. R. Miller & N. Heather (Eds.), *Treating addictive behaviors* (2nd ed., pp. 203–216) New York: Springer.

Miller, W. R., Benefield, G., & Tonigan, J. S. (1993). Enhancing motivation for change in problem drinking: A controlled comparison of two therapist styles. *Journal of Consulting and Clinical Psychology, 61*, 455–461.

Miller, W. R., Leckman, A. L., Delaney, H. D., & Tinkcom, M. (1992). Long-term follow-up of behavioral self-control training. *Journal of Studies on Alcohol, 53,* 249–261.

Miller, W. R., Meyers, R. J., & Tonigan, J. S. (1999). Engaging the unmotivated in treatment for alcohol problems: A comparison of three strategies for intervention through family members. *Journal of Consulting and Clinical Psychology, 67,* 688–697.

Miller, W. R., Meyers, R. J., Tonigan, J. S., & Hester, R. K. (1992). *Effectiveness of the community reinforcement approach. Final progress report to the National Institute on Alcohol Abuse and Alcoholism.* Albuquerque: University of New Mexico Center on Alcoholism, Substance Abuse, and Addictions.

Miller, W. R., & Rollnick, S. (1991). *Motivational interviewing: Preparing people to change addictive behavior.* New York: Guilford.

Miller, W. R., & Rollnick, S. (2002). *Motivational interviewing: Preparing people for change* (2nd ed.). New York: Guilford.

Miller, W. R., & Tonigan, J. S. (1996). Assessing drinkers' motivation for change: The stages of change readiness and treatment eagerness scale (SOCRATES). *Psychology of Addictive Behaviors, 10,* 81–89.

Miller, W. R., Westerberg, V. S., Harris, R. J., & Tonigan, J. S. (1996). What predicts relapse? Prospective testing of antecedent models. *Addiction, 91* (Suppl.), 155–172.

Miller, W. R., Yahne, C. E., Moyers, T. B., Martinez, J., & Pirritano, M. (2004). A randomized trial of methods to help clinicians learn motivational interviewing. *Journal of Consulting and Clinical Psychology, 72,* 1050–1062.

Miller, W. R., Yahne, C. E., & Tonigan, J. S. (2003). Motivational interviewing in drug abuse services: A randomized trial. *Journal of Consulting and Clinical Psychology, 71,* 754–763.

Moak, D. H., & Anton, R. F. (1999). Alcohol. In B. S. McCrady & E. E. Epstein (Eds.), *Addictions: A comprehensive handbook* (pp. 75–94). New York: Oxford University Press.

Molina, B. S. G., Bukstein, O. G., & Lynch, K. G. (2002). Attention-deficit/hyperactivity disorder and conduct disorder symptomatology in adolescents with alcohol use disorder. *Psychology of Addictive Behaviors, 16,* 161–164.

Montgomery, H.A., Miller, W. R., & Tonigan, J. S. (1995). Does Alcoholics Anonymous involvement predict treatment outcome? *Journal of Substance Abuse Treatment, 12,* 241–246.

Monti, P. M., Abrams, D. B., Binkoff, J. A., Zwick, W. R., Liepman, M. R., Nirenberg, T. D., et al. (1990). Communication skills training, communication skills training with family and cognitive-behavioral mood management training for alcoholics. *Journal of Studies on Alcohol, 51,* 263–270.

Monti, P. M., Abrams, D. B., Kadden, R. M., & Cooney, N. L. (1989). *Treating alcohol dependence: A coping skills training guide in the treatment of alcoholism.* New York: Guilford.

Monti, P., & Rohsenow, D. J. (1999). Coping skills training and cue exposure therapy in the treatment of alcoholism. *Alcohol Research and Health, 23,* 107–115.

Monti, P. M., Rohsenow, D. J., Michalec, E., Martin, R. A., & Abrams, D. B. (1997). Brief coping skills treatment for cocaine abuse: substance use outcomes at 3 months. *Addiction, 92,* 1717–1728.

Monti, P. M., Rohsenow, D. J., Rubonis, A. V., Niaura, R. S., Sirota, A. D., & Colby, S. M. (1993). Alcohol cue reactivity: Effects of detoxification and extended exposure. *Journal of Studies on Alcohol, 54,* 235–245.

Monti, P. M., Rohsenow, D. J., Swift, R. M., Gulliver, S. B., Colby, S. M., Mueller, T. I., et al. (2001). Naltrexone and cue exposure with coping and communication skills training for alcoholics: Treatment process and 1-year outcomes. *Alcoholism: Clinical and Experimental Research, 25,* 1634–1647.

Moos, R. H., Finney, J. W., Ouimette, P. C., & Suchinsky, R. T. A. (1999). A comparative evaluation of substance abuse treatment: 1. Treatment orientation, amount of care, and 1 year outcomes. *Alcoholism: Clinical and Experimantal Research, 25,* 529–536.

Moos, R. H., & Moos, B. S. (2004). The interplay between help-seeking and alcohol-related outcomes: Divergent processes for professional treatment and self-help groups. *Drug and Alcohol Dependence, 75,* 155–164.

Morgenstern, J., Labouvie, E., McCrady, B. S., Kahler, C. W., & Frey, R. M. (1997). Affiliation with Alcoholic Anonymous after treatment: A study on its therapeutic effects and mechanisms of action. *Journal of Consulting and Clinical Psychology, 65,* 768–777.

Morgenstern, J., & Longabauch, R. (2000). Cognitive-behavioral treatment for alcohol dependence: A review of evidence for its hypothesized mechanisms of action. *Addiction, 95,* 1475–1490.

Moser, A., & Annis, H. (1995). The role in coping in relapse crisis outcome: A prospective study of treated alcoholics. *Addiction, 91,* 1101–1114.

Moyers, T. B., & Waldorf, V. A. (2004). Motivational interviewing: Destination, direction, and means. In F. Rotgers, J. Morgenstern, & S.T. Walters (Eds.), *Treating substance abuse: Theory and technique* (pp. 298–313). New York: Guilford.

Mugford, S. K. (1994). Recreational cocaine use in three Australian cities. *Addiction Research, 2*, 95–108.

Najavits, L. J. (2002a). Clinicians' views on treating posttraumatic stress disorder and substance use disorder. *Journal of Substance Abuse Treatment, 22*, 79–85.

Najavits, L. J. (2002b). *Seeking safety: Cognitive-behavioral therapy for PTSD and substance abuse.* New York: Guilford.

Najavits, L. J., Weiss, R., & Liese, B. (1996). Group cognitive-behavioral therapy for women with PTSD and substance use disorder. *Journal of Substance Abuse Treatment, 13*, 13–22.

National Survey on Drug Use and Health (2001). Retrieved October 20, 2005, from http://oas.samhsa.gov/nhsda2k2.htm#2k1NHSDA.

Newcomb, M. D., Scheier, L. M., & Bentler, P. M. (1993). Effects of adolescent drug use on adult mental health: A prospective study of a community sample. *Experimental and Clinical Psychology, 1*, 215–241.

Niaura, R. S., Rohsenow, D. J., Binkoff, J. A., Pedraza, M., & Abrams, D. B. (1988). Relevance of cue reactivity to understanding alcohol and smoking relapse. *Journal of Abnormal Psychology, 97*, 133–152.

Nigam, R., Schottenfeld, R., & Kosten, T. R. (1992). Treatment of dual diagnosis patients: A relapse prevention group approach. *Journal of Substance Abuse Treatment, 9*, 305–309.

Nisbith, P., Mueser, K. T., Srcic, C. S., & Beck, A.T. (1997). Differential response to cognitive therapy in parolees with primary and secondary substance use disorders. *Journal of Nervous Disease, 185*, 763–766.

Noel, N. E., & McCrady, B. S. (1993). Alcohol-focused spouse involvment with behavioral marital therapy. In T. J. O'Farrell (Ed), *Treating alcohol problems: Marital and family inverventions* (pp. 229–235). New York: Guilford.

Noonan, W., & Moyers, T. (1997). Motivational interviewing. *Journal of Substance Misuse, 2*, 8–16.

Noone, M. N., Dua, J., & Markham, R. (1999). Stress, cognitive factors, and coping resources as predictors of relapse in alcoholics. *Addictive Behaviors, 24*, 687–693.

Nowinsky, J. (1999). Self-help groups for addictions. In B. S. McCrady & E. E. Epstein (Eds.), *Addictions: A comprehensive guidebook* (pp. 328–346). New York: Oxford University Press.

Nowinsky, J. (2004). Facilitating 12-steps recovery from substance abuse and addiction. In F. Rotgers, J. Morgenstern, & S. T. Walters (Eds.), *Treating substance abuse: Theory and technique* (pp. 31–66). New York: Guilford.

Nowinsky, J., Baker, S., & Carroll, K. (1992). *Twelve-step facilitation therapy manual* (DHHS Publication No. ADM 92-1893). Rockville, MD: National Institute on Alcohol Abuse and Alcoholism.

Nunes, E., Quitkin, F., Brady, R., & Post-Koenig, T. (1994). Antidepressant treatment in methadone maintenance patients. *Journal of Addictive Diseases, 13*, 13–24.

Nunes, E. V., & Levin, F. R. 2004). Treatment of depression in patients with alcohol or other drug dependence: A meta-analysis. *Journal of the American Medical Association, 29*, 1887–1896.

Nurnberger, J. I., Wiegand, R., Bucholz, K., O'Connor, S., Meyer, E.T., Reich, T.,et al. (2004). Family study of alcohol dependence: Co-aggregation of multiple disorders in relatives of alcohol-dependent probands. *Archives of General Psychiatry, 61*, 1246–1256.

O'Brien, C., Childress, A. R., McLellan, A. T., & Ehrman, R. (1990). Integrating systematic cue exposure with standard treatment in recovering drug dependent patients. *Addictive Behavior, 15*, 355–365.

O'Brien, C. P. (1996). Recent developments in the pharmacotherapy of substance abuse. *Journal of Consulting and Clinical Psychology, 64*, 677–686.

O'Farrell, T. J. (1993). A behavioral marital therapy couples program for alcoholics and their spouses. In T. J. O'Farrell (Ed.), *Treating alcohol problems: Marital and family interventions* (pp. 170–209). New York: Guilford.

O'Farrell, T. J., & Birchler, G. R. (1987). Marital relationships of alcoholic, conflicted, and nonconflicted couples. *Journal of Marital and Family Therapy, 13*, 259–285.

O'Farrell, T. J., Choquette, K. A., Cutter, H. S. G., Brown, E. D., & McCourt, W. F. (1993). Behavioral marital therapy with and without additional couples relapse prevention sessions for alcoholics and their wives. *Journal of Studies on Alcohol, 54*, 652–666.

O'Farrell, T. J., Cutter, H. S. G., Choquette, K. A., Floyd, F. J., & Bayog, R. D. (1992). Behavioral marital therapy for male alcoholics: Marital and drinking adjustment during the two years after treatment. *Behavior Therapy, 23*, 529–549.

O'Farrell, T. J., Cutter, H. S. G., & Floyd, F. J. (1985). Evaluating behavioral marital therapy for male alcoholics: Effects on marital adjustment and communication from before to after therapy. *Behavior Therapy, 16*, 147–167.

O'Farrell, T. J., Fals-Stewart, W., Murphy, M., & Murphy, C. M. (2003). Partner violence before and after individually-based alcoholism treatment for male alcoholic patients. *Journal of Consulting and Clinical Psychology, 71*, 92–102.

O'Farrell, T. J., Kleinke, C., & Cutter, H. S. G. (1998). Sexual adjustment of male alcoholics: Changes from before to after receiving alcoholism counseling with and without marital therapy. *Addictive Behaviors, 23*, 419–425.

O'Farrell, T. J., & Murphy, C. M. (1995). Marital violence before and after alcoholism treatment. *Journal of Consulting and Clinical Psychology, 63*, 256–262.

O'Farrell, T. J., Murphy, C. M., Hoover, S., Fals-Stewart, W., & Murphy, M. (2004). Domestic violence before and after couples-based alcoholism treatment: The role of treatment involvement and abstinence. *Journal of Consulting and Clinical Psychology, 72*, 202–217.

Öjehagen, A., Berglund, M., & Hansson, L. (1997). The relationship between helping alliance in outpatient treatment of alcoholics: A comparative study of psychiatric treatment and multimodal behavioural therapy. *Alcohol and Alcoholism, 32*, 241–249.

O'Malley, S. S., Jaffe, A. J., Chang, G., Rode, S., Schottenfeld, R. S., Meyer, R. E., et al. (1996). Six month follow-up of naltrexone and coping skills therapy for alcohol dependence. *Archives of General Psychiatry, 53*, 217–224.

O'Malley, S. S., Jaffe, A., Chang, G., Witte, G., Schottenfeld, R. S., & Rounsaville, B. (1992) Naltrexone and coping skills therapy for alcohol dependence: A controlled study. *Archives of General Psychiatry, 49*, 881–887.

O'Malley, S. S., Jaffe, A. J., Rode, S., & Rounsaville, B. J. (1996). Experience of a "slip" among alcoholics treated with naltrexone or placebo. *American Journal of Psychiatry, 153*, 281–283.

Otto, M. W., & Pollack, M. H. (2004). Internal cue exposure and the treatment of substance use disorders. *Journal of Anxiety Disorders, 18*, 69–87.

Ouimette, P. C., Brown, P. J., & Najavits, L. M. (1998). Course and treatment of patients with both substance use and posttraumatic stress disorders. *Addictive Behaviors, 23*, 785–795.

Ouimette, P. C., Finney, J. W., & Moos, R. H. (1997). Twelve-step and cognitive-behavioral treatment for substance abuse: A comparison of treatment effectiveness. *Journal of Consulting and Clinical Psychology, 65*, 230–240.

Ouimette, P. C., Gima, K., Moos, R. H., & Finney, J. W. (1999). A comparative evaluation of substance abuse treatment IV: The effect of comorbid psychiatric diagnoses on amount of treatment, continuing care and-year outcomes. *Alcoholism: Clinical and Experimental Research, 23,* 552–557.

Ouimette, P. C., Moos, H., & Finney, J. W. (1998). Influence of outpatient treatment and 12-step group involvement on one-year substance abuse treatment outcomes. *Journal of Studies on Alcohol, 59,* 513–522.

Pendery, M. L., Maltzman, I. M., & West, L. J. (1982). Controlled drinking by alcoholics? New findings and a reevaluation of a major affirmative study. *Science, 217,* 169–175.

Penn, P. E., & Brooks, A. J. (2000). Five years, twelve-steps, and REBT in the treatment of dual diagnosis. *Journal of Rational Emotive and Cognitive Behavior Therapy, 18,* 197–208.

De los Cobos, J.P., Trujols, J., Ribalta, E., & Casas, M. (1997). Cocaine use imediately prior to entry in an inpatient heroin detoxification unit as a predictor of discharges against medical advice. *American Journal of Drug and Alcohol Abuse, 23,* 43–59.

Petrakis, I., Carroll, K. M., Nich, C., Gordon, L. T., McCance-Katz, E. F., Frankforter, T. L., et al. (2000). Disulfiram treatment for cocaine dependence in methadone-maintained opioid addicts. *Addiction, 95,* 219–228.

Petry, N. M. (2000). A comprehensive guide to the application of contingency management procedures in clinical settings. *Drug and Alcohol Dependence, 58,* 9–25.

Petry N. M., & Martin, B. (2002). Low-cost contingency management for treating cocaine- and opioid abusing methadone patients. *Journal of Consulting and Clinical Psychology, 70,* 398–405.

Petry, N. M., Martin, B., Cooney, J. L., & Kranzler, H. R. (2000). Give them prizes and they will come: Contingency management treatment of alcohol dependence. *Journal of Consulting and Clinical Psychology, 68,* 250–257.

Petry, N. M., Martin, B., & Simcic, F. (2005). Prize reinforcement contingency management for cocaine dependence. *Journal of Consulting and Clinical Psychology, 73,* 354–359.

Petry, N. M., Tedford, J., Austin, M., Nich, C., Carroll. K. M., & Rounsaville, B. J. (2004). Prize reinforcement contingency management for treating cocaine users: How low can we go, and with whom? *Addiction, 99,* 349–360.

Petry, N. M., Tedford, J., & Martin, B. (2001). Reinforcing compliance with non-drug-related activities. *Journal of Substance Abuse Treatment, 20,* 33–44.

Pettinati, H. M., Pierce, J. D., Wolf, A. L., Rukstalis, M. R., & O'Brien, C. P. (1997). Gender differences in comorbidly depressed alcohol-dependent outpatients. *Alcoholism: Clinical and Experimental Research, 21,* 1742–1746.

Pirard, S., Sharon, E., Kang, S. K., Angarita, G. A., & Gastfriend, D. R. (2005). Prevalence of physical and sexual abuse among substance abuse patients and impact on treatment outcome. *Drug and Alcohol Dependence, 78,* 57–64.

Poling, J., Oliveto, A., Petry, N., Sofuoglu, M., Gonsai, M., Gonzalez, G., et al. (2006). Six-month trial of bupropion with contingency management for cocaine dependence in a methadone-maintained population. *Archives of General Psychiatry, 63,* 219–228.

Powell, T., Bradley, B., & Gray, J. (1993). Subjective craving for opiates: Evaluation of a cue-exposure protocol for use with detoxified opiate addicts. *British Journal of Clinical Psychology, 32,* 39–53.

Preston, K.L., Ubricht, A., Wong, C.J., & Epstein, D.H. (2001). Shaping cocaine abstinence by successive approximation. *Journal of Consulting and Clinical Psychology, 69,* 643–654.

Prochaska, J. O., & DiClemente, C. C. (1982). Transtheoretical therapy: Toward a more integrative model of change. *Psychotherapy, Theory, Research, and Practice, 19,* 276–288.

Prochaska, J. O., & DiClemente, C. C. (1992). Stages of change in the modification of problem behaviors. In R. M. E. Hersen, R. M. Eisler, & P. M. Miller (Eds.), *Progress in behavior modification* (Vol. 28, pp. 184–218). Sycamore, IL: Sycamore.

Prochaska, J. O., DiClemente, C. C., & Norcross, J. C. (1992). In search of how people change: Applications to addictive behaviors. *American Psychologist, 47,* 1102–1114.

Project MATCH Research Group (1997a). Matching alcoholism treatments to client heterogeneity: Project MATCH posttreatment drinking outcomes. *Journal of Studies on Alcohol, 58,* 7–29.

Project MATCH Research Group (1997b). Project MATCH secondary a priori hypotheses. *Addiction, 92,* 1671–1698.

Project MATCH Research Group (1998). Matching alcoholism treatments to client heterogeneity: Project MATCH three-year drinking outcomes. *Journal of Studies on Alcohol, 58,* 7–29.

Randall, C. L., Thomas, S., & Thevos, A. K. (2001). Concurrent alcoholism and social anxiety disorder: A first step toward developing effective treatments. *Alcoholism: Clinical and Experimental Research, 25,* 210–220.

Rankin, H., Hodgson, R., & Stockwell, T. (1983). Cue exposure and response prevention with alcoholics: A controlled trial. *Behaviour Research and Therapy, 21,* 435–446.

Rawson, R.A., Huber, A., McCann, M., Shoptaw, S., Farabee, D., Reiber, C., et al (2002). A comparison of contingency management and cognitive-behavioral approaches during methadone maintenance treatment for cocaine dependence. *Archives of General Psychiatry, 59*, 817–824.

Raytek, H. S., McCrady, B. S., Epstein, E. E., & Hirsch, L. S. (1999). Therapeutic alliance and the retention of couples in conjoint alcoholism treatment. *Addictive Behaviours, 24*, 317–330.

Regier, D. A., Farmer, M. E., Rae, D. S., Locke, B. Z., Keith, S. J., & Judd, L. L. (1990). Comorbidity of mental disorders with alcohol and other drug abuse. *Journal of the American Medical Association, 264*, 2511–2518.

Rey, J. M., Martin, A., & Krabman, P. (2004). Is the party over? Cannabis and juvenile psychiatric disorders: The past 10 years. *Journal of the American Academy of Child and Adolescent Psychiatry, 43*, 1194–1205.

Reynolds, M., Mezey, G., Chapman, M., Wheeler, M., Drummond, C., & Baldacchino, A. (2005). Co-morbid post-traumatic stress disorder in a substance misusing clinical population. *Drug and Alcohol Dependence, 77*, 251–258.

Ritsher, J. B., Moos, R. H., & Finney, J. (2002). Relationship of treatment orientation and continuing care to remission among substance abuse patients. *Psychiatric Services, 53*, 595–601.

Robins, L., & Helzer, J. E. (1994). The half-life of a structured interview: The NIMH Diagnostic Interview Schedule (DIS). *International Journal of Methods in Psychiatric Research, 4*, 95–102.

Robins, L., Helzer, J. E., Croughan, J., & Ratcliff, K. S. (1981). NIMH Diagnostic Interview Schedule: Its history, characteristics, and validity. *Archives of General Psychiatry, 38*, 381–389.

Robins, L. N., Wing, J. K., & Helzer, J. E. (1983). *Composite International Diagnostic Interview (CIDI)*. Geneva: World Health Organization.

Rogers, C. (1961). *On becoming a person*. London: Constable.

Rogers, R. D., & Robbins, T. W. (2001). Investigating the neurocognitive deficits associated with chronic drug misuse. *Current Opinion in Neurobiology, 11*, 250–257.

Rohsenow, D. J., Colby, S. M., Monti, P. M., Swift, R. M., Martin, R. A., Mueller, T. I., et al. (2000). Predictors of compliance with naltrexone among alcoholics. *Alcohol Clinical and Experimental Research, 24*, 1542–1549.

Rohsenow, D. J., Martin, R. A., & Monti, P. M. (2005). Urge-specific and lifestyle coping strategies of cocaine abusers: Relationships to treatment outcomes. *Drug and Alcohol Dependence, 78*, 211–219.

Rohsenow, D. J., Monti, P. M., Binkoff, J. A., Leipman, M. R., Niren-berg, T. D., & Abrams, D. B. (1991). Patient-treatment matching for alcoholic men in communication skills versus cognitive-behavioral mood management training. *Addictive Behaviors, 16*, 63–69.

Rohsenow, D. J., Monti, P. M., Martin, R. A., Colby, S. M., Myers, M. G., Gulliver, S. B., et al. (2004). Motivational enhancement and coping skills training for cocaine abusers: Effects on substance use outcomes. *Addiction, 99*, 862–874.

Rohsenow, D. J., Monti, P. M., Rubonis, A. V., Gulliver, S. B., Colby, S. M., Binkhoff, J. A., et al. (2001). Cue exposure with coping skills training and communication skills training for alcohol dependence: 6 and 12 month outcomes. *Addiction, 96*, 1161–1174.

Rohsenow, D. J., Monti, P. M., Rubonis, A. V., Sirota, A. D., Niaura, R. S., Colby, S. M., et al. (1994). Cue reactivity as a predictor of drinking among male alcoholics. *Journal of Consulting and Clinical Psychology, 62*, 620–626.

Room, R. (1993). Alcoholics Anonymous as a social movement. In B. S. McCrady & W. R. Miller (Eds.), *Research on Alcoholics Anonymous: Opportunities and alternatives* (pp. 167–188). New Brunswick, NJ: Rutgers Center of Alcohol Studies.

Roozen, H. G., Boulogne, J. J., Van Tulder, M. W., Van Den Brink, W., De Jong, C. A., & Kerkhof, A. J. (2004). A systematic review of the effectiveness of the community reinforcement approach in alcohol, cocaine and opioid addiction. *Drug and Alcohol Dependence,74*, 1–13.

Rosenberg, H., & Davis, L. A. (1994) Acceptance of moderate drinking by alcohol treatment services in the United States. *Journal of Studies on Alcohol, 55*, 167–172.

Rosenberg, H., Melville, J., Levell, D., & Hodge, J. E. (1992) A 10-year follow-up survey of acceptability of controlled drinking in Britain. *Journal of Studies on Alcohol, 53*, 441–446.

Rosenberg, S. D., Drake, R. E.,Wolford, G. L., Muester, T. K., Oxman, T. E., Vidaver, R. M., et al. (1998). The Dartmouth Assessment of Lifestyle Inventory (DALI): A substance use screen for people with severe mental illness. *American Journal of Psychiatry, 153*, 232–238.

Rosenblum, A., Cleland, C., Magura, S., Mahmood, D., Kosanke, N., & Foote, J. (2005). Moderator of effects of motivational enhancements to cognitive behavioral therapy. *American Journal of Drug and Alcohol Abuse, 1*, 35–58.

Ross, S., Dermatis, H., Levounis, P., & Galanter, M. (2003). A comparison between dually diagnosed inpatients with and without Axis II comorbidity and the relationship to treatment outcome. *American Journal of Drug and Alcohol Abuse, 29,* 263–279.

Rounsaville, B. J. (2004). Treatment of cocaine dependence and depression. *Biological Psychiatry, 56,* 803–809.

Rounsaville, B. J., Dolinsky, Z. S., Babor, T. F., & Meyer, R. E. (1987). Psychopathology as a predictor of treatment outcome in alcoholics. *Archives of General Psychiatry, 44,* 505–513.

Rounsaville, B. J., Kranzler, H. R., Ball, S. A., Tennen, H., Poling, J., & Triffleman, G. E. (1998). Personality disorders in substance abusers: Relation to substance use. *Journal of Nervous and Mental Disease, 186,* 87–95.

Rowe, C. L., Liddle, H. A., Greenbaum, P. E., & Henderson, C. E. (2004). Impact of psychiatric comorbidity on treatment of adolescent drug abusers. *Journal of Substance Abuse Treatment, 26,* 129–140.

Roy, A., DeJong, J., Lamparski, D., Adinoff, B., George, T., Moore, V., Garnett, D.. et al. (1991). Mental disorders among alcoholics: Relationship to age of onset and cerebrospinal fluid neuropeptides. *Archives of General Psychiatry, 48,* 423–427.

Rubio, G., Jimenez-Arriero, M. A., & Ponce, G. (2001). Naltrexone versus acamprosate: One year follow-up of alcohol dependence tratment. *Alcohol and Alcoholism, 36,* 419–425.

Safren, S. A., Otto, M. W., Sprich, S., Winett, C. L., Wilens, T. E., & Biederman, J. (2005). Cognitive-behavioral therapy for ADHD in medication treated adults with continued symptoms. *Behaviour Research and Therapy, 43,* 831–842.

Saunders, J. B., Wilkinson, C., & Phillips, M. (1995). The impact of a brief motivational intervention with opiate users attending a methadone program. *Addiction, 90,* 415–424.

Schadé, A., Marquenie, L. A., Van Balkom, A. J. L. M., De Beurs, E., Van Dyck, R., & Van den Brink, W. (2003). Do comorbid anxiety disorders in alcohol dependent patients need specific treatment to prevent relapse? *Alcohol and Alcoholism, 38,* 255–262.

Schadé, A., Marquenie, L. A., Van Balkom, A. J. L. M., Koeter, M. W. J., De Beurs, E., Van den Brink, W., et al. (2004). Alcohol-dependent patients with comorbid phobic disorders: A comparison between comorbid patients, pure alcohol-dependent and pure phobic patients. *Alcohol and Alcoholism, 39,* 241–246.

Schadé, A., Marquenie, L. A., Van Balkom, A. J. L. M., Koeter, M. W. J., De Beurs, E., Van Dyck, R., et al. (2005). The effectiveness of anxiety treatment on alcohol-dependent patients with a comorbid phobic disorder: A randomized controlled trial. *Alcoholism: Clinical and Experimental Research, 29,* 794–800.

Schmitz, J. M., Averill, P., Stotts, A. L., Moeller, F. G., Rhoades, H. M., & Grabowski, J. (2001). Fluoxetine treatment of cocaine-dependent patients with major depressive disorder. *Drug and Alcohol Dependence, 63,* 207–214.

Schneider, U., Altmann, A., Baumann, M., Bernzen, J., Bertz, B., Bimber, U., et al. (2001). Comorbid anxiety and affective disorder in alcohol-dependent patients seeking treatment: The first multicentre study in Germany. *Alcohol and Alcoholism, 36,* 219–223.

Schneider, R. J., Casey, J., & Kohn, R. (2000). Motivational versus confrontational interviewing: A comparison of substance abuse assessment practices at employee assistance programs. *Journal of Behavioural Health Services and Research, 27,* 60–74.

Schoener, E. P., Madeja, C. L., Henderson, M. J., Ondersma, S. J., & Janisse, J. J. (in press). Effects of motivational interviewing training on mental health therapist behavior. *Drug and Alcohol Dependence.*

Schottenfeld, R. S., Chawarski, M. C., Pakes, J. R., Pantalon, M. V., Carroll, K. R., & Kosten, T. R. (2005). Methadone versus buprenorphine with contingency management or performance feedback for cocaine and opioid dependence. *American Journal of Psychiatry, 162,* 340–349.

Schubiner, H. (2005). Substance abuse in patients with attention-deficit hyperactivity disorder: Therapeutic implications. *CNS Drugs, 19,* 643–655.

Schubiner, H., Saules, K. K., Arfken, C. L., Johanson, C.E., Schuster, C.R., Lockhart, N., et al. (2002). Double-blind placebo-controlled trial of methylphenidate in the treatment of adult ADHD patients with comorbid cocaine dependence. *Experimental Clinical Pharmacology, 10,* 286–294.

Schuckit, M., Tipp, J., Bergman, M., Reich, W., Hesselbrock, V., & Smith, T. (1997). Comparison of induced and independent major depressive disorders in 2,945 alcoholics. *American Journal of Psychiatry, 154,* 948–957.

Schumacher, J. E., Usdan, S., Milby, J. B., Wallace, D., & McNamara, C. (2000). Abstinent-contingent housing and treatment retention among crack-cocaine-dependent homeless persons. *Journal of Substance Abuse Treatment, 9,* 81–88.

Scott, C. K., Dennis, M. L., & Foss, M. A. (2005). Utilizing Recovery Management Checkups to shorten the cycle of relapse, treatment reentry, and recovery. *Drug and Alcohol Dependence, 78,* 325–338.

Scott, J., Gilvarry, E., & Farrell, M. (1998). Managing anxiety and depression in alcohol and drug dependence. *Addictive Behaviors, 23,* 919–931.

Secades-Villa, R., Fernande-Hermida, J. R., & Arnaez-Montaraz, C. (2004). Motivational interviewing and treatment retention among drug user patients: A pilot study. *Substance Use and Misuse, 39,* 1369–1378.

Shafer, J, & Brown, S. A. (1991). Marijuana and cocaine effect expectancies and drug use patterns. *Journal of Consulting and Clinical Psychology, 59,* 558–565.

Sheehan, T., & Owen, P. (1999). The disease model. In B. S. McCrady & E. E. Epstein (Eds.), *Addictions: A comprehensive guidebook* (pp. 268–286). New York: Oxford University Press.

Sheeren, M. (1988). The relationship between relapse and involvement in Alcoholics Anonymous. *Journal of Studies on Alcohol, 49,* 104–106.

Sherwood Brown, E., Suppes, T., Adinoff, B., & Rajan Thomas, N. (2001). Drug abuse and bipolar disorder: Comorbidity or misdiagnosis? *Journal of Affective Disorders, 65,* 105–115.

Shewman, D., & Dalgarno, P. (2005). Evidence for controlled heroin use? Low levels of negative health and social outcomes among non-treatment heroin users in Glasgow (Scotland). *British Journal of Health Psychology, 10,* 33–48.

Siegel, S. (1983). Classical conditioning, drug tolerance, and drug dependence. In R. G. Smart, F. B. Glaser, Y. Israel, H. Kalant, R. E. Popham, & W. Schmidt (Eds.), *Research advances in alcohol and drug problems* (Vol. 7, pp. 207–246). New York: Plenum.

Silverman, K., Chutuape, M. A. D., Bigelow, G. E., & Stitzer, M. L. (1996). Voucher-based reinforcement of attendance by unemployed methadone patients in a job skills training program. *Drug and Alcohol Dependence, 41,* 197–207.

Silverman, K., Chutuape, M. A. D., Bigelow, G. E., & Stitzer, M. L. (1999). Voucher-based reinforcement of cocaine abstinence in treatment-resistant methadone patients: Effects of reinforcement magnitude. *Psychopharmacology, 146,* 128–138.

Silverman, K., Higgins, S. T., Brooner, R. K., Montoya, I. D., Cone, E. J., Schuster, C. R., et al. (1996). Sustained cocaine abstinence in methadone maintenance patients through voucher-based reinforcement therapy. *Archives of General Psychiatry, 53,* 409–415.

Silverman, K., Svikis, D., Robles, E., Stitzer, M. L., & Bigelow, G. E. (2001). A reinforcement-based therapeutic workplace for the treatment of drug abuse: Six-month abstinence outcomes. *Experimental and Clinical Psychopharmacology, 9*, 14–23.

Silverman, K., Svikis, D. S., Wong, C. J., Hampton, J., Stitzer, M. L., & Bigelow, G. E. (2002). A reinforcement-based therapeutic workplace for the treatment of drug abuse: Three year abstinence outcomes. *Experimental and Clinical Psychopharmacology, 10*, 228–240.

Silverman, K., Wong, C. J., Higgins, S. T., Brooner, R. K., Montoya, I. D., Contoreggi, C., et al. (1996). Increasing opiate abstinence through voucher-based reinforcement therapy. *Drug and Alcohol Dependence, 41*, 157–165.

Silverman, K., Wong, C. J., Umbricht-Schneiter, A., Montoya, I. D., Schuster, C. R., & Preston, K. L. (1998). Broad beneficial effects of cocaine abstinence reinforcement among methadone patients. *Journal of Consulting and Clinical Psychology, 66*, 811–824.

Sinha, R., Fuse, T., Aubin, L. R., & O'Malley, S. S. (2000). Psychological stress, drug-related cues and cocaine craving. *Psychopharmacology, 152*, 140–148.

Sisson, R. W., & Azrin, N. H. (1986). Family-member involvement to initiate and promote treatment of problem drinkers. *Journal of Behavior Therapy and Experimental Psychiatry, 17*, 15–21.

Sitharthan, T., Sitharthan, G., Hough, M., & Kavanagh, D. J. (1997). Cue-exposure in moderation drinking: A comparison with cognitive-behavior therapy. *Journal of Consulting and Clinical Psychology, 65*, 878–882.

Skinner, H. (1982). The Drug Abuse Screening Test. *Addictive Behaviors, 7*, 363–371.

Skinner, H. A., & Sheu, W. (1982). Reliability of alcohol use indices: The Lifetime Drinking History and the MAST. *Journal of Studies on Alcohol, 43*, 1157–1170.

Sklar, S. M., Annis, H. M., & Turner, N. E. (1997). Development and validation of the drug-taking confidence questionnaire: A measure of coping self-efficacy. *Addictive Behaviors, 22*, 655–670.

Sklar, S. M., & Turner, N. E. (1999). A brief measure for the assessment of coping self-efficacy among alcohol and other drug users. *Addiction, 94*, 723–729.

Smit, F., Bolier, L., & Cuijpers, P. (2004). Cannabis use and the risk of later schizophrenia: A review. *Addiction, 99*, 425–430.

Smith, G. T., Goldman, M. S., Greenbaum, P. E., & Christiansen, B. A. (1995). Expectancy for social facilitation from drinking: The divergent paths of high-expectancy and low-expectancy adolescents. *Journal of Abnormal Psychology, 104*, 32–40.

Smith, J. W. (2000). Addiction medicine and domestic violence. *Journal of Substance Abuse Treatment, 19*, 329–338.

Sobell, L. C., & Sobell, M. B. (1992). Timeline followback: A technique for assessing self-reported alcohol consumption. In R. Z. Litten & J. Allen (Eds.), *Measuring alcohol consumption* (pp. 41–47). Totowa, NJ: Humana.

Sobell, L. C., & Sobell, M. B. (1996). *Timeline FollowBack user's guide: A calendar method for assessing alcohol and drug use.* Toronto: Addiction Research Foundation.

Sobell, L. C., Toneatto, T., & Sobell, M. B. (1994). Behavioral assessment and treatment planning for alcohol, tobacco, and other drug problems: Current status with an emphasis on clinical applications. *Behavior Therapy, 25*, 533–580.

Sobell, M. B., & Sobell, L. C. (1984). The aftermath of heresy: A response to Pendery et al.'s (1982) critique of "individualized behavior therapy for alcoholics." *Behavior Research and Therapy, 22*, 413–440.

Sofuoglu, M., & Kosten, T. R. (2005). Novel approaches to the treatment of cocaine addiction. *CNS Drugs, 19*, 13–25.

Sørensen, H. J., Jepsen, P. W., Haastrup, S., & Juel, K. (2005). Drug-use pattern, comorbid psychosis and mortality in people with a history of opioid addiction. *Acta Psychiatrica Scandinavia, 111*, 244–249.

Spencer, T., Wilens, T., Biederman, J., Faraone, S. V., Ablon, J. S., & Lapey, K. (1995). A double-blind, cross-over comparison of methylphenidate and placebo in adults with childhood-onset attention-deficit/hyperactivity disorder. *Archives of General Psychiatry, 52*, 434–443.

Staiger, P. K., Greeley, J. D., & Wallace, S. D. (1999). Alcohol exposure therapy: Generalisation and changes in responsivity. *Drug and Alcohol Dependence, 57*, 29–40.

Stasiewicz, P. R., & Maisto, S. A. (1993). Two-factor avoidance theory: The role of negative affect in the maintenance of substance use and substance use disorder. *Behavior Therapy, 24*, 337–356.

Stephens, R. S., Roffman, R. A., & Curtin, L. (2000). Comparison of extended versus brief treatments for marijuana use. *Journal of Consulting and Clinical Psychology, 68*, 898–908.

Stephens, R. S., Roffman, R. A., & Simpson, E. E. (1994). Treating adult marijuana dependence: A test of the relapse prevention model. *Journal of Consulting and Clinical Psychology, 62*, 92–99.

Stewart, S.H. (1996). Alcohol abuse in individuals exposed to trauma: A critical review. *Psychological Bulletin, 120*, 83–112.

Stewart, S. H., Pihl, R. O., Conrod, P. J., & Dongier, M. (1998). Functional associations among trauma, PTSD, and substance-related disorders. *Addictive Behaviors, 23,* 797–812.

Stitzer, M. L., Iguchi, M. Y., & Felch, L. J.(1992). Contingency take-home incentive: Effects on drug use of methadone maintenance patients. *Journal of Consulting and Clinical Psychology, 60,* 972–934.

Stockwell, T. R., Hodgson, R. J., Edwards, G., Taylor, C., & Rankin, H. (1979). The development of a questionnaire to measure severity of alcohol dependence. *British Journal of Addiction, 74,* 79–87.

Stockwell, T. R., Murphy, D., & Hodgson, R. (1983). The Severity of Alcohol Dependence Questionnaire: Its use, reliability and validity. *British Journal of Addiction, 78,* 145–155.

Stotts, A. L., Schmitz, J. M., Rhoades, H. M., & Grabowski, J. (2001). Motivational interviewing with cocaine-dependent patients: A pilot study. *Journal of Consulting and Clinical Psychology, 69,* 858–862.

Strakowski, S. M., DelBello, M. P., Fleck, D. E., Adler, C. M., Anthenelli, R. M., Keck, P. E., Jr., et al. (2005). Effects of co-occurring alcohol abuse on the course of bipolar disorder following a first hospitalization for mania. *Archives of General Psychiatry, 62,* 851–858.

Straus, M.A., Hamby, S.L., Boney-McCoy, S., & Sugarman, D. (1996). The revised conflict-tactics scale (CTS2): Development and preliminary psychometric data. *Journal of Family Issues, 17,* 283–316.

Street, K., Harrington, J., Chiang, W., Cairns, P., & Ellis, M. (2004). How great is the risk of abuse in infants born to drug-using mothers? *Child: Care, Health and Development, 30,* 325–330.

Streeton, C., & Whelan, G. (2001). Naltrexone, a relapse-prevention maintenance treatment of alcohol dependence: A meta-analysis of randomized controlled trials. *Alcohol and Alcoholism, 36,* 544–552.

Substance Abuse and Mental Health Services Administration (2001). *National House survey on drug abuse.* Rockville, MD: U.S. Department of Health and Human Services, Public Health Services.

Substance Abuse and Mental Health Services Administration (2002). *National survey on drug use and health.* Online at http://oas.samsha.gov.

Sullivan, M. A., & Rudnik-Levin, F. (2001). Attention deficit/hyperactivity disorder and substance abuse: Diagnostic and therapeutic considerations. *Annals of the New York Academy of Sciences, 931,* 251–270.

Swanson, A. J., Pantalon, M. V., & Cohen, K. R. (1999). Motivational interviewing and treatment adherence among psychiatric and dually diagnosed patients. *Journal of Nervous and Mental Diseases, 187,* 630–635.

Swendsen, J. D., & Merikangas, K. R. (2000). The comorbidity of depression and substance use disorders. *Clinical Psychology Review, 20,* 173–189.

Swendsen, J. D., Merikangas, K. R., Canino, G. J., Kessler, R. C., Rubio-Stipec, M., & Angst, J. (1998). The comorbidity of alcoholism with anxiety and depressive disorders in four geographic communities. *Comprehensive Psychiatry, 39,* 176–184.

Teichner, G., Horner, M. D., Roitzsch, J. C., Herron, J., & Thevos, A. (2002). Substance abuse treatment outcomes for cognitively impaired and intact outpatients. *Addictive Behaviour, 27,* 751–763.

Teitelbaum, L., & Carey, K. B. (2000). Temporal stability of alcohol screening measures in a psychiatric setting. *Psychology of Addictive Behaviors, 14,* 401–404.

Teitelbaum, L., & Mullen, B. (2000). The validity of the MAST in psychiatric settings: A meta-analytic integration. *Journal of Studies on Alcohol, 61,* 254–26.

Thevos, A. K., Roberts, J. S., Thomas, S. E., & Randall, C. L. (2000). Cognitive behavioral therapy delays relapse in female socially phobic alcoholics. *Addictive Behaviors, 25,* 333–345.

Thomas, S. E., Randall, C. L., & Carrigan, M. H. (2003). Drinking to cope in socially anxious individuals: A controlled study. *Alcoholism: Clinical and Experimental Research, 27,* 1937–1943.

Thomson, A. D., Cook, C. C. H., Touquet, R., & Henry, J. A. (2002). The Royal College of Physicians report on alcohol: Guidelines for managing Wernicke's encephalopathy in the accident and emergency department. *Alcohol and Alcoholism, 37,* 513–521.

Tiffany, S. T., & Conklin, C. A. (2000). A cognitive processing model of alcohol craving and compulsive alcohol use. *Addiction, 95*(Suppl.), S145–S153.

Timmerman, I. G. H., & Emmelkamp, P. M. G. (2006). The relationship between attachment styles, Cluster B personality disorders in prisoners and forensic inpatients. *International Journal of Law and Psychiatry, 29,* 48–56.

Tohen, M., Waternaux, C. M., & Tsuang, M. T. (1990). Outcome in mania: A 4-year prospective follow-up of 75 patients utilizing survival analysis. *Archives of General Psychiatry, 47,* 1106–1111.

Tomasson, K., & Vaglum, P. (1996). Psychopathology and alcohol consumption among treatment seeking alcoholics: A prospective study. *Addiction, 91,* 1019–1030.

Tonigan, J. S., Connors, G. J., & Miller, W. R. (2002). Participation and involvement in Alcoholics Anonymous. In T. F. Babor & F. K. Del Boca (Eds.), *Matching alcoholism treatments to client heterogeneity: The results of Project MATCH* (pp. 184–204). New York: Cambridge University Press.

Tonigan, J. S., & Hiller-Strumhofel, S. (1994). Alcoholics Anonymous: Who benefits. *Alcohol Health and Research World, 18,* 308–310.

Tonigan, J. S., Miller, W. R., Juarez, P., & Villanueva, M. (2002). Utilization of AA by Hispanic and non-Hispanic white clients receiving outpatient alcohol treatment. *Journal of Studies on Alcohol, 63,* 215–218.

Tonigan, J. S., Toscova, R., & Miller, W. R. (1996). Meta-analysis of the literature on Alcoholics Anonymous: Sample and study characteristics moderate findings. *Journal of Studies on Alcohol, 57,* 65–72.

Torrens, M., Fonseca, F., Mateu, G., & Farre, M. (2005). Efficacy of antidepressants in substance use disorders with and without comorbid depression: a systematic review and meta-analysis. *Drug and Alcohol Dependence, 78,* 1–22.

Torresani, S., Favaretto, E., & Zimmermann, C. (2000). Parental representations in drug-dependent patients and their parents. *Comprehensive Psychiatry, 41,* 123–129.

Toumbourou, J. W., Hamilton, M., U'Ren, A., Stevens-Jones, P., & Storey, G. (2002). Narcotics Anonymous participation and changes in substance use and social support. *Journal of Substance Abuse Treatment, 23,* 61–66.

Tracy, M., Piper, T. M., Ompad, D., Bucciarelli, A., Coffin, P. O., Vlahov, D., & Galea, S. (2005). Circumstances of witnessed drug overdose in New York City: Implications for intervention. *Drug and Alcohol Dependence, 79,* 181–190.

Triffleman, E., Carroll, K., & Kellogg, S. (1999). Substance dependence posttraumatic stress disorder therapy: An integrated cognitive-behavioral approach. *Journal of Substance Abuse Treatment, 17,* 3–14.

Trull, T. J., Sher, K. J., Minks-Brown, C., Durbin, J., & Burr, R. (2000). Borderline personality disorder and substance use disorders: A review and integration. *Clinical Psychology Review, 20,* 235–253.

Tsuang, J. W., Irwin, M. R., Smith, T. L., & Schuckit, M. A. (1994). The clinical course of alcoholism in 636 male inpatients. *American Journal of Psychiatry, 150,* 786–792.

Tucker, K. A., Potenza, M. N., Beauvais, J. E., Browndyke, J. N., Gottschalk, P. C., & Kosten, T. R. (2004). Perfusion abnormalities and decision making in cocaine dependence. *Biological Psychiatry, 56,* 527–530.

Turner, N. E., Annis. H. M., & Sklar, S. M. (1997). Measurement of antecedents to drug and alcohol use: Psychometric properties of the Inventory of Drug-Taking Situations (IDTS). *Behaviour Research and Therapy, 35,* 465–483.

Tyler, K. A., Whitbeck, L. B., Hoyt, D. R., & Johnson, K. D. (2003). Self-mutilation and homeless youth: The role of family abuse, street experiences, and mental disorders. *Journal of Research on Adolescence, 13,* 457–474.

Vaillant, G. E. (1996). A long-term follow-up of male alcohol use. *Archives of General Psychiatry, 53,* 243–249.

Van den Bosch, L. M. C., Verheul, R., Schippers, G. M., & Van den Brink, W. (2002). Dialectical behavior therapy of borderline patients with and without substance use problems, implementation and long term effects. *Addictive Behaviors, 27,* 911–923.

Van den Brink, W., & Van Ree, J. (2003). Pharmacological treatments for heroin and cocaine addiction. *European Neuropsychopharmacology, 13*(6), 476–487.

Van der Oord, S., Prins, P.J.M., Oosterlaan, J., and Emmelkamp, P.M.G. (2006). Efficacy of methylphenidate, psychosocial treatments, and there combination in school-aged children with ADHD: A meta-analysis (submitted).

Van Etten, M. L., & Taylor, S. (1998). Comparative efficacy of treatments for post-traumatic stress disorder: A meta-analysis. *Clinical Psychology and Psychotherapy, 5,* 126–144.

Van Nimwegen, L., De Haan, L., Van Beveren, N., Van Den Brink, W., & Linszen, D. (2005). Adolescence, schizophrenia and drug abuse: A window of vulnerability. *Acta Psychiatrica Scandinavica, 111*35–42.

Van Velzen, C., & Emmelkamp, P. M. G. (1996). The assessment of personality disorders: Implications for cognitive and behavior therapy. *Behaviour Research and Therapy, 34,* 655–668.

Vedel, E., & Emmelkamp, P. M. G. (2004). Behavioral couple therapy in the treatment of a female alcohol dependent patient with comorbid depression, anxiety and personality disorders. *Clinical Case Studies, 3*(2), 187–205.

Vedel, E., Emmelkamp, P. M. G., & Schippers, G. M. (2006). Behavioral couple therapy versus individual cognitive behavior therapy in the treatment of alcohol dependence: A randomized clinical trail. Manuscript in preparation.

Verheul, R., Lehert, P., Geerlings, P. J., Koeter, M.W.J., & Van Den Brink, W. (2005). Predictors of acamprosate efficacy: Results from a pooled analysis of seven European trials including 1485 alcohol dependence patients. *Psychopharmacology, 178,* 167–173.

Verheul, R., Van den Bosch, L. M. C., Koeter, M. W. J., De Ridder, A. W., Stijnen, T., & Van den Brink, W. (2005). A 12-month randomized clinical trial of dialectical behaviour therapy for women with borderline personality disorder in the Netherlands. *British Journal of Psychiatry, 182,* 135–140.

Verheul, R., Van den Brink, W., & Hartgers, C. (1998) Personality disorders predict relapse in alcoholic patients. *Additive Behaviors, 23,* 869–882.

Vervaeke, G. A. C., & Emmelkamp, P. M. G. (1998) Treatment selection: What do we know? *European Journal of Psychological Assessment, 14,* 50–59.

Vik, P. W., Celluci, T., Jarchow, A., & Hedt, J. (2004). Cognitive impairment in substance abuse. *Psychiatric Clinics of North America, 27,* 97–109.

Vocci, F. J., Acri, J., & Elkashef, A. (2005). Medication development for addictive disorders: The state of the science. *American Journal of Psychiatry, 162,* 1432–1440.

Volkow, N. D., Fowler, J. S., & Wang, G. J. (2003). Positron emission tomography and single-photon emission computed tomography in substance abuse research. *Seminars in Nuclear Medicine, 33,* 114–128.

Volkow, N. D., Fowler, J. S., & Wang, G. J. (2004). The addicted human brain viewed in the light of imaging studies. *Neuropharmacology, 47,* 3–13.

Volpicelli, J. R., Clay, K. L., Watson, N. T., & O'Brien, C. P. (1995). Naltrexone in the treatment of alcoholism: Predicting response to naltrexone. *Journal of Clinical Psychiatry, 56,* 39–44.

Walitzer, K. S., & Dermen, K. H. (2004). Alcohol-focused spouse involvement and behavioral couples therapy; evaluation of enhancement to drinking reduction treatment for male problem drinkers. *Journal of Consulting and Clincial Psychology, 72,* 944–955.

Wallace, J. (2004). Theory of 12-step-oriented treatment. In F. Rotgers, J. Morgenstern, & S. T. Walters (Eds.), *Treating substance abuse: Theory and technique* (pp. 9–29). New York: Guilford.

Walters, G. D. (2000). Behavioral self-control training for problem drinkers: A meta-analysis of randomized control studies. *Behavior Therapy, 31,* 135–149.

Weaver, M. F., & Schnoll, S. H. (1999). Stimulants: Amphetamines and cocaine. In B. S. McCrady & E. E. Epstein (Eds.), *Addictions: A comprehensive guidebook* (pp. 105–120). New York: Oxford University Press.

Weiss, R. D., Griffin, M. L., Gallop, R. J., Najavits, L. M., Frank, A., Crits-Christoph, P., et al. (2005). The effect of 12-step self-help group attendance and participation on drug use outcomes among cocaine-dependent patients. *Drug and Alcohol Dependence, 77*, 177–184.

Weiss, R. D., Griffin, M. L., Greenfield, S. F., Najavits, L. M., Wyner, D, Soto, J. A., et al. (2000). Group therapy for patients with bipolar disorder and substance dependence: Results of a pilot study. *Journal of Clinical Psychiatry, 61*, 361–367.

Weiss, R. D., Najavits, L. M., & Greenfield, S. F. (1999). A relapse prevention group for patients with bipolar and substance use disorders. *Journal of Substance Abuse Treatment, 16*, 47–54.

Wells, E. A., Peterson, P. L., Gainey, R. R., Hawkins, J. D., & Catalano, R. F. (1994). Outpatient treatment for cocaine abuse: A controlled comparison of relapse prevention and twelve-step approaches. *American Journal of Drug and Alcohol Abuse, 20*, 1–17.

West, S. L., O'Neal, K. K., & Graham, C. W. (2000). A meta-analysis comparing the effectiveness of buprenorphine and methadone. *Journal of Substance Abuse, 12*, 405–414.

Widiger, T. A., & Corbitt, E. M. (1997). Comorbidity of antisocial personality disorder with other personality disorders. In D. M. Stoff, J. Breiling, & J. D. Maser (Eds.), *Handbook of antisocial behavior* (pp. 75–82). New York: Wiley.

Wilcox, H. C., Conner, K. K., & Caine, E. D. (2003). Association of alcohol and drug use disorders and completed suicide. *Drug and Alcohol Dependence, 76*(Suppl.), S11–S19.

Wilens, T., Biederman, J., & Mick, E. (1998). Does ADHD affect the course of substance abuse? Findings from a sample of adults with and without ADHD. *American Journal on Addictions, 7*, 156–163.

Wilens, T., Faraone, S. V., Biederman, J., & Gunawardene, S. (2003). Does stimulant therapy of attention deficit hyperactivity disorder beget later substance abuse? *Pediatrics, 111*, 179–185.

Willinger, U., Lenzinger, K., Hornik, K., Fischer, G., Schoenbeck, G., Aschauer, H. N., et al. (2002). Anxiety as a predictor of relapse in detoxified alcohol-dependent patients. *Alcohol and Alcoholism, 37*, 609–612.

Wills, T. A., McNamara, G., Vaccaro, D., & Hirky, A. E. (1996). Escalated substance use: A longitudinal grouping analysis from early to middle adolescence. *Journal of Abnormal Psychology, 105*, 166–180.

Winokur, G., Coryell, W., Akiskal, H. S., Maser, J.D., Keller, M.B., Endicott, J., et al. (1995). Alcoholism in manic-depressive (bipolar) illness. *American Journal of Psychiatry, 152*, 365–372.

Winters, J., Fals-Stewart, W., O'Farrell, T. J., Birchler, G. R., & Kelly, M. L. (2002). Behavioral couples therapy for female substance abusing patients: effects on substance use and relationship adjustment. *Journal of Consulting and Clinical Psychology, 70*, 344–355.

Winzelberg, A., & Humphreys, K. (1999). Should patients' religiosity influence clinicians' referral to 12-step self-help groups? Evidence from a study of 3018 male substance abuse patients. *Journal of Consulting and Clinical Psychology, 67*, 790–794.

Wise, B. K., Cuffe, S. P., & Fischer, T. (2001). Dual diagnosis and successful participation of adolescents in substance abuse treatment. *Journal of Substance Abuse Treatment, 21*, 161–165.

Woody, G. E., McLellan, A. T., Luborsky, L., & O'Brien, C. (1987). Twelve-month follow-up of psychotherapy for opiate dependence. *American Journal of Psychiatry, 144*, 590–596.

Woody, G. E., McLellan, A. T., Luborsky, L., & O'Brien, C. (1995). Psychotherapy in community methadone programs: A validation study. *American Journal of Psychiatry, 152*, 1302–1308.

Yen, C. F., Wu, H. Y., Yen, J. Y., & Ko, C. H. (2004). Effects of brief cognitive-behavioral interventions on confidence to resist the urges to use heroin and methamphetamine in relapse-related situations. *Journal of Nervous and Mental Disease, 192*, 788–791.

Zanarini, M. C., & Gunderson, J. G. (1997). Differential diagnoses of antisocial behavior and borderline personality disorder. In D. M. Stoff, J. Breiling, and J. D. Maser (Eds.), *Handbook of antisocial behavior* (pp. 83–91). New York: Wiley.

Zanarini, M. C., Vujanovic, A. A., Parachini, E. A., Boulanger, J. L., Frankenburg, F. R., & Hennen, J. (2003). A screening measure for BPD: The McLean Screening Instrument for Borderline Personality Disorder (MSI-BPD). *Journal of Personality Disorders, 17*, 568–573.

Ziedonis, D. M., Smelson, D., Rosenthal, R. N., Batki, S. L., Green, A. I., Henry, R. J., et al. (2005). Improving the care of individuals with schizophrenia and substance use disorders: Consensus recommendations. *Journal of Psychiatric Practice, 11*, 315–339.

Zimmermann, G., Pin, M. A., Krenz, S., Bouchat, A., Favrat, B., Besson, J., et al. (2004). Prevalence of social phobia in a clinical sample of drug dependent patients. *Journal of Affective Disorders, 83*, 83–87.

APPENDIX

GENERAL INFORMATION ABOUT SUBSTANCE-USE DISORDERS

National Institute on Alcohol Abuse and Alcoholism (NIAAA). Online at http://www.niaaa.nih.gov.
National Institute on Drug Abuse (NIDA). Online at http://www.drugabuse.gov
Substance Abuse and Mental Health Services Administration (SAMHSA). Online at http://www.samhsa.gov.

SELF-HELP SUPPORT GROUPS

Al-anon/Alateen. Online at http://www.al-anon.alateen.org/. Family support based on Alcoholics Anonymous principals.
Alcoholics Anonymous. Online at http://www.aa.org.
Rational Recovery System. Online at http://www.rational.org/recovery.
Secular Organization for Sobriety (SOS). Online at http://www.sossobriety.org.
SMART Recovery. Online at http://www.smartrecovery.org.

TREATMENT MANUALS

Budney, A. J.,Higgins, S.T., Mercer, D.E., & Carpenter, G. (1998). *A community reinforcement plus vouchers approach: Treating cocaine addiction.* Online at http://www.drugabuse.gov/drugpages/treatment_all.html
Carroll, K. M. (1998). *A cognitive behavioral approach: Treating cocaine addiction.* Online at http://www.drugabuse.gov/drugpages/treatment_all.htm.
Daley, D. C., & Woody, G.E. (1999). *Drug counseling for cocaine addiction: A collaborative cocaine treatment study model.* Online at http://www.drugabuse.gov/drugpages/treatment_all.html
    Addiction and the Family Research Group treatment manuals. Online at http://www.addictionandfamily.org/htm_pages/manuals.htm.
    Behavioral couples therapy (BCT) for drug abuse and alcoholism: A 12-session manual.

Brief BCT for drug abuse and alcoholism: A 6-session manual.

Group BCT for drug abuse and alcoholism: A 10-session manual.

Group BCT with HIV risk reduction plan for drug abuse and alcoholism: A 9-session manual.

Parent skills BCT for drug abuse: A 12-session manual.

Parent skills BCT for alcoholism: A 12-session manual

The psycho-education attentions control treatment PACT: A 12-session lecture series

Mercer, D. E., & Woody, G. E. *An individual drug counseling approach to treat cocaine addiction: The collaborative cocaine treatment study model.* Online at http://www.drugabuse.gov/drugpages/treatment_all.html

Miller, W. R. (1995). *Motivational enhancement therapy with drug abusers manual.* Online at http://casaa.unm.edu/pubs.html.

Project MATCH Treatment manuals. Ordering information online at http://pubs.niaaa.nih.gov/publications/match.htm#ordering.

Cognitive-behavioral coping skills therapy manual: A clinical research guide for therapist treating individuals with alcohol abuse and dependence.

Twelve-step facilitation therapy manual: A clinical research guide for therapist treating individuals with alcohol abuse and dependence.

Motivational enhancement therapy manual: A clinical research guide for therapist treating individuals with alcohol abuse and dependence.

Substance Abuse & Mental Health Services Administration. Brief counseling for marijuana dependence: A manual for treating adults. Online at http://kap.samhsa.gov/products/manuals/index.htm.

Substance Abuse & Mental Health Services Administration. Cannabis youth treatment (CYT) series manuals. Online at http://kap.samhsa.gov/products/manuals/cyt/index.htm.

Motivational enhancement therapy and cognitive behavioral therapy for adolescent cannabis users: 5 sessions

Motivational enhancement therapy and cognitive behavioral therapy supplement: 7 sessions

Multidimensional family therapy for adolescent cannabis users.

Family Support Network for Adolescent Cannabis Users.

The Adolescent Community Reinforcement Approach for Adolescent Cannabis Users.

Substance Abuse & Mental Health Services Administration. Substance abuse relapse prevention for older adults: A group treatment approach. Online at http://kap.samhsa. gov/products/manuals/index.htm.

Szapocznik, J., Hervis, O., & Schwartrz, S. (2003). *Brief strategic family therapy for adolescent drug abuse.* Online athttp://www.drugabuse.gov/drugpages/treatment_all.html.

GUIDEBOOKS AND GUIDELINES

Addiction and the Family Research Group. *Behavioral Couples Therapy: A 3-day training and facilitators guide.* Online at http://www.addictionandfamily.org/htm_pages/manuals.htm.

Addiction and the Family Research Group. *The TLFB for substance use and spousal violence: A user's guide.* Online at http://www.addictionandfamily.org/htm_pages/manuals.htm.

National Institute on Alcohol Abuse and Alcoholism. *Helping patients who drink too much: A clinician's guide.* Online at http://pubs. niaaa.nih.gov/publications/niaaa-guide/index.htm.

National Institute on Alcohol Abuse and Alcoholism. *A guide for marriage and family therapists.* Online at http://pubs.niaaa.nih.gov/publications/niaaa-guide/index.htm.

National Institute on Drug Abuse (1997). *Beyond the therapeutic alliance: Keeping the drug-dependent individual in treatment.* Online at http://www.drugabuse.gov/drugpages/treatment_all.html.

National Institute on Drug Abuse (1999). *Principles of drug addiction treatment: A research-based guide.* Online at http://www.drugabuse.gov/drugpages/treatment_all.html .

Substance Abuse & Mental Health Services Administration. *Treatment improvement protocol (TIP) series.* Online at http://kap.samhsa. gov/products/manuals/tips/index.htm. Best-practice guidelines for the treatment of substance abuse:

Assessment and treatment of cocaine-abusing methadone-maintained patients.

Brief interventions and brief therapies for substance abuse.

Comprehensive case management for substance abuse treatment.

Enhancing motivation for change in substance abuse treatment.

A guide to substance abuse services for primary care clinicians.

Screening and assessing adolescents with substance use disorders.
Substance abuse treatment and domestic violence.
Substance abuse treatment and family therapy.
Substance abuse treatment for persons with co-occurring disorders.
Substance use disorder treatment for people with physical and cognitive disabilities.
Treatment of adolescents with substance use disorders.

ASSESSMENT INSTRUMENTS

Addiction Severity Index (ASI). Online at http://www.tresearch.org; click on *Quick Link: Addiction Severity Index.*

Alcohol Use Disorder Identification Test (AUDIT). Online at http://www.projectcork.org/clinical_tools/index.html. Online in Spanish at http://www.nova.edu/gsc; click on *Online Forms.*

Blood Alcohol Concentration Calculation System. Online at http://casaa.unm.edu; click on *Downloads: Free Software.*

Brief Drinking Profile (BDP). Online at http://casaa.unm.edu/inst.html.

Brief Michigan Alcoholism Screening Test (BMAST). Online at http://www.projectcork.org/clinical_tools/index.html.

Brief Situational Confidence Questionnaire (BSCQ). Online at http://www.nova.edu/gsc; click on *Online Forms.* Also available in Spanish at the same website.

CAGE alcoholism assessment test. Online at http://www.projectcork.org/clinical_tools/index.html.

Comprehensive Drinking Profile (BDP). Online at http://casaa.unm.edu/inst.html.

CRAFFT substance abuse screening instrument indented for adolescents. Online at http://www.projectcork.org/clinical_tools/index.html.

Drinker Inventory of Consequences (DrInC). Online at http://casaa.unm.edu/inst.html.

Drug Abuse Screening Test (DAST). Online at http://www.projectcork.org/clinical_tools/index.html. Michigan Alcoholism Screening Test (MAST). Online at http://www.projectcork.org/clinical_tools/index.html.

DSM-IV Diagnostic Checklist for Alcohol and Drug Abuse and Dependence. Online at http://www.projectcork.org/clinical_tools/index.html.

Form 90. Online at http://casaa.unm.edu/inst.html.

Inventory of Drug Use Consequences (inDUC). Online at http://casaa.
unm.edu/inst.html.
Short Michigan Alcoholism Screening Test (SMAST) Online at http://
www.projectcork.org/clinical_tools/index.html.
SOCRATES (Drug or Alcohol). Online at http://casaa.unm.edu/inst.
html.
T-ACE alcoholism assessment test. Online at http://www.projectcork.org/
clinical_tools/index.html.
The Timeline Followback Interview for Alcohol and Drug Use (TLFB).
Online at http://www.nova.edu/gsc; click on *Online Forms*. Also
available in Spanish at the same website.
TWEAK alcoholism assessment test. Online at http://www.projectcork.
org/clinical_tools/index.html.

OTHER RESOURCES

Alcohol Alerts. Quarterly bulletin that disseminates important research
findings on a single aspect of alcohol abuse and alcoholism. Online at
http://www.niaaa.nih.gov/Publications/AlcoholAlerts/default.htm.
Alcohol Research and Health. Quarterly, peer-reviewed scientific journal. Online at http://www.niaaa.nih.gov/Publications/AlcoholRe-
search/default.htm.
Behavioral Couples Therapy. Free online training through the Addiction Technology Transfer Center Network. Online at http://www.
neattc.org/training.htm.
Guide to Self-Change Exercises (GSC). Online at http://www.nova.edu/
gsc; click on *Online Forms*.
NIDA InfoFacts. Science-based facts on drug abuse and addiction.
Online at http://www.nida.nih.gov/Infofacts/Infofaxindex.html.
NIDA Research Reports. Reports on research findings for the public,
educational groups, and practitioners. Online at http://www.nida.
nih.gov/ResearchReports/ResearchIndex.html.
NIDA Science and Practice Perspectives Journal. Initiative to combine
drug abuse science and clinical practice. Online at http://www.
nida.nih.gov/Perspectives/index.html.
Wolfe, B.L., and Miller, W.R. (1994). *Program evaluation: A do-it-
yourself manual for substance abuse programs.* Online at http://
casaa.unm.edu; click on *Downloads: Publication List*.

SUGGESTED READING: SUBSTANCE ABUSE

Barnes, K. H., Mueser, K. T., Noordsy, D. L., Drake, R. E., & Fox, L. (2003). *Integrated treatment for dual disorders: A guide to effective practice.* New York: Guilford.

Donovan, D. M., & Marlatt, G. A. (Eds.) (2005). *Assessment of addictive behaviors* (2nd ed.). New York: Guilford.

Edwards, G., Marshall, E. J., & Cook, C. C. H. (2003). *The treatment of drinking problems: A guide for the helping professions.* Cambridge: Cambridge University Press.

Essau, C. A. (Ed.) (2002). *Substance abuse and dependence in adolescence.* New York: Brunner-Routledge.

Higgins, S. T., & Katz, J.L. (Eds.) (1998). *Cocaine abuse: Behavior pharmacology and clinical applications.* San Diego, CA: Academic.

Marlatt, G. A., & Gordon, J. R. (Eds.) (2005). *Relapse prevention: Maintenance strategies in the treatment of addictive behaviors* (2nd ed.). New York: Guilford.

McCrady, B. S., & Epstein, E. E. (Eds.) (1999). *Addiction.* New York: Oxford University Press.

Meyers, R. J., & Smith, J. E. (1995). *Clinical guide to alcohol treatment: The community reinforcement approach.* New York: Guilford.

Miller, W. R., & Carroll, K. M. (Eds.) (2006). *Rethinking substance abuse: What the science shows and what we should do about it.* New York: Guilford.

Miller, W. R., & Rollnick, S. (Eds.) (2002). *Motivational interviewing: Preparing people for change* (2nd ed.). New York: Guilford.

Monti, P. M., Abrams, D. B., Kadden, R. M., Cooney, N. L., & Rohsenow, D.J. (2002). *Treating alcohol dependence: A coping skills training guide* (2nd ed.). New York: Guilford.

Najavits, L. M. (2001). *Seeking safety: A treatment manual for PTSD and substance abuse.* New York: Guilford.

O'Farrell, T. J. (Ed.) (1993). *Treating alcohol problems: Marital and family interventions.* New York: Guilford.

Pagliaro, A. M., & Pagliaro, L. A. (2000). *Substance abuse among women.* New York: Routledge.

Strang, J., & Tober, G. (Eds.) (2003). *Methadone matters: Evolving community methadone treatment of opiate addiction.* New York: Taylor and Francis.

SUGGESTED READING: SELF-HELP

Klingeman, H., Sobell, L.C.., Barker, J., Blomqvist, J., Cloud, W., Ellins-tad, T., et al . (2001). *Promoting self-change for problem substance use*. Dordrecht, Netherlands: Kluwer Academic.

Miller, W. R., & Muñoz, R. F. (2005). *Controlling your drinking: Tools to make moderation work for you*. New York: Guilford.

Sobell, M. B., & Sobell, L. C. (1996). *Problem drinkers: Guided self-change treatment*. New York: Guilford.

INDEX

A

Abandonment issues, in borderline personality disorder, 162
Abstinence. *See also* Treatment goals
alternative treatment goals to, 203
vs. controlled substance use, 108–110, 125–126
as goal for PTSD patients, 175
increased motivation with failed controlled experiments, 126
internal *vs.* external drives for, 125
superiority of 12-step enhancement programs for, 93
as treatment goal, 142
Abstinence-contingent housing, 66, 67–68
Abstinence violation effect, 28, 56–57
Acamprosate, 81, 112, 114
Accidental death, risk with substance abuse, 35
Acid, 9
Action stage, 204
appropriateness of cognitive-behavioral methods for, 50
in stages-of-change model, 44
A'dam, 9
Addiction, 1
neurobiology of, 23–24
Addiction centers, segregation from mental health centers, 168, 187
Addiction Severity Index, 38, 264
Addictive personality, 26
ADHD, and comorbid substance abuse, 20
Adolescents
cannabis and risk of later psychosis, 15

contingency management in, 66–67
Adverse family upbringing, 19
Affectionless control, 26
Age, and incidence of substance abuse, 29
Aggression-control treatment, 160
Aggressiveness, in antisocial personality disorder, 165
Agoraphobia, 16, 140
in case study, 139
AIDS, risk in drug abuse, 34
Al-anon/Alateen, 261
Alcohol abuse, ix
12-step approach effectiveness in, 104–105
anticraving medication in, 81
association with murders, rapes, car accidents, 31
behavioral couple therapy effectiveness for, 100–102
with cannabis, 11
case study with anxiety disorder, 170–171
case study with domestic violence, 159
case study with interpersonal violence, 157
coping-skills training effectiveness in, 51, 90–91
cue exposure therapy effectiveness in, 94–95
dangers during pregnancy, 33
disruptions to homeostasis in, 126–127
disulfiram as aversive deterrent in, 80
enhancement of psychotherapy by medication in, 114–115
epidemiology of, 10
genetic vulnerability to, 21–22
impaired sexual performance and, 30

enhancing with booster sessions,
196–197
links to dialectical behavior
therapy, 164
misconceptions about therapeutic
relationship in, 189–190
and model of relapse process, 56
in psychotic patients, 169
in PTSD, 173
Cognitive deficits
association with substance abuse,
32
in chronic cocaine abusers, 34
as complicating factor in
treatment, 191–192
Cognitive restructuring, in cannabis
abuse case study, 137
Coke, 8
Collaborative Cocaine Treatment
Study, 105
Combined Pharmacotherapies and
Behavioral Interventions
(COMBINE) study, 113
Communication training
in alcohol abuse case study, 151
in behavioral couple therapy,
70–71
Community reinforcement, 67–68
clinical guidelines, 68–69
meta-analysis of, 100
research-based clinical
effectiveness, 98–100
Comorbid psychiatric disorders, 1,
11–12, 152
antisocial personality disorder, 20
anxiety disorders, 15–17
borderline personality disorder,
19–20
case study, 152–156
childhood disorders, 20–21
co-occurring Axis I disorders,
167–168
and Double Trouble in Recovery
self-help, 200
etiological models for, 13–14
mood disorders, 17–19

psychosis, 14–15
Compliance, 132
with homework assignments, 124
and vulnerability to relapse, 194
Complicating factors, 157
antisocial personality disorder,
165–167
anxiety disorders, 170–172
attention deficit hyperactivity
disorder, 184–187
bipolar disorder, 182–184
borderline personality disorder,
162–165
co-occurring Axis I disorders,
167–168
cognitive deficits, 191–192
comorbid personality disorders,
162, 167–168
dysthymia, 176–182
homelessness, 192
interpersonal violence, 157–160
intimate partner violence,
158–160
major depression, 176–182
obstacles to therapeutic
relationship, 188–191
post-traumatic stress disorder,
172–176
psychotic disorders, 168–169
self-harm, 160–161
suicidal ideation, 160–161
Composite International Diagnostic
Interview (CIDI), 38
Compulsive sex, 19
Conditioning, in etiology of
substance abuse, 24–26
Conduct disorders, 13, 20, 165
and contingency management for
adolescents, 66–67
and interpersonal violence, 157
preceding alcohol abuse, 21
Confabulation, in alcohol amnestic
disorder, 33
Confrontational counseling, *vs.*
motivational interviewing in
alcohol-use disorders, 86–87

time limited nature of, 126
in withdrawal, 4
Criminal behavior
reduced with methadone, 111
and substance abuse, 31
and unemployment, 64
Crystal, 8
Cue avoidance, 53–54
Cue exposure therapy, 60–63, 109
context-specific effects of, 96
effectiveness in alcohol-use
disorders, 94–95
effectiveness in drug-use disorders,
95–96
research-based clinical
effectiveness, 94
therapeutic processes research in,
96
Cue-reactivity paradigm, 24

D

Daily sobriety trust contract, 70
Dartmouth Assessment of Lifestyle
Instrument, 37
Decision making deficits, in chronic
cocaine abusers, 34
Dehydration, with ecstasy use, 8
Delirium tremens, 32
Demographics, of substance abuse/
dependence, 2
Denial, recognition in Minnesota
Model, 75
Depression, 121, 140, 141, 145, 146.
See also Major depression
impact on relapse, 194
management in alcohol abuse case
study, 150–151
relapse risk in, 194–195
and suicide risk, 161
treatment attendance vs. relapse
rates in, 176–177
Detoxification
in alcohol dependence case study,
141–143

cannabis abuse case study,
129–137
as necessary prelude to treatment
and assessment, 120
persistence of anxiety/depression
and treatment outcome, 194
pharmacotherapy in, 79
Diagnostic Interview Schedule (DIS),
38
Diagnostic issues, 35–36
assessment of high-risk situations,
motives, coping, 40–41
biological markers, 36
expectancies, 41
questionnaires, 39
screening instruments, 36–37
stages of change, 39–40
structured interviews, 37–39
Dialectical behavior therapy, 187–188
efficacy in borderline personality
disorder, 164
Diary forms, 122, 123
Directive style, 190
Discrepancy, developing in
motivational interviewing,
48
Disorientation, in alcohol
withdrawal, 32
Distorted beliefs, changing, 56
Distraction techniques, 54
Distrust, in antisocial personality
disorder, 166
Disulfiram, 114, 139, 144, 183
as aversive deterrent in alcohol
use, 80
context of effectiveness, 113
and decreased cocaine use, 83
efficacy in cocaine dependency,
113–114
as enhancement to psychotherapy
in alcoholics, 114–115
Domestic violence, 69
and behavioral couple therapy,
102
as complicating factor in
treatment, 158–160

of cannabis abuse, 10
of cocaine abuse, 10
of methamphetamine abuse, 11
of opioid abuse, 11
of poly drug use, 11
Etiology, 1
   conditioning and craving, 24–26
   genetic vulnerability to substance
       abuse, 21–22
   neurobiology of addiction, 23–24
   psychological vulnerability, 26
   social learning theory, 26–28
Euphoria, with alcohol use, 5
Eve, 9
Evidence-based treatments, ix, x, 85
Expectancy, 27, 39
   and outcome of cue exposure
       therapy, 96
   in substance use, 41
Exposure therapy
   in alcohol dependence case study,
       143
   in PTSD with substance abuse,
       174
External cues, 62, 131
   in alcohol dependence case study,
       142
   in cannabis abuse case study, 135

F

Fearful attachment style, in antisocial
   personality disorder, 166
Feedback, in social skills
   enhancement, 59
Fetal alcohol syndrome, 33
Financial problems, 121
Fire, 8
Fishbowl lottery, 66
Flake, 8
Follow-up visits, 197–199. See also
   Maintenance strategies
Freebase, 8
Friends, therapist support for changes
   in, 78

Frontal cortex, changes with
   substance abuse, 2323
Functional analysis
   in alcohol dependence case study,
       142, 143
   in behavioral couple therapy, 70
   in cannabis abuse case study, 135
   in clinical assessment, 122, 124
   in coping-skills training, 52–53

G

Gender differences
   alcohol dependence, 10
   in BAC levels, 5
   in comorbid alcoholism and
       antisocial personality
       disorder, 20
   genetic alcohol abuse tendencies,
       21–22
   response to 12-step programs, 202
   results of child abuse/neglect, 31
Genetic vulnerability, to substance
   abuse, 21–22
GHB, effect on sexual functioning,
   30
Glass, 8
Go fast, 8
Goal setting. See also Treatment
   goals
   abstinence vs. controlled use,
       124–126
   in alcohol abuse case study,
       147–148
   for dual-diagnosis patients, 168
   realistic, 151
Grass, 7
Gravel, 8
Group therapy. See also Self-help
   groups
   in psychotic disorders with
       substance abuse, 169
Guidebooks, information sources,
   263–264

Q

Questionnaires
  in clinical assessment, 119
  for substance abuse diagnosis, 39

R

Randomized controlled studies, 85.
  See also Evidence-based
  treatments; Research basis
  of treatments
  clinical interventions proven in, 43
Rational emotive therapy, 200
Rational Recovery System, 261
Rationalization, recognition in
  Minnesota Model, 75
Readiness to change, 39
  and ease of therapeutic
    relationship, 189
  as function of therapeutic
    relationship, 45
Reasons for Drinking Scale, 40
Recovery management checkup
  model, 197–198
  improved outcomes with, 199
Reflective listening, in motivational
  interviewing technique, 47
Refusal skills, 55–56
  in alcohol dependence case study,
    144
Reinforcement, 63
  for depressed patients with
    substance abuse, 181
  use of escalating reinforcement
    schedule, 68
Relapse, 34–35
  after detoxification, 79
  among previously hospitalized
    homeless patients, 192
  with anxiety and depression,
    194–195
  and continued cannabis use, 195
  early detection through recovery
    relapse checkup model, 198

  emotional and attributional
    response to, 28
  high with pharmacotherapy alone,
    84
  maintenance strategies for,
    193–194
  preparing in cannabis abuse case
    study, 138
  preventing in coping-skills
    training, 56–58
  preventing with telephone-based
    continuing care, 199
  role of craving in, 25
  violence prevention in, 160
Relapse prevention plan, 57
  in alcohol abuse case study,
    151–152
  in alcohol dependence case study,
    144
  in behavioral couple therapy, 71
  for bipolar patients with substance
    abuse, 183
  for depressed substance abuse
    patients, 177–178
  manual-based, 152
  in PTSD, 175
Relationship problems, 121
  associated with substance abuse,
    29
  in substance abuse, 30
Relaxation training, 76
Religious beliefs, assessing before 12-
  step referral, 201–202
Remorselessness, 165
Research basis of treatments, 85.
  See also Evidence-based
  treatments
  12-step approaches, 104–108
  behavioral couple therapy,
    100–104
  community reinforcement, 98–100
  contingency management, 96–98
  controlled substance use *vs.*
    abstinence, 108–110
  coping-skills training, 83–94
  cue exposure, 94–96